PLEASURE ACTIVISM

The Politics of Feeling Good

Written and Gathered by adrienne maree brown

T0003089

PRESS

Pleasure Activism: The Politics of Feeling Good
By adrienne maree brown
Emergent Strategy Series No. 1

© 2019 AK Press (Chico, Edinburgh)
ISBN: 978-1-84935-326-7
E-ISBN: 978-1-84935-327-4
Library of Congress Control Number: 2018932264

AK Press   AK Press
370 Ryan Ave. #100   33 Tower St.
Chico, CA 95973   Edinburgh EH6 7BN
USA   Scotland
www.akpress.org   www.akuk.com
akpress@akpress.org   ak@akedin.demon.co.uk

The above addresses would be delighted to provide you with the latest AK Press
distribution catalog, which features books, pamphlets, zines, and stylish apparel
published and/or distributed by AK Press. Alternatively, visit our websites for the
complete catalog, latest news, and secure ordering.

Cover design by Herb Thornby
Interior design by Margaret Killjoy | birdsbeforethestorm.net
Printed in the USA

I dedicate this book to Alana Devich Cyril (April 17, 1976–October 27, 2018), who I loved and learned from during the journey of creation and pleasure research for this book (and include as a teacher in these pages). She said, "Drink in beauty. Pleasure is a practice. Practice pleasure like your life depends on it."

I also dedicate this book to Prince for the awakening. He said "I only wanted one time to see you laughing."

CONTENTS

19
Section One: Who Taught You to Feel Good?

103
Section Two: The Politics of Radical Sex

125
Section Three: A Circle of Sex

Sub-Section:
Skills for Sex in the #MeToo Era 190

235
Section Four: The Politics of Radical Drug Use

Section Five: Pleasure as Political Practice

Sub-Section:
The Politics of Liberated Relationships 399

435
Section Six: Outro, Thank Yous

INTRODUCTION

The role of the artist is to make the
revolution irresistible.
—Toni Cade Bambara

Hello. Welcome to *Pleasure Activism: The Politics of Feeling Good.*[1]

My name is adrienne maree brown. I am a facilitator, emergent strategist, doula, healer, auntie extraordinaire, and pleasure activist. I am your host in this sensual space, your learning companion on this pleasure journey, possibly even an arrow pointing to your erotic awakening. I have gathered here everything I know so far about pleasure activism in the form of essays, interviews, profiles, poems, and tools.

My intentions for readers of this book are that you

- recognize that pleasure is a measure of freedom;
- notice what makes you feel good and what you are curious about;
- learn ways you can increase the amount of feeling-good time in your life, to have abundant pleasure;
- decrease any internal or projected shame or scarcity thinking around the pursuit of pleasure, quieting any voices of trauma that keep you from your full sacred sensual life;
- create more room for joy, wholeness, and aliveness (and less room for oppression, repression, self-denial and unnecessary suffering) in your life;
- identify strategies beyond denial or repression for navigating pleasure in relationship to others; and
- begin to understand the liberation possible when we collectively orient around pleasure and longing.

---

1   If you can, I suggest that you have an orgasm before diving into this book and at the beginning of each new section. I am not joking—an orgasm a day keeps the doctor away and the worries at bay.

- Bonus: realize you are a pleasure activist!

Trust is a crucial part of the intimacy that yields pleasure for ourselves and others. Most likely you don't know me, so whatever trust can exist between us will come from how well I can share and how much you can open yourself to what I share. In that spirit, it feels important that you know a bit about my identity, contradictions, practices, and desires as they relate to pleasure.

I have a Black father and a white mother with a big love story, and I grew up in all of the possibility of that. My family has not escaped white supremacy, racism, internalized racism, or colorism, but we have experienced those patterns and sicknesses from a position of love that can see through them to the humans beneath the socialization. Mostly.

I identify as a Black mixed person in the particular racial construct of this country at this time. I understand that race is a social construct, not a biological one—and in this life I experience a lot of pleasure in being Black. I love Black girl magic, Black joy, Black love, and work toward Black liberation. I feel unapologetic glee at the ways in which we subvert white supremacy, dominate culture, and "coolness," often inviting people to the pleasures we have constructed from dreams and thin air.

And … I understand this to be temporary—that there were, among my ancestors, feelings of love to be of tribes whose names I will never know or from nations no longer on any maps. In the future, there may be a time when the term "Black" feels to my nibblings' nibblings the way the terms "Negro" or "Quadroon" sound to me now;[2] perhaps these future nibblings will invent new terminology indicating some way of understanding themselves that I cannot comprehend. There may be a time beyond these borders, beyond these racial constructs, beyond this planet even. I

---

2   "Nibblings" is a gender-neutral word for referring to the children of your sibling, introduced to me by Tanuja Jagernauth.

feel humble in the face of all that time. And, in this time, it's a gift to be Black.

Similarly, I am learning that much of how we experience and practice gender is a social construct—and I love the particular pleasures of being a woman. I love being of women who transform the brutal conditions we survive, who are upending rape culture, knowing we are inferior to no one, weaving our suffering into a fierce togetherness, into homes, chosen families, radical sisterhood, and tomorrows.

And I'm a woman with some boy in me and haven't found the language for that.

I know it is a privilege to feel aligned with the gender assignment I was given at birth. I love the bodies I was born from and with. And I love the wildly diverse spectrum of bodies I have gotten to hold, kiss, doula, and love in my lifetime.

I imagine there have been periods in my ancestry when gender was held very differently, maybe didn't matter so much, or was less binary. And I imagine there will be a future with a multitude of widely known and understood genders. In this moment, I get to be part of the expansion of possible genders that can live and love safely on this planet.

This book will center the experiences of Black women pursuing and related to pleasure, because these are the particular experiences with which I am both most familiar and most in community. But I am also always human and take seriously the truth that I am connected to all humans. I do not subscribe to any politics of reduction. I may see the humor in stereotypes, but I do not live my life or desires through the lens or limitation of anyone else's construction of power, identity, or supremacy. This book includes a few voices that are not Black or woman-identified but that I trust in the human experience of finding pleasure beyond oppression.

I have been a student of facilitation since my late teens, learning how to make it easier for people to be with each other. Along this journey I have been asked to facilitate people at a lot of different levels, each request teaching me more about what facilitation can do—coach, healer, doula, relationship supporter, grief supporter and death doula, breakup guide, and confidante for sexual adventures, as well as an organizational, network, and coalition/alliance facilitator.[3] I have often said yes, sometimes with trepidation, often with enthusiasm, because I am fascinated by how we interact with each other.

This book comes about partially because I realized that I have supported thousands of people in taking steps they crafted, articulated, and needed to take—steps closer to pleasure and liberation. I have seen, over and over, the connection between tuning into what brings aliveness into our systems and being able to access personal, relational and communal power.

Conversely, I have seen how denying our full, complex selves—denying our aliveness and our needs as living, sensual beings—increases the chance that we will be at odds with ourselves, our loved ones, our coworkers, and our neighbors on this planet.

I enter this book with a lot of experience pursuing pleasure and power in human systems and a ton of hope and curiosity about what might be possible if we were all living our full pleasure potential. What would happen if we aligned with a pleasure politic, especially as people who are surviving long-term oppressive conditions?

In the writing and gathering process, whenever I came to one of my edges or limitations, I reached out and gathered in a comrade who knows more than I do—about sex work, BDSM, burlesque, legalizing marijuana, pleasure during gender transition, recovering pleasure after childhood sexual abuse, pleasure while battling cancer, pleasure over age sixty, and parenting to generate pleasure-oriented children. I think the tapestry of voices here shows how many people are orienting toward and around radical pleasure in this political moment and just how many ways there are to do that.

Some other things to know:

3　People also ask me for directions a lot, even when I am in a new place and feel lost.

If I were living purely from my mind, I might have become a nun. And I don't mean a naughty nun with no panties under my habit—I really love routines and quiet. I can get a ton of pleasure from precision, rigor, and discipline (those who have experienced me as a teacher may have an inkling of this). I like being of service. And I feel a thrumming, full aliveness when in conversation with the divine. I think a lot about what god is, how god is, and where we are relating to and running from and surrendering to god. My answers are always shifting, but that conversation has been continuous in my life.

But! If I were living purely from my body, I might have achieved some world record for sexual activity, or at least be the belle of some wild bordello. Perhaps a Black Moulin Rouge singer[4]—I love seduction, I love sex, I love an exposed shoulder, the curves of the hip, the moment of realizing that under the top layer of clothing there's no bra or boxers containing the body I am observing. I love the unspeakable heat of romance. I love all the ways we are sensual. I like to smell good, taste everything yummy, feel how alive skin is, listen to sounds of breath and pleasure, see the beauty of flesh and bones. Laugh uncontrollably. Play. Feel alive. My body has the capacity to sense immense pleasure, and as I get older I keep intentionally expanding my sensual awareness and decolonizing it so that I can sense more pleasure than capitalism believes in.

I am a hermit nudist at heart. It has taken me a while to learn this, but I feel most at home when I am alone and naked. Or with someone where we can be alone/together, naked.

I know that my body could never be inappropriate. If I walk around naked all the time, or wear a muumuu slit to the moon to show my big dimpled thighs, or let my tummy hang soft and low, it's right. I am of nature. I have cycles in my body that reflect the cycles of day and night, of the seasons, of the

---

4 You might be thinking that movies aren't real life. I am thinking that the line between the real and the imagined is a construct.

moon and the tides. My body is a gorgeous miracle. I know it is only conditioning and shame, particularly fat shame, that keeps me covered (especially when I am in places where it's too hot to wear a top and men are running around shirtless).

For now, I wear clothes because I enjoy fashion and to get warm during colder parts of the year. But as I get older, it's hard to keep clothing on at home, and what I do wear needs to flow and not make a big deal against my skin or it can't stay. I also feel this way about the company I keep—that I need people around me who can adapt, have a gentle bright presence, who make me feel free, creative … and beautiful in every aspect.

And even though I have this hermit nature, I get down with people and love it. If I am forced to choose labels to describe the ways I move toward people, I say I am pansexual to express who I am attracted to and/or queer for how I relate to sex and the world. Pansexual means my desire is not limited by the biological sex, gender, or gender identity of a potential lover. I would add species, just in case new hot aliens arrive in my lifetime. So far, I have been most attracted to gender-fluid beings, particularly masculine women, effeminate men, and trans men.

And I am queer, in the grandest sense of the word. I buck the norms in my sexual life and in the rest of my life. For instance, while I enjoy a solid dose of masculinity in my lovers, it only intrigues me if I can top, bottom, and sideways them, and if they can see the woman and the boy in me.

I have tried on monogamy, open relationships, polyamory, and solitude. Nonmonogamy tends to suit me best, even if I am occasionally focused on one lover. A recent lover shared a framework with me called relationship anarchy, which is the most precise articulation I've come across so far of my approach to love and sex, basing connection in trust, freedom, change, and honest communication.[5]

---

5   See the essays "Love as Political Resistance" (p. 59) and "On Nonmonogamy" (p. 409) in this book for more on relationship anarchy.

So that's the sex and relationship landscape ... now, onto the drugs!

Before I share my drug history, I want to say that I believe that most drugs should be legalized and that there should be safe spaces to use them. I have been privileged and fortunate to safely move through my explorations. Those who are currently incarcerated for getting medicine to people should be released and given opportunities to actually lead in their industry.

I have been an active drug user since my sophomore year of college, when I first smoked weed. I have smoked, vaped, salved, and eaten cannabis products since that fateful day and really enjoy the moderation I have been slowly growing, as well as the cultural shift toward legalization that is sweeping the United States.

I also love mushrooms! I think they are truly magical, and I have had some delightful weird experiences of perceiving the world's aliveness while tripping on mushrooms on multiple continents.[6] In general, the role that fungi play in nature is wonderful—they are communicators, they process toxins, they break down dead material and make it serve life. I think fungi are a crucial part of any functional ecosystem, including our human ecosystems. But I also like to imagine mushrooms giving trees and squirrels hallucinations, for kicks.

I went through a period in my twenties where I was doing ecstasy all the time, and I believe it saved my life, to be able to buy and swallow happiness when I could not figure it out internally.[7] My pleasure goddess self definitely began to burst the seams of my post-sexual-trauma-frumpy-girl disorder during those years.

I haven't gone much further in the realm of drugs—a sniff or tab here, a recreational Vicodin or Percocet there. But I was once hospitalized with vampire bites,[8] and they put me

---

6   I recommend putting them in a fruity smoothie or dark chocolate.

7   See the essay "Ecstasy Saved My Life" in this book (p. 263).

8   I feel your doubt. It was three sets of paired bite marks on my left arm and two sets on the right. The hospital didn't believe me and said it was from dangerous urban composting. Like vampires don't like leaves.

on an IV with Benadryl and Dilaudid. Within a day, I was lying about the amount of pain I was in so they would give me more of whichever one was making everything feel like a cloud. When I left the hospital, I understood that I could never play with injection drugs, not if I also wanted to do things with my life. I think of this as harm reduction (which you will learn a lot about in this book), basically reducing or limiting the harmful impact of drug use on my life.

I love sex and drugs. I have an addictive personality, a gift and learning edge I inherited from my paternal grandmother, so I've learned to only engage those activities in substances I can moderate. Except sugar—so far that one tends to be all or nothing.

Beliefs

The other thing I want to share with y'all are a few foundational beliefs that shape everything else that will flow from me.

I believe that all organizing is science fiction—that we are shaping the future we long for and have not yet experienced. I believe that we are in an imagination battle, and almost everything about how we orient toward our bodies is shaped by fearful imaginations. Imaginations that fear Blackness, brownness, fatness, queerness, disability, difference. Our radical imagination is a tool for decolonization, for reclaiming our right to shape our lived reality. *Octavia's Brood: Science Fiction from Social Justice Movements* explores these ideas in depth.[9]

I believe that we are part of a natural world that is constantly changing, and we need to learn to adapt together and stay in relationship if we hope to survive as a species. *Emergent Strategy: Shaping Change, Changing Worlds* explores these concepts in depth.[10]

---

9   Walidah Imarisha and adrienne maree brown, eds., *Octavia's Brood: Science Fiction from Social Justice Movements* (Oakland, CA: AK Press, 2015).

10 adrienne maree brown, *Emergent Strategy: Shaping Change, Changing Worlds* (Chico, CA: AK Press, 2017).

I believe in transformative justice—that rather than pun-ishing people for surface-level behavior, or restoring condi-tions to where they were before the harm happened, we need to find the roots of the harm, together, and make the harm impossible in the future. I believe that the roots of most harm are systemic, and we must be willing to disrupt vicious sys-tems that have been normalized. I believe that we are at the beginning of learning how to really practice transformative justice in this iteration of species and society. There is ancient practice, and there will need to be future practices we can't yet foresee. But I believe that with time it must become an in-credible pleasure to be able to be honest, expect to be whole, and to know that we are in a community that will hold us accountable and change with us.

I am in this practice in as many spaces as I can be in my life. I believe that transformative justice is actually a crucial element in moving toward the kind of large-scale societal healing we need—transformative justice is a way we can be-gin to believe that the harm that has come to us won't keep happening, that we can uproot it, and that we can seed some new ways of being with each other.

I also believe that I am not creating the ideas in this book but observing a beautiful pattern of pleasure shifting the ground beneath us, inside us, and transforming what is possible between us. I have learned from so many teachers living and dead. To that end, I have an extended section of this book that is lineage, tracing the streams that are flowing into this particular river in ways that I hope create common ground, even a common titillation, between you and me.

Finally, I am constantly discovering new parts of myself to bring into the light, and that feels like an essential aspect of pleasure activism. I am discovering things as I write this book, and I will keep discovering things afterward.

As I gather this book together I am sitting in a quiet house, off season, on Martha's Vineyard. Right now, I am watching two massive swans slowly extend their long necks, bobbing in icy water, reaching toward each other, equal parts tentative and persistent. It is that energy in me as I take the tentative steps into this realm of the erotic, of the sensual, and ask us to explore together all of the power we potentially wield together.

In these pages, I am intentionally bringing academics into conversation with experiential experts, to show the patterns of aligned interest and learning happening across the language barriers that exist between us. I am bringing together a lot of different styles of expression in order to weave this tale. I asked contributors to share themselves as whole people, in the spirit of the Combahee River Collective, who taught me that "from the personal, the striving toward wholeness individually and within the community, comes the political, the struggle against those forces that render individuals and communities unwhole. The personal is political, especially for Black women."[11] Each person in this text is whole, complex, and brave in how they are shaping the world around them.

We are in a time of fertile ground for learning how we align our pleasures with our values, decolonizing our bodies and longings, and getting into a practice of saying an *orgasmic* yes together, deriving our collective power from our felt sense of pleasure.

I think a result of sourcing power in our longing and pleasure is abundant justice—that we can stop competing with each other, demanding scarce justice from our oppressors. That we can instead generate power from the overlapping space of desire and aliveness, tapping into an abundance that has enough attention, liberation, and justice for all of us to have plenty.

We're going to keep learning together. These pages are a space to ask shameless questions, to love what we love and explore why we love it, to increase the pleasure we feel when we are doing things that are good for the species and the planet,

---

11 Combahee River Collective, "The Combahee River Collective Statement," in *Home Girls: A Black Feminist Anthology*, edited by Barbara Smith (New York: Kitchen Table: Women of Color Press, 1983), 264–74.

to cultivate our interest in radical love and pleasure, and to nourish the orgasmic yes in each of us.

What Is Pleasure Activism?

Pleasure is a feeling of happy satisfaction and enjoyment. Activism consists of efforts to promote, impede, or direct social, political, economic, or environmental reform or stasis with the desire to make improvements in society. Pleasure activism is the work we do to reclaim our whole, happy, and satisfiable selves from the impacts, delusions, and limitations of oppression and/or supremacy.

Pleasure activism asserts that we all need and deserve pleasure and that our social structures must reflect this. In this moment, we must prioritize the pleasure of those most impacted by oppression.

Pleasure activists seek to understand and learn from the politics and power dynamics inside of everything that makes us feel good. This includes sex and the erotic, drugs, fashion, humor, passion work, connection, reading, cooking and/or eating, music and other arts, and so much more.

Pleasure activists believe that by tapping into the potential goodness in each of us we can generate justice and liberation, growing a healing abundance where we have been socialized to believe only scarcity exists.

Pleasure activism acts from an analysis that pleasure is a natural, safe, and liberated part of life—and that we can offer each other tools and education to make sure sex, desire, drugs, connection, and other pleasures aren't life-threatening or harming but life-enriching.

Pleasure activism includes work and life lived in the realms of satisfaction, joy, and erotic aliveness that bring about social and political change.

Ultimately, pleasure activism is us learning to make justice and liberation the most pleasurable experiences we can have on this planet.

Pleasure Principles

- *What you pay attention to grows.* This will be familiar to those who have read *Emergent Strategy*. Actually, all the emergent strategy principles also apply here! (Insert eggplant emoji). Tune into happiness, what satisfies you, what brings you joy.

- *We become what we practice.* I learned this through studying somatics! In his book *The Leadership Dojo*, Richard Strozzi-Heckler shares that "300 repetitions produce body memory … [and] 3,000 repetitions creates embodiment."[12]

- *Yes is the way.* When it was time to move to Detroit, when it was time to leave my last job, when it was time to pick up a meditation practice, time to swim, time to eat healthier, I knew because it gave me pleasure when I made and lived into the decision. Now I am letting that guide my choices for how I organize and for what I am aiming toward with my work—pleasure in the processes of my existence and states of my being. Yes is a future. When I feel pleasure, I know I am on the right track. Puerto Rican pleasure elder Idelisse Malave shared with me that her pleasure principle is "If it pleases me, I will."

- *When I am happy, it is good for the world.*[13]

- *The deepest pleasure comes from riding the line between commitment and detachment.*[14] Commit yourself fully to the process, the journey, to bringing the best you can bring. Detach yourself from ego and outcomes.

- *Make justice and liberation feel good.*

---

12 Richard Strozzi-Heckler, *The Leadership Dojo: Build Your Foundation as an Exemplary Leader* (Berkeley, CA: Frog Books, 2007), 59.

13 I owe this one to my incomparable, brave, and brilliant Canadian woe, Jodie. Folks who are rooted in sensing and seeking pleasure, and bring that energy into their work and relationships, are shining a light for others—there is another path that isn't full of stress, self-doubt, pain, victimization, and suffering. There is a path in which everything is learning, playing, practicing, doing things anew.

14 This is true in sex; it's true in work; it's just true.

- *Your no makes the way for your yes.* Boundaries create the container within which your yes is authentic. Being able to say no makes yes a choice.
- *Moderation is key.*[15] The idea is not to be in a heady state of ecstasy at all times, but rather to learn how to *sense* when something is good for you, to be able to feel what enough is. Related: pleasure is not money. Pleasure is not even related to money, at least not in a positive way. Having resources to buy unlimited amounts of pleasure leads to excess, and excess totally destroys the spiritual experience of pleasure.

A Word on Excess

Pleasure activism is not about generating or indulging in excess. I want to say this early and often, to myself and to you. Sometimes when I bring up this work to people, I can see a bacchanalia unfold in their eyes, and it makes me feel tender. I think because most of us are so repressed, our fantasies go to extremes to counterbalance all that contained longing. Pleasure activism is about learning what it means to be satisfiable, to generate, from within and from between us, an abundance from which we can all have enough.[16]

Part of the reason so few of us have a healthy relationship with pleasure is because a small minority of our species hoards the excess of resources, creating a false scarcity and then trying to sell us joy, sell us back to ourselves. Some think it belongs to them, that it is their inheritance. Some think it a sign of their worth, their superiority. On a broad level, white people and men have been the primary recipients of this delusion, the belief that they deserve to have excess, while the majority of others don't have enough ... or further, that the majority of the world exists in some way to please them.

---

15 But as Maya Angelou once told Oprah, even moderation needs moderation.

16 My first memory of this concept, of being satisfiable, was from Staci Haines.

And so many of us have been trained into the delusion that we must accumulate excess, even at the cost of vast inequality, in order to view our lives as complete or successful.

A central aspect of pleasure activism is tapping into the natural abundance that exists within and between us, and between our species and this planet. Pleasure is not one of the spoils of capitalism. It is what our bodies, our human systems, are structured for; it is the aliveness and awakening, the gratitude and humility, the joy and celebration of being miraculous.

So rather than encouraging moderation over and over, I want to ask you to relinquish your own longing for excess and to stay mindful of your relationship to enough. How much sex would be enough? How high would be high enough? How much love would feel like enough? Can you imagine being healed enough? Happy enough? Connected enough? Having enough space in your life to actually live it? Can you imagine being free enough?

Do you understand that you, as you are, who you are, is enough?

Glossary

Why a glossary? Language changes so quickly these days. The right way to speak about people, about identities, about gender, about geography—everything is in motion on a regular basis. I know that in writing this book I am creating something instantly dated. Given that god is change, there are some terms in this book that I want to be super clear about.

Bitch is one of my favorite words. When I say it, I mean you are fierce, I love you, wow, that's the boss, be yourself, yes yes yes.

Fat is a word I am reclaiming for myself, especially when connected to sexy, #sexyfat. I am thick, I am big, but most of what gives me this outstanding shape and feel is actual fat.

Somatics is

> a path, a methodology, a change theory, by which we can embody transformation, individually and collectively. Embodied transformation is foundational change that shows in our actions, ways of being, relating, and perceiving. It is transformation that sustains over time. Somatics pragmatically supports our values and actions becoming aligned. It helps us to develop depth and the capacity to feel ourselves, each other and life around us. Somatics builds in us the ability to act from strategy and empathy, and teaches us to be able to assess conditions and 'what is' clearly. Somatics is a practice-able theory of change that can move us toward individual, community and collective liberation. Somatics works through the body, engaging us in our thinking, emotions, commitments, vision and action.[17]

I teach and reference somatics often in these pages.

Pleasure is "a feeling of happy satisfaction or enjoyment" and "to give sexual enjoyment or satisfaction to another."

Erotic is "relating to or tending to arouse sexual desire or excitement."

Finally, I believe we are actively moving toward a nonbinary gender future—one in which gender is understood as a spectrum instead of a binary with two options to move between. I write as someone raised in, interacting with, and

---

17 "What is Somatics?," Generative Somatics, accessed July 23, 2018, http://www.generativesomatics.org/content/what-somatics.

intentionally disrupting the gender binary. I respect how people identify themselves, what they know themselves to be.

When I use *women* in this text I mean any and all people who identify as women. This includes those who identify as cis, non-trans, trans, and anyone else who identifies with the words "woman" and "women." The same is true for *men*—I include any and all who identify with the language of "man" and "men." *Nonbinary* and *gender nonconforming* in this text refers to people who don't identify with women/men binary terminology. If the content requires a distinction that draws on a specific *trans* experience—which includes the experiences of those who identify as transsexual or transgender, with or without surgery—then I (or the writer of that piece) will make that distinction. In this text, the pronouns will reflect the identity of the subjects being discussed—he, she, they, et cetera. If this is being read in a future in which this language has evolved, then please know I would be evolving right along with you.

SECTION ONE

WHO TAUGHT YOU TO FEEL GOOD?

May you devour life.
—the late Kevin Estrada, as a blessing to
the children of Elizabeth Mendez Berry

Lineage, an Overview

I am the granddaughter of a woman who had seven children with a few men. She raised the children with the help of her family. She drank and kept a freezer full of pops that all the neighborhood kids could visit. I was never sure about how to think of my grandmother growing up. I felt kinship for her. I thought she was beautiful, fly, smelled good, felt soft. I remember her being generous. As I get older, I realize how sexually liberated she was for her time. She didn't give up on sex or love, even though it was a struggle for her. She kept finding lovers, kept finding ways to feel good as a southern Black hotel maid. I want to honor her as the first person in my personal pleasure lineage.

The next person of significance is Octavia Butler. This book is the third one I've worked on that roots back into Butler's work. The first was *Octavia's Brood: Science Fiction from Social Justice Movements,* in which I worked with Walidah Imarisha to gather visionary fiction in the lineage of Butler—fiction that understands it is not neutral, that seeks to evolve the status quo by centering those communities traditionally marginalized by white supremacy, patriarchy, and capitalism.

The second book was *Emergent Strategy: Shaping Change, Changing Worlds,* in which a lot of my comrades and I explored the adaptive, relational leadership that so many of Butler's protagonists displayed, finding models in complex science and the natural world.

This third book is inspired in part by the ways in which Butler's characters often find the way beyond evolutionary obstacles with physical pleasure and symbiotic communities.

It's also inspired by the sheer pleasure I get reading and rereading Butler and other science fiction writers, stretching my imagination out beyond the horizon. I write more later in this book about the ways Butler turns me on.

While Butler is a core root of this work, I had to include, in full, with some of my own annotation, Audre Lorde's life-changing essay "Uses of the Erotic: The Erotic as Power." This essay was published a few days before I was born, on August 25, 1978. I first read and heard it in college.[1] Lorde shared what she had learned about the ways the power of the erotic makes us "give up, of necessity, being satisfied with suffering, and self-negation."[2]

I am aware that Lorde uses the language of the erotic, which specifies the pleasures and aliveness associated with sex. I love the erotic, and it's all over this book, but I also wanted to broaden the scope to all the experiences that bring us happiness, aliveness, transcendence—which is why this is *pleasure* activism and not *erotic* activism.

The place where it all comes together, for me, is the orgasmic yes.

Lorde made me look deeply at my life to find the orgasmic, full-bodied "yes!" inside of me, inside of the communities I love and work with, and inside our species in relationship to our home planet. Through her writing here and in other places—Lorde was prolific—I became attuned to the ways erotic and other pleasures shaped and healed me. It helped me to understand that there is no way to repress pleasure and expect liberation, satisfaction, or joy. With Lorde's guidance, I reflected on how my experiences with sex had opened doors to loving my body in spite of what society had taught me about big Black glasses-wearing queer girls being undesirable.

---

1   Yes, I said "heard"—get your life by searching for the video in which you can hear Audre Lorde read the essay while looking at her incredible face.

2   See Audre Lorde, "Uses of the Erotic: The Erotic as Power," this volume, p. 27.

I began to move toward my own yes, my satisfaction. I examined how my experiences of deep political alignment with people who wanted to collaborate had taught me more than years of battling with people who wanted to dominate me or compete against me.

I began to make decisions about whether I wanted to do things in my life and in the movements I am part of by checking for my orgasmic yes. And to feel for resistance inside, the small place in my gut that knows before I do that something is not a fit for me and will not increase my aliveness. This exploration led me to some core questions that have shaped my work:

What would I be doing with my time and energy if I made decisions based on a feeling of deep, erotic, orgasmic yes?

How do I find balance in the things that give me pleasure, especially the things that tend to be misunderstood and manipulated by racialized capitalism, such as drugs, sex, drink, sugar?

How do we learn to harness the power and wisdom of pleasure, rather than trying to erase the body, the erotic, the connective tissue from society?

How would we organize and move our communities if we shifted to focus on what we long for and love rather than what we are negatively reacting to?

Is it possible for justice and pleasure to feel the same way in our collective body? Could we make justice and liberation the most pleasurable collective experiences we could have?

Again, most of my work has been facilitation—making it easy for those transforming the world to be with each other, be impactful together. As I facilitate these movements for social and environmental transformation, with a focus on Black liberation, I always prioritize how people feel.[3] Is it a pleasure to be with each other? Does the agenda or space allow for aliveness, connection, and joy? Is there a "yes!" at the center

---

3 Learn more about my facilitation and training work at www.allied media.org/esii.

of the work? There are so many things that are violent, offensive, unbearable. An embodied "no" is so justified—but I don't believe it moves us forward.

"Yes!" has a future. Witnessing an embodied yes in the body of a historically oppressed person is irresistible to me.

Which brings us to Toni Cade Bambara. She taught us many things, but I keep coming back to her task to writers/ artists to "make the revolution irresistible."[4] Bambara taught us to say yes to ourselves, to a future that included our whole selves. She did this by being intact in public: complex and multitalented and vulnerable. Alexis Pauline Gumbs will help us all see the wholeness of Bambara.

To round out the lineage, I am including two pieces on pleasure philosophy. The first is a piece on pleasure politics from Joan Morgan. I remember hearing that Morgan was rocking with a crew called the Pleasure Ninjas and then learning that they were the badass Black academics that I wanted to be when I grew up, even though I lacked the particular gene that makes one pursue advanced degrees and teaching. This piece feels foundational to the work we'll explore in these pages.

Years later, I heard my Detroit afrofuturist comrade Ingrid LaFleur speak to an aligned approach to life, a pleasure philosophy that was shaping her choices, family, fashion, and future. So there's a brief interview with her.

There are some other people I just need to mention in the pleasure activism lineage.

- Writers like Anaïs Nin, Erica Jong, Andrea Dworkin, and Alice Walker changed my mind about what sex could be, what my body was for, shifting the very definition of being sexually liberated outside of a framework of wanting or needing men. But at the same time, I learned from Samuel R. Delany to

---

4   "An Interview with Toni Cade Bambara," by Kay Bonetti, in *Conversations with Toni Cade Bambara*, ed. Thabiti Lewis, (Jackson: University Press of Mississippi, 2012), 35–47.

engage the future through desire, through the queer body. Delany has had thousands of lovers and has written some of the most sensual otherworldly sex that has ever been put on a page.

- I learned from Frida Kahlo the pleasure of public self-love. Kahlo taught me to find my own beautiful, to be curious about my own face, to be unafraid to stand out, and to be true to my and our capacity for genius.
- I learned from my aunt Margaret about the pleasures of fashion and home decor, bringing and colliding the brightest patterns and colors into everything—socks, textiles, shower curtains, muumuus.
- Keith Cylar, cofounder of Housing Works, was the first person I remember hearing the term pleasure activism from and also the person to show me that even in "professional" spaces you could be a sexual, drug-using grown-up who danced with your whole body every time you heard music. And that flirtation could be a part of great friendships.

The other teachers I have on this path are in the pages that follow, as authors of essays, interviewees, or references.

HOT AND HEAVY HOMEWORK

Write up *your* pleasure activism lineage! Who awakened your senses? Who politicized your experiences of body, identity, sensation, feeling good? If they are still living, have you thanked them properly? If yes, good, do it again. If not, reach out. If they are ancestors, honor them with a pleasure altar covered in sticky fruit, sweet smells, sacred water, and thick earth, centered around fire. Gratitude is part of pleasure too.

USES OF THE EROTIC

The Erotic as Power

Audre Lorde

There are many kinds of power, used and unused, acknowledged or otherwise.[1] The erotic is a resource within each of us that lies in a deeply female and spiritual plane, firmly rooted in the power of our unexpressed or unrecognized feeling.[2] In order to perpetuate itself, every oppression must corrupt or distort those various sources of power within the culture of the oppressed that can provide energy for change. For women, this has meant a suppression of the erotic as a considered source of power and information within our lives.

We have been taught to suspect this resource, vilified, abused, and devalued within western society. On the one hand, the superficially erotic has been encouraged as a sign of female inferiority; on the other hand, women have been

---

1   Paper delivered at the fourth Berkshire Conference on the History of Women, Mount Holyoke College, August 25, 1978. Published as a pamphlet by Out & Out Books (available from the Crossing Press), annotations and emphasis by adrienne maree brown.

2   amb: In this book, I will explore nonbiological feminine erotic power, which I believe all bodies can tap into.

made to suffer and to feel both contemptible and suspect by virtue of its existence.

It is a short step from there to the false belief that only by the suppression of the erotic within our lives and consciousness can women be truly strong. But that strength is illusory, for it is fashioned within the context of male models of power.

As women, we have come to distrust that power which rises from our deepest and nonrational knowledge. We have been warned against it all our lives by the male world, which values this depth of feeling enough to keep women around in order to exercise it in the service of men, but which fears this same depth too much to examine the possibilities of it within themselves. So women are maintained at a distant/inferior position to be psychically milked, much the same way ants maintain colonies of aphids to provide a life-giving substance for their masters.

But the erotic offers a well of replenishing and provocative force to the woman who does not fear its revelation, nor succumb to the belief that sensation is enough.

The erotic has often been misnamed by men and used against women. It has been made into the confused, the trivial, the psychotic, the plasticized sensation. For this reason, we have often turned away from the exploration and consideration of the erotic as a source of power and information, confusing it with its opposite, the pornographic. But pornography is a direct denial of the power of the erotic, for it represents the suppression of true feeling. Pornography emphasizes sensation without feeling.[3]

The erotic is a measure between the beginnings of our sense of self and the chaos of our strongest feelings. It is an internal sense of satisfaction to which, once we have experienced it, we know we can aspire. For having experienced the fullness of this depth

---

3   amb: There are a few pieces in this book that explore pornography—as a potentially liberating technology or as a problem.

of feeling and recognizing its power, in honor and self-respect we can require no less of ourselves.[4]

It is never easy to demand the most from ourselves, from our lives, from our work. To encourage excellence is to go beyond the encouraged mediocrity of our society. But giving in to the fear of feeling and working to capacity is a luxury only the unintentional can afford, and the unintentional are those who do not wish to guide their own destinies.[5]

This internal requirement toward excellence which we learn from the erotic must not be misconstrued as demanding the impossible from ourselves nor from others. Such a demand incapacitates everyone in the process. For the erotic is not a question only of what we do; it is a question of how acutely and fully we can feel in the doing. Once we know the extent to which we are capable of feeling that sense of satisfaction and completion, we can then observe which of our various life endeavors bring us closest to that fullness.

The aim of each thing which we do is to make our lives and the lives of our children richer and more possible. Within the celebration of the erotic in all our endeavors, my work becomes a conscious decision—a longed-for bed which I enter gratefully and from which I rise up empowered.

Of course, women so empowered are dangerous. So we are taught to separate the erotic demand from most vital areas of our lives other than sex. And the lack of concern for the erotic root and satisfactions of our work is felt in our disaffection from so much of what we do. For instance, how often do we truly love our work even at its most difficult?

The principal horror of any system which defines the good in terms of profit rather than in terms of human need, or

---

4   amb: This paragraph is one of the essential concepts that will guide and shape this entire book. Feel free to read it several times.

5   amb: I would also argue that the unintentional may include those who do not realize that guiding their own destinies is a possibility. For this reason, throughout this work, I will encourage us to come out again and again, to live our pleasure and power out loud.

which defines human need to the exclusion of the psychic and emotional components of that need—the principal horror of such a system is that it robs our work of its erotic value, its erotic power and life appeal and fulfillment. Such a system reduces work to a travesty of necessities, a duty by which we earn bread or oblivion for ourselves and those we love. But this is tantamount to blinding a painter and then telling her to improve her work, and to enjoy the act of painting.[6] It is not only next to impossible, it is also profoundly cruel.

As women, we need to examine the ways in which our world can be truly different. I am speaking here of the necessity for reassessing the quality of all the aspects of our lives and of our work, and of how we move toward and through them.

The very word *erotic* comes from the Greek word *eros*, the personification of love in all its aspects—born of Chaos, and personifying creative power and harmony. When I speak of the erotic, then, I speak of it as an assertion of the lifeforce of women; of that creative energy empowered, the knowledge and use of which we are now reclaiming in our language, our history, our dancing, our loving, our work, our lives.

There are frequent attempts to equate pornography and eroticism, two diametrically opposed uses of the sexual. Because of these attempts, it has become fashionable to separate the spiritual (psychic and emotional) from the political, to see them as contradictory or antithetical. "What do you mean, a poetic revolutionary, a meditating gunrunner?" In the same way, we have attempted to separate the spiritual and the erotic, thereby reducing the spiritual to a world of flattened affect, a world of the ascetic who aspires to feel nothing. But nothing is farther from the truth. For the ascetic position is one of the highest fear, the gravest immobility. The severe abstinence of the ascetic becomes the ruling obsession. And it is one not of self-discipline but of self-abnegation.

---

6   I want to note the ableism of this metaphor, even if we can't be in a
    conversation with Lorde about it anymore.

The dichotomy between the spiritual and the political is also false, resulting from an incomplete attention to our erotic knowledge. For the bridge which connects them is formed by the erotic—the sensual—those physical, emotional, and psychic expressions of what is deepest and strongest and richest within each of us, being shared: the passions of love, in its deepest meanings.[7]

Beyond the superficial, the considered phrase, "It feels right to me," acknowledges the strength of the erotic into a true knowledge, for what that means is the first and most powerful guiding light toward any understanding. And understanding is a handmaiden which can only wait upon, or clarify, that knowledge, deeply born. The erotic is the nurturer or nursemaid of all our deepest knowledge.

The erotic functions for me in several ways, and the first is in providing the power which comes from sharing deeply any pursuit with another person. *The sharing of joy, whether physical, emotional, psychic, or intellectual, forms a bridge between the sharers which can be the basis for understanding much of what is not shared between them, and lessens the threat of their difference.*

Another important way in which the erotic connection functions is the open and fearless underlining of my capacity for joy. In the way my body stretches to music and opens into response, hearkening to its deepest rhythms, so every level upon which I sense also opens to the erotically satisfying experience, whether it is dancing, building a bookcase, writing a poem, examining an idea.

That self-connection shared is a measure of the joy which I know myself to be capable of feeling, a reminder of my capacity for feeling. *And that deep and irreplaceable knowledge of my capacity for joy comes to demand from all of my life that it be lived within the knowledge that such satisfaction is possible, and does not have to be called* marriage, *nor* god, *nor* an afterlife.

---

7   amb: I will explore learning to actually recognize and read our own sensations in the essay "The Sensuality of Somatics."

This is one reason why the erotic is so feared, and so often relegated to the bedroom alone, when it is recognized at all. *For once we begin to feel deeply all the aspects of our lives, we begin to demand from ourselves and from our life-pursuits that they feel in accordance with that joy which we know ourselves to be capable of.* Our erotic knowledge empowers us, becomes a lens through which we scrutinize all aspects of our existence, forcing us to evaluate those aspects honestly in terms of their relative meaning within our lives. And this is a grave responsibility, projected from within each of us, not to settle for the convenient, the shoddy, the conventionally expected, nor the merely safe.

During World War II, we bought sealed plastic packets of white, uncolored margarine, with a tiny, intense pellet of yellow coloring perched like a topaz just inside the clear skin of the bag. We would leave the margarine out for a while to soften, and then we would pinch the little pellet to break it inside the bag, releasing the rich yellowness into the soft pale mass of margarine. Then taking it carefully between our fingers, we would knead it gently back and forth, over and over, until the color had spread throughout the whole pound bag of margarine, thoroughly coloring it.

I find the erotic such a kernel within myself. When released from its intense and constrained pellet, it flows through and colors my life with a kind of energy that heightens and sensitizes and strengthens all my experience.

We have been raised to fear the yes within ourselves, our deepest cravings. But, once recognized, those which do not enhance our future lose their power and can be altered. The fear of our desires keeps them suspect and indiscriminately powerful, for *to suppress any truth is to give it strength beyond endurance.* The fear that we cannot grow beyond whatever distortions we may find within ourselves keeps us docile and loyal and obedient, externally defined, and leads us to accept many facets of our oppression as women.

When we live outside ourselves, and by that I mean on external directives only rather than from our internal knowledge and needs, when we live away from those erotic guides from within ourselves, then our lives are limited by external and alien forms, and we conform to the needs of a structure that is not based on human need, let alone an individual's. But when we begin to live from within outward, in touch with the power of the erotic within ourselves, and allowing that power to inform and illuminate our actions upon the world around us, then we begin to be responsible to ourselves in the deepest sense. *For as we begin to recognize our deepest feelings, we begin to give up, of necessity, being satisfied with suffering and self-negation, and with the numbness which so often seems like their only alternative in our society. Our acts against oppression become integral with self, motivated and empowered from within. In touch with the erotic, I become less willing to accept powerlessness, or those other supplied states of being which are not native to me, such as resignation, despair, self-effacement, depression, self-denial.*

And yes, there is a hierarchy. There is a difference between painting a back fence and writing a poem, but only one of quantity. And there is, for me, no difference between writing a good poem and moving into sunlight against the body of a woman I love.

This brings me to the last consideration of the erotic. To share the power of each other's feelings is different from using another's feelings as we would use a Kleenex. When we look the other way from our experience, erotic or otherwise, we use rather than share the feelings of those others who participate in the experience with us. And use without consent of the used is abuse.

In order to be utilized, our erotic feelings must be recognized. The need for sharing deep feeling is a human need. But within the european-american tradition, this need is satisfied by certain proscribed erotic comings-together. These occasions are almost always characterized by a simultaneous looking away, a pretense of calling them something else, whether a religion, a fit, mob violence, or even playing doctor. And this misnaming of the need and the deed give rise to that distortion which results in pornography and obscenity—the abuse of feeling.

When we look away from the importance of the erotic in the development and sustenance of our power, or when we look away from ourselves as we satisfy our erotic needs in concert with others, we use each other as objects of satisfaction rather than share our joy in the satisfying, rather than make connection with our similarities and our differences.[8] To refuse to be conscious of what we are feeling at any time, however comfortable that might seem, is to deny a large part of the experience, and to allow ourselves to be reduced to the pornographic, the abused, and the absurd.

The erotic cannot be felt secondhand. As a Black lesbian feminist, I have a particular feeling, knowledge, and understanding for those sisters with whom I have danced hard, played, or even fought. This deep participation has often been the forerunner for joint concerted actions not possible before.

But this erotic charge is not easily shared by women who continue to operate under an exclusively european-american male tradition. I know it was not available to me when I was trying to adapt my consciousness to this mode of living and sensation.

Only now, I find more and more women-identified women brave enough to risk sharing the erotic's electrical charge without having to look away, and without distorting the enormously powerful and creative nature of that exchange.[9]

---

8   amb: I believe this is also how we can use each other in movements for social justice, use each other as numbers, as followers, as a mass of bodies rather than a solidarity of many unique bodies with unique needs choosing to be together because it brings us joy and liberation.

9   amb: I am not able to ask Audre Lorde her intended distinctions here, but I can ask that you as readers consider the text through the lens of her time rather than ours—in this day and age, when I hear "women-identified women," I can bristle in search of transphobia. This book will in no way support any identity of woman that does not include cis and trans women. The way I want to explore pleasure includes everyone of any gender and all genders who is looking for

Recognizing the power of the erotic within our lives can give us the energy to pursue genuine change within our world, rather than merely settling for a shift of characters in the same weary drama.

For not only do we touch our most profoundly creative source, but we do that which is female and self-affirming in the face of a racist, patriarchal, and anti-erotic society.

a different way to be in power with each other and willing to experiment with a feminine, erotic use of power.

THE LEGACY OF "USES OF THE EROTIC"

A Conversation with Cara Page

Cara Page is a striking human being. She's quite tall, her smile is bright, her eyes look like they miss nothing, and when she speaks her voice is mountains and dark liquor. For the years I was dreaming and writing this book, Cara was executive director of the Audre Lorde Project. Before that, I'd known Cara as a healer weaving the threads between other healers and the social/ environmental justice movements. We once took a car ride where she was responsible for giving the directions to the driver, possibly me ... and as she spoke, "go right, rerouting," it became a sensual experience. We spoke by video call for this interview.[1]

amb. *You're one of the first people that leapt to mind for this project. I want your voice in here for lots of different reasons. Outside of the Audre Lorde Project (ALP),[2] just as a healer, as someone who has been shaping the way people who do change work think*

---

1   This conversation took place on April 13, 2017, transcription by ill Weaver.

2   Cara was the executive director of the Audre Lorde Project for five years.

*about being in their bodies, and being in our collective bodies,
for a long time. It feels like, yes, Cara. I literally heard your voice.
I was, like, who do I want to read this audiobook? Cara.[3]*

And then Audre Lorde.

*"Uses of the Erotic" is a seed text for this book. It's the first thing
I read and heard that was like, "Holy shit! You can talk about
that?" Just the fact you could talk about it was my first response.
And it really stuck with me. That metaphor she talks about, the
little golden color pellet inside the margarine, and kneading it,
and feeling like, oh, you've been spread all through with actual
aliveness. You can't go back to suffering. I just thought, oh, that's
actually what we need to be doing. That's what our movements
should be doing.*

*It's such a core text, and I'm interested in how her work has
echoed through time in your work. Before you came even to the
Audre Lorde Project. What are the ways that you feel she's inter-
acted with you?*

Cara. In 1991 when I was twenty-one years old, I met Audre
Lorde. I was one of the organizers on the Audre Lorde Cele-
Conference. We embraced her while she was alive; it was very
intentional, to celebrate her while she was living. And that
was very powerful, right? And then my senior year, which
would have been the following year, I did a series of performances, and one of them (my whole thesis in undergrad)
was "Uses of the Erotic: The Erotic as Power," using political theater and performance to claim body and spirit.[4] And
it was very much infused with that entire essay, "The Uses
of the Erotic," because it was my medicine. Alongside Toni
Cade Bambara, especially *The Salt Eaters*. I would say *Sister
Outsider* and *The Salt Eaters* changed my life.[5] And around

---

3   There will be an audiobook! I hope it will include Cara's voice.
4   See Audre Lorde, "Uses of the Erotic: The Erotic as Power," this volume, p. 27.
5   Toni Cade Bambara, *The Salt Eaters* (New York: Penguin Random
House, 1980); Audre Lorde, *Sister Outsider* (Berkeley: Ten Speed
Press, 1984).

that time I met Toni Cade Bambara and Audre Lorde. I spent a long day in Iowa with Toni Cade Bambara in the airport. And we talked about sex and pleasure! So, going back to Audre Lorde, yes, I became very moved by the relationship to transforming your fear into erotic power. And transforming desire into transformative action.

So we could say on the spectrum of pleasure, yes, I like to get touched, I like to get fucked, but also, what about for my community, for my people? What is pleasurable in finding a place of grace and well-being and transcending oppression? If we're not imagining where we're going, then it will constantly just be pushing back outside from inside of cages, as opposed to imagining what's happening outside of cages. So I feel incredibly indebted to this essay in particular … wow, there are just so many good quotes.

One in particular, "Giving into the fear of feeling and working to capacity is a luxury only the unintentional can afford. And the unintentional are those that do not wish to guide their own destinies."[6] And I wrote, as my live, ripe, twenty-one-year-old self, "Our lives have mapped our destinies for generations." You know, I was writing a conversation with Audre Lorde. I was like, "Here, Audre. This is what I think about what you just said."

But how do we map our destiny and desire? By understanding where we've come from and where we want our generations to go? [Writing] our destinies and desires, that has been my life since the early nineties. I believed, I'm going to live like a writer. I'm going to be a writer. I desire to be, and I am a writer. I desired to say to my family, "I'm going be a writer," even when, in the early nineties, many of us still didn't choose that as a job.

My whole life was filled with desire and destiny. I grew up around jazz musicians, and my mom raised me around theater and the folk festival scene. I also had queer family— three generations of Black queer family. So I was very used to

---

6   See Lorde, "Uses of the Erotic," this volume, p. 27.

a gender spectrum, a cultural reality that was very performative and queer, that was very full of life and desire. I was not devoid of that as a child.

And yet, as a survivor and a bystander of family violence, desire was hard to trust. When I was young, before he was in recovery from violence, my father was—this term is limited—a batterer and caused great harm; my mom was a survivor, and I was a survivor/bystander. So all of my erotic self was wrapped in "how do I associate with pleasure and desire without fear, without losing control, without being harmed?" I really had to walk out of a space that allowed for me to unravel and unpack those things as separate so I could define my sexuality and my erotic self in relationship to something that did not have to be violent, to understand that the desire to be loved and to love your family wasn't always mired with violent pasts but could begin again with new, healing destinies.

And then my work expanded in my twenties. It wasn't just about family violence. This is about structural violence too and about how I relate to myself through desire when I am deeply undesirable, I am expendable, and I am only here for labor or reproduction? And ... then what is my erotic self in that, when you're devoid of being able to define yourself outside of capitalism and white supremacy?

So she touches on all of these things, right? I mean this is a fucking mantra. Because it says, first, how can I be a creator? How can I trust that I am worthy of defining desire and pleasure and liberation as myself or in relationship to other Black lesbians, Black queer women of color, trans and gender-nonconforming folks of color? That reality seemed untouchable when I was coming into my own, until she spoke these words. My truth.

In my late teens, I found the Audre Lordes and the James Baldwins and the Toni Cade Bambaras and the Essex Hemphills and the Marlon Riggses, the Pat Parkers, the Cherríe Moragas, Gloria Anzaldúas, Jewelle Gomezes, and more. All these, they were more than people. They were saints in my reality. Black lesbian leaders like Fran White were my teachers, literally my teachers, who I had the opportunity to learn from, to see them embody power and transformation as my teachers in college. And I was amazingly anointed by the breadth of a canon of Black lesbian feminism that I came into, one that is very much defined by pleasure and power in relationship to our lived experience.

And of course, Barbara Smith lives and breathes this too.

amb. *That's the lineage! It feels kind of like you had been this stream making your way through the boulders and down the mountain, to this very fast-moving river. I can feel that rolling along into this ... Black and Brown brilliance. Decolonizing. Deconstructing.*

Cara. And it felt like they were constellations. We were constellations. I've written several pieces using that analogy of maps and constellations and being cartographers. Harriet Tubman as an architect and a cartographer. Audre Lorde as an architect and a cartographer. And what's that called—when you read the stars? ... an astrologer. Yes, astrologers for life.

So I don't know if that answers your question. I want to say also: when I did performance theater, political theater in the nineties, there wasn't a lot out there. You had, of course, Ntozake Shange's *For Colored Girls*.[7] That changed my fucking life. That changed all little Black girls' lives. Right? Then I met her and realized, oh, you could talk like that too. You could talk like poetry. Who cares if anyone doesn't understand you. Roll with it. I was like, go 'head with your bad self. And I found my place of power and righteousness in language.

And I was very much raised by a lineage of, a generation of, Black women who came from Georgia, North Carolina sharecroppers, and the Black Seminole Nation. They really

---

7   Ntozake Shange, *For Colored Girls Who Consider Suicide When the Rainbow Is Enuf* (New York: Scribner Poetry, 1997).

embodied truth. They were very much my orators and taught me, very much so, how to love myself.

I used to say, "I don't know if I love myself." And one of my aunts put me in front of the mirror at age six and seven, and she said, "You are gonna look at yourself in the mirror and say 'I love myself.' And then you're going to say 'I love Black people.'" And at first I resisted, but then I was like, "OK. Let's do this." And she was committed to that practice every time I saw her. Until it rolled off the tongue and there was no pause and she could say, "OK, go to the mirror, and love yourself." And I would, knowingly, lovingly. You feel me?

amb. *I love that. I literally just told someone to do that today. I told them they need to look at themselves in the mirror and say they love themselves. And do it every day.*

Cara. These are not small things. They changed my life. And in this quote here, from "Uses of the Erotic," Lorde says, "Our erotic knowledge empowers us. Becomes a lens through which we scrutinize all aspects of our existence, forcing us to evaluate those aspects honestly, in terms of their relative meaning within our lives."[8] I based my whole political theatrical process around the question of how to acknowledge erotic power. I did a whole performance around this and the historical oppressive violence against us and the state of Black women.

amb. *Do you have a copy?*

Cara. Yes, I have a copy of it. I'm going send it to you when I unpack these boxes from my move.[9] It's so cool. It's so young and ripe, I should say. My early writing days. Lorraine Hansberry was the narrator. And it traced, oh, you'll appreciate

---

8   See Lorde, "Uses of the Erotic," this volume, p. 27.
9   amb note to self: Make sure you hound Cara until you actually get to see this cool young ripe performance!

this, there's a Black queer woman of mixed ancestry trying to understand her sexuality, gender identity, race and ethnicity in relationship to a world full of violence against Black women. And she has a chorus of Black women very much informed by James Baldwin's play *The Amen Corner.*[10] His character gets visited by a choir in the bathtub while he's in the bathroom. I realized I often felt like I had this choir of Black women in my ear. So at the time, I was also studying international lesbians of color. Very informed by South Asian women of color doing some badass shit in India around sex work. My world was just getting blown apart. But I was like, where is my relationship to my own Blackness? And historically, who are the Black bodies, the Black women bodies, female bodies, that have taken violence, taken on violence, and experience it? And where is their resiliency? And how do you speak to that? And so Lorraine Hansberry was guiding the story for the mixed-race Black girl trying to find herself and listening to a chorus of Black women ancestors who had all been vilified and violated by state violence—starting with the Hottentot Venus all the way up to a Black woman sex worker who had just been murdered in Boston by her john, whose father came out publicly and said she deserved to die because she was a sex worker.

And that was 1991, girl! And I thought, what the fuck? She had been stabbed like fifty-two times by her john. And (her father) basically stood in front of that camera and said she was expendable. And don't pay no mind, she deserved it. So I took it all the way from Hottentot to her story, in relationship to this Black woman trying to find herself. And it was very much about acknowledging and empowering a lens through which we scrutinize all aspects of our lived experience as Black women.

amb. *And so you're moving in this creative mode. You're writing.*

---

10   James Baldwin, *The Amen Corner: A Drama in Three Acts* (New York: Samuel French, 1961).

Cara. On fire.

amb. *A performance artist. And you're waking up into this political sense of wholeness. And your whole self. And then you come into your healing. What's the awakening?*

Cara. I don't know where she is now, but Andrea Hairston [note: amb squealed] was also one of my teachers. She was at Smith College. How do you know her?

amb. *I know her because she writes Black speculative fiction. She wrote a couple of books I thought were amazing. She does this really gorgeous Black and Indigenous love story stuff.*

Cara. Wow. Get the fuck out. Get out. I always wondered where she was. That's amazing. So I was studying with her. And she very much embodied "Uses of the Erotic: The Erotic as Power." She really put us in the practice of knowing our bodies. As part of theatrical performance. How do you explore, as big bodies, small bodies, Black bodies, queer bodies? How do you expand and contract? And take up space, and show pleasure, show fear, show anger?

And then, very much, Rhodessa Jones. I had an inkling of time with her, who very similarly pushed me to my edges.

And Adrienne Kennedy. She's a Black British playwright. And she was really getting popular during the nineties.

And Aishah Rahman. Just incredible Black playwrights and poets. And you could see how they were integrating the spiritual, the spirit, with Black women's narratives. And it felt very healing. To not only lift up the story but to understand that we are surrounded by ancestors and to ask, where is our practice and our connection to holding a generational history of trauma? I didn't have a language for it, but, boy, was I writing it. I was writing about how we unpack, unravel, how we disassociate from ourselves with these incredible histories of colonialist violence and genocide.

And I think that when I came into theater, I walked

through it and came out on the other side, and was like, oh, this is about something else. This is about vibration. This is about how we transform the frequencies we're living inside.

I started doing work in my mid-twenties with Black women who had tumors because I was steeped in reproductive health and justice and it made sense to me: Let us honor what is happening to our bodies, the histories of trauma we are holding in our bodies that block us from desire. I worked with some women with diabetes, or different illnesses, asking that we consider these illnesses as manifestations of oppression and slavery, self-hatred, and attempted genocide. And how do you transform these very dense masses in the body into feeling that you can fly, and you can move, and have different shapes?

I know you know working with shapes in the body.[11] And I started to work with sound. In particular with Black women. And, mind you, I was also very cognizant that we had a lot of folks, in many different cultures, in Asia, in Latin America, using sound. I didn't practice, I didn't have a teacher. I just kind of went with it using my performance to lead me into, oh, vibration is vibration.

Whether or not you're telling the story of the healing of your body, that's release. Whether or not you're literally learning how to make sound with your voice. If you have different abilities and you're not able to do it with your voice, how do you make shape with your body, that repeats pattern, that can transform pattern into a new metamorphosis?

amb. *That's fucking incredible.*

Cara. Yeah. And I did some really good work with different healers along the path. I don't even know all the names, where we all are. Imani Uzuri and I, we started doing sound circles. In the Bay Area in the mid-nineties with women of

---

11   Here, Cara is referencing my work as a healer, somatic teacher, and
      bodyworker.

color. Out in the East Bay, standing at the shoreline of the water doing sound circles and improvisational sound. That was awesome. And that energy work, that collective healing sound work, rooted me and took me into my pathway of thinking about healing and trauma and transformation from oppression and colonization to our collective healing.

amb. *That makes a lot of sense. So then you enter this period of life where healer becomes a more central role. I feel like I met you in that time. And then, how long have you been at the Audre Lorde Project (ALP)?*

Cara. I'm going into my fifth year at ALP. And I'm actually transitioning out. To move to a different role in movement. And I'm returning to movement to do more intensive work on the medical-industrial complex. Because I really feel like that work is critical, and it's still a gap, paying testimonial to the ways our bodies have been experimented on, tested on, and continue to be under surveillance and policed in the medical-industrial complex.

amb. *Where does "Uses of the Erotic" come into the work you do? How do you see that showing up in current movement work?*

Cara. We're inside of a new political regime, that's what I like to call it. And understanding that, it's not that things were all perfect. In the constellation of stars, we were already resisting. And I think we were winning, and we became more threatening because we were winning. And there was a lot still happening in the past administration that was challenging as well.

So we recently just celebrated ALP's twentieth anniversary. There we talked about the erotic as a resource within each of us that lies in a deeply spiritual plane. How is it firmly rooted, the erotic as power, and an unexpressed or unrecognized feeling? How do we transcend the oppression? Every oppression must correct or distort those very sources of power; for us, this is oppression of the erotic as a considered source of power. How do we love ourselves in liberation?

That's what we took from Audre Lorde's words: how do we live, love, suck, fuck, and liberate ourselves? How come we're not talking about sex or desire anymore in relationship to liberation? And Audre Lorde was all about it, in a positive, consensual, erotic, fully embodied way. With cancer, without cancer, with physical disability, with different ways of living your life. And we thought, oh shit, where is this in the vision of how are we naming self-love, collective love, and desire and pleasure, as consensual, as transformative? How does this become our liberatory practice?

We brought poets and burlesque performers and musicians together. And we did a ring-shout that Adaku Utah led at the beginning, because I said, "Girl, can we have a ring-shout?"[12] Adaku looked at some recordings, and we did a fucking ring-shout. So it's, like, how do we call ourselves in and call each other to see ourselves and bring testimony to each other? And there was a hot erotic photo booth. I was fascinated by how long it took us to get to the erotic. To get to a level of comfort and sexy when folks let it all hang out … much later into the night. I was like, oh, it probably needed more time. It needed to get a little bit later into the evening.

amb. *Those low lights …*

Cara. We had a fabulous photographer, who was dressed in leather and wearing leather suspenders, with toys and things for us to unravel with. He brought pleasure. Anyway, I just think the intention was there, and I thought, what if we had done this event into the wee hours of the morning? Who knows what would have come undone?

But the burlesque dancers were off the chain. And we had fabulous gifts that we gave—dildos, vibrators, harnesses—as

---

12   Adaku Utah is the founder and a collective member of Harriet's Apothecary.

the raffle. Alongside archival pieces from Audre Lorde's collection, donated by her daughter. And what was there? The conference program for the Audre Lorde Cele-Conference. Full circle. And prints of poems that she had on her wall. Gifts given to her. Cloths from Barbados. Just everything? To have that integrated with the hot burlesque and to understand all of these things and to name Audre Lorde inside of "what is the political positioning in twenty years, to fight for freedom?"—despite all odds that still say we're expendable, cannot be loved, cannot be desired, cannot be powerful. We flipped that shit on its ass. We must continue to do that. And we celebrated that.

And to me, the Audre Lorde Project is very much centering wellness and safety. And I think it is the same question to keep asking ourselves: how do we center creation and desire as integral to liberation? That is a question we're going to have to keep asking ourselves. Because this world begs of us to be, to move out of scarcity, move out of fear, move out of crisis, and not imagine anything abundant or transformed, not to move out of desiring one another and being desired as powerful, fully living beings.

amb. *Yes. There's this concept of suffering central to so many of us as whatever, activists, organizers, anyone trying to change the world ... so much of how we get pulled into community and kept in community is a solidarity built around our suffering ... which is not liberatory. That's just not it. It's not us. The suffering is not what we're called to attend to. That's happening all the time. What does it mean to transcend it and make it so that: I can't settle for this? This has nothing to do with me. This doesn't have anything to do with us. I think about that a lot: what does it take to actually shift the feel of organizing? The way we feel our existence? We're not meant to suffer alone. We're meant to experience pleasure and togetherness.*

So I just wanted to ask you, how are we present in our collective bodies? How are we present and excited and letting the erotic come open in us today? Especially when it makes sense to respond with a lot of fear right now, and yet the call of the erotic, of the yes, is still clarion. It's still so available. Even now. Even as the suffering gets bigger. I keep saying, I don't think things are getting worse, I think they're getting uncovered. This is the unveiling, and at the end of the unveiling, we have nakedness. And that nakedness calls for new desire. So how do we perceive what this is, what we are as humans right now? And how can we really feel the love for what we are now? I guess the main question inside all of that, when you think about setting down suffering work, or awakening something that is more compelling than suffering, where do you see that happening in your world and work today?

Cara. I know that I have been talking a lot about fascism and dictatorships and that all of these things existed before Trump, during Trump, after Trump, so how are we pushed to our edges to imagine creation? How is desire about full-on creation?

Despite what I think is an accelerated pace. Like you said, it's uncovering, it's being revealed, it was always right there at the surface. I think it's a little more accelerated too because some of these right-wing people are getting righteous. They're like, I've been waiting to just show you my real colonizer self.[13]

But what I've been most moved by, especially working at an intergenerational political organizing center in New York City, is a newer generation of organizers and an older generation of organizers coming together and saying, "What are we going to build? What are we going to create?" And that to me is the erotic as power. That is understanding that we are collectively capable of calling on ancestral traditions for our resilience and also building some new shit. Knowing that we have made mistakes, what we have learned from them, how do we transform sexual violence, how do we transform state violence, how do we transform criminal violence? And no,

---

13   When Cara said this, I snapped and heard the snaps of a million ancestors, who also at that moment said, "Oh, snap!"

wait, let's take a moment to reflect, to release what we want to release and understand that we can choose what we desire. And we could choose what we want to build. And it doesn't have to come from this place of scarcity and fear. And I've seen it. I've seen it in the imagination and creation of our organizing. Of our political work. Of putting our bodies on the line against fascism, our queer bodies, trans, lesbian, gay, bi, two-spirit bodies. I feel inspired.

amb. *I do too. And having a different level of conversation about risk. I don't think that she even uses the word "risk." But Audre Lorde talks about how we are providing energy for change. And considering the erotic as a source of power and information. Like this is, we are, constantly communicating what is possible. And people are also identifying the level of risk they are willing to take. It does feel different to me, a different kind of measurement or temperature check, or assessment of who can be up front, who's in the back, who's in the middle, who's on the side. And that can transform. You can alternate. You can shift roles. You don't have to be the same person, in the same line, every time. We can metamorphosize as we're doing this. This feels very powerful to me. This is what I'm witnessing. I'm not saying it hasn't happened before. But it's happening now. This is a moment.*

The thing that I've been loving is that I'm sure this has happened before. But the difference is, I didn't see it. So what this looks and feels like, all these narratives of these charismatic leaders and these moments, this shit is so complicated. I am realizing it must have been complicated in earlier movements too. I bet those people were beefing. Now I'm starting to look back at history and be like, those motherfuckers were not getting along. Cause it is so hard to find people who actually get along, even if the work is in conversation. What I'm seeing is people who want to fracture and separate.

And, fortunately, there are so many people who are like, no. We have to find our way to each other—to me that's a felt finding. Like maybe our words are not right, but deeper than that, I can feel that your spirit is trying to be on this right path. And we're gonna figure out a way to get there. And we have to have a broader sense of our species. Cause we are species. On a species level, I can feel there's not a story for our survival in the cards and in ourselves right now. We need to generate that. Desire and pleasure are two ways that we assert that there's something worth living for. And the more we remind ourselves of that together, the more we generate together. How do we move from a dying body to a reproductive body?

Cara. I used the word "risk," but now I'm realizing it's really levels of intimacy that we're able to explore with each other consensually. Because what I do see is people jumping into movement in this moment, in this heightened moment, and they want everything. They want all the energy, all the love, all the liberation. And I'm like, oh, this takes time. This is relationship building. And this is building trust. And consensually understanding how to be moved and inspired by each other without sometimes assuming that energy has to be sexual. That maybe that's just an erotic exchange that's actually about sharing knowledge, memory, power, and that to me is understanding levels of intimacy in relationship to liberation.

amb. *It's important to say, we don't all have to love or want each other. Your clear "no" makes the way for your "yes." Being able to say what we don't want allows us to clear the path.*

And we need more tolerance. If you want to break through to the multi-orgasmic level, you have to be willing to kind of push through something that feels like discomfort the first few times. You're like, "Can I get there?" And you're like "yes, I can." It's just like, if you do, then something else is going to become possible.

And can I let people into where my visioning happens? Can we be intimate at the level of our longings? What as a society can we truly long for? Can I truly say out loud? So yes, all of that.

Cara. And before we close, I do want to say that my work with Southerners on New Ground really was transformative in how we moved work.[14] I'm talking like ten years ago or eight years ago. I was living in the South for seventeen years. Our organizing was moved by the questions: How do we move toward liberation with our longing and desire? And what do we long for? And these questions were a beautiful realization that "what do we long for?" to me holds "what do we remember? What can we imagine? What do we desire?" And that's a very different language from "protect and defend," which is critical too, but we're on a spectrum of understanding, our heart must be in this. Our spirit must be in this. Our memory is in this. Our collective bodies and desires must be in this. And all of that is integral to our transformation.

amb. *Fuck yes. Thank you for taking this time.*

Cara. Thank you so much. Keep doing what you do. Peace.

---

14 Southerners on New Ground (SONG) is a regional queer liberation organization made up of people of color, immigrants, undocumented people, people with disabilities, working-class and rural and small town LGBTQ people in the South.

A SPOILERIFIC GUSH ON HOW OCTAVIA BUTLER TURNS ME ON

I once sat on Octavia Butler's face.

It was stitched onto a pillow in a tent in Dubai, and we were in public, but I still flush at the sheer longing I felt in that moment.

I met her once and saw her smile. Sometimes I think about how tall she was, her broad shoulders, that jaw, the way her cheeks folded into her smile, those focused skeptical eyes. The lack of social niceties, that laugh.

Octavia Butler was crushable.

I truly think that we could have had a very dynamic sexual connection if I had been bold enough to flirt with her when I met her. I don't know her sexuality (although there are others who have argued every position vehemently with me), but I know that Octavia Butler had a beautifully freaky mind and that she, like me, used masturbation to move through her creative blocks.

Age, race, gender, species, time—nothing familiar could limit or otherwise dictate the kind of intimacy in which her characters could engage. Reading her work, which was offered up to me as dystopian writing, absolutely terrified me. But it also opened my young mind to a realm of aliveness and sexual adventure that I am still pursuing.

I have a hypothesis that Octavia believed pleasure to be one of the most important strategies and activities for long-term survival. And that she knew how complicated it was to let pleasure be, to let it lead us. I even think she understood that the moral essence of the species was unveiled in these complications around what we desire and how we follow it or deny it.

There are two levels at which I need to examine the sensual realm of Octavia Butler. On one level are the actual sexy encounters she wrote, to examine them with focus and rigid...rigor. At the same time, I'm interested in the time that sex, pleasure, and relationship play in each of her projections of human systems in the future.

Let's examine Octavia's work:

Interspecies sex. Some might call it bestiality, but that's only if you assume aliens are beasts. Octavia had *Wild Seed's* shapeshifting Anyanwu in a full-out love affair with a dolphin, as a dolphin! Anyanwu also spent time as a shark, eagle, leopard, and wolf.[1] And then when we meet the Oankali in Butler's Xenogenesis series, all mating has to happen through their third gender ooloi, who have big elephant-trunk-like "sensory tentacles." In the Patternist series, the Clayarks are a hybrid species with animalistic qualities that some humans still desire and mate with.

Threesomes. The only way to get down with the aforementioned Oankali! It's gonna be you, me, and our ooloi friend here.

Shapeshifting/Body Snatching/Gender Switching Sex. Yeah, so Octavia taught me that if you can shapeshift into any

---

1   Octavia Butler, *Wild Seed* (New York: Warner Books, 2001).

form, including other sexes, and your boo-nemy can snatch whatever bodies are out there, then y'all can experience some gender-switching sex.

Male bodies in receptive mode. In the title story of the *Bloodchild* short story collection, male bodies are impregnated and then completely reliant on their alien masters to remove the baby because there is no other way for it to leave the body.[2] In a different way, in both the Lilith's Brood and Xenogenesis series, men are part of a sexual encounter in which they play the same role as women—they are pleasured while something is extracted from their bodies, sperm or egg.

Old/young affairs. In *Parable of the Sower*, Olamina is not yet twenty when she meets and falls into a sexual and romantic relationship with Bankole, who is in his sixties.[3] The way the relationship is written, what matters is the world they are facing together, passion, and enough of a shared worldview to move forward. I think Octavia was saying something about how apocalypse ages and equalizes us, but this gap, when I consider it in my own life, still gives me pause. Then there's Shori, in *Fledgling*, who is an ancient being in a body that looks like a young girl, with lovers of all ages and backgrounds.[4] Octavia enjoyed fucking with the technicalities!

Incest. In the Patternist series, ancient body snatcher Doro is trying to generate an evolved species, in part by breeding himself with his own gifted offspring. One of his children asks if she should call him Daddy, and he advises her not to, as it will make things difficult later. Eek! And sure enough, before the end of the second book in the series, he has bred with her. (I'd say this contributes mightily to the incredible rage and righteousness at the ending of the book.) Doro

2   Octavia Butler, *Bloodchild* (New York: Seven Stories Press, 1996).
3   Octavia Butler, *Parable of the Sower* (New York: Four Walls Eight Windows Press, 1993).
4   Octavia Butler, *Fledgling* (New York: Seven Stories Press, 2005).

operates outside of time, leaping from body to body, so while the bodies that copulate are not related, Doro is nevertheless sleeping with, and forcing the interbreeding of, his offspring.

Symbiotic sexual experiences and communities. Octavia's young vampire Shori pleases those who share their blood with her, and her lovers share a kind of compersion as a circle of people in relationship with her.[5] In the Patternist series, Mary is the heart of the First Family, a first group of humans linked telepathically, many of whom have intimate relations. In the *Parables* the survivors that live longest are the ones that pair up as lovers.[6] In *Clay's Ark*, the hybrids quickly form into a pack, to survive.[7] And Xenogenesis is all about family structures created through relationship and multi-adult procreation.

Before moving on, I want to say that when I have gone back and reread her books, I see that she is often very complex, not presenting these ideas as purely sensual or easy. I have to say that because a lot of it still lodged in my mind as sensual, as a longing, as a turn on. I wanted to move in the body of a dolphin and feel the tentacular love of the Ooloi. I wanted to find a vampire who would make me feel good and be super healthy in exchange for a little taste of me.

And I think so many of us would be nourished by the sort of symbiotic communities that Octavia envisioned, where connection wasn't necessarily based on visual attraction but other kinds of longing and need. Where being attracted to someone wasn't the first step of a path toward a singular ownership but could be a move into community and a future. Where interdependence was a given and there was no shame in seeking to learn the right ways to enter and stay in community. And where the truth could be perceived by the physical or telepathic connection, so instead of wasting time on projecting and lying to each other, we would spend our time

5   Butler, *Fledgling*.
6   Butler, *Parable of the Sower*.
7   Octavia Butler, *Clay's Ark* (New York: St. Martin's Press, 1984).

lifting each other up, generating futures based on our truest selves, truest needs.

Octavia Butler will always be my lover outside of time, a sensual mind of my mind. I am grateful for all the seeds she cast into my young erotic mind and will explore what has burst forth from them with rigor and curiosity in these pages.

LOVE AS POLITICAL RESISTANCE

Audre Lorde taught us that caring for ourselves is "not self-indulgence, it is self-preservation, and that is an act of political warfare."[1] And although we know how to meme and tweet those words, living into them is harder. We have a deeper socialization to overcome, one that tells us that most of us don't matter—our health, our votes, our work, our safety, our families, our lives don't matter—not as much as those of white men. We need to learn how to practice love such that care—for ourselves and others—is understood as political resistance and cultivating resilience.

We don't learn to love in a linear path, from self to family to friends to spouse, as we might have been taught. We learn to love by loving. We practice with each other, on ourselves, in all kinds of relationships.

And right now we need to be in rigorous practice, because we can no longer afford to love people the way we've been loving them.

---

1   Essay reprinted from adrienne maree brown, "Love as Political Resistance: Lessons from Audre Lorde and Octavia Butler," February 14, 2017, *Bitch Media* (blog), https://www.bitchmedia.org/article/love-time-political-resistance/transform-valentines-day-lessons-audre-lorde-and-octavia. Quote is from Audre Lorde, *A Burst of Light and Other Essays* (Ithaca, NY: Firebrand, 1988), 130.

Who have we been loving?
- the people who cross our physical or virtual paths, spark the flame of our interest, earn our devotion and respect and protection
- our own family, because blood
- people we are committed to but don't like anymore

How have we been loving?
- defining love by obligation
- celebrating love on externally marked holidays
- keeping the realities of love behind closed doors
- framing love as a fairy tale on social media
- framing love as a product we give each other
- framing love as a limited resource that gets swallowed and used up, tied in plastic when we're done and piled up out of sight
- prioritizing romantic love over self, comrade, and friend love

This kind of love is not sufficient, even if it is the greatest love of our lives. The kind of love that we will be forced to celebrate or escape on Valentine's Day is too small.

We're all going to die if we keep loving this way, die from isolation, loneliness, depression, abandoning each other to oppression, from lack of touch, from forgetting we are precious. We can no longer love as a secret or a presentation, as something we prioritize, hoard for the people we know. Prioritizing ourselves in love is political strategy, is survival.

From religious spaces to school to television shows to courts of law, we are socialized to seek and perpetuate private, even corporate, love. Your love is for one person, forever. You celebrate it with dying flowers and diamonds. The largest celebration of your life is committing to that person. Your family and friends celebrate you with dishes and a juicer. You need an income to love. If something doesn't work out with your love, you pay a lot of money to divide your lives, generally not telling people much unless it's a soap opera dramatic ending. This way of approaching love strangles all the good out of it.

What we need right now is a radical, global love that grows from deep within us to encompass all life.

No big deal.

To help make this a true day of love, here is brief radical love manifesto.

Radical Honesty

We begin learning to lie in intimate relationships at a very early age. Lie about the food your mother made, to avoid punishment, as you swallow your tears, about loving this Valentine's Day gift, about the love you want and how you feel. Most of this is taught as heteropatriarchy 101: men love one way, women another, and we have to lie to impress and catch each other. Women are still taught too often to be submissive, diminutive, obedient, and later nagging and caregiving—not to be peers, emotionally complex powerhouses, loving other women and trans bodies. These mistruths in gender norms are self-perpetuating, affirmed by magazines and movies, girded at family dinner tables.

We also learn that love is a limited resource and that the love we want and need is too much, that we are too much. We learn to shrink, to lie about the whole love we need, settling with not quite good enough in order to not be alone.

We have to engage in an intentional practice of honesty to counter this socialization. We need radical honesty—learning to speak from our root systems about how we feel and what we want. Speak our needs and listen to others' needs. To say, "I need to hear that you miss me." "When you're high all the time it's hard for me to feel your presence." "I lied." "The way you talked to that man made me feel unseen." "Your jealousy makes me feel like an object and not a partner." The result of this kind of speech is that our lives begin to align with our longings, and our lives become a building block for authentic community and ultimately a society that is built around true need and real people, not fake news and bullshit norms.

Healing

Trauma is the common experience of most humans on this planet. Love too often perpetuates trauma, repeating the patterns of intimacy and pain so many of us experienced growing up in racist and/or hetero-patriarchal environments. Shame might be the only thing more prevalent, which leads to trauma being hidden, silenced, or relegated to a certain body of people. If we can't carry our trauma and act normal, if we have a breakdown or lose our jobs/homes/children, there is something wrong with us. What we need is a culture where the common experience of trauma leads to a normalization of healing. Being able to say: I have good reasons to be scared of the dark, of raised voices, of being swallowed up by love, of being alone. And being able to offer each other: "I know a healer for you." "I'll hold your hand in the dark." "Let's begin a meditation practice." "Perhaps talk therapy is not enough." We should celebrate love in our community as a measure of healing. The expectation should be: I know we are all in need of healing, so how are we doing our healing work?

Learn How to Change

Most of us resist changes we didn't spark. We feel victimized, so we try to hold tight to whatever we figure out as a way to survive. We spend too much time watching change happen with our jaws dropped, writing "what the fuck?" over and over. It is time to learn Octavia Butler's lessons—both that "the only lasting truth is Change" and that we can, and must, "shape change."[2] So we need to observe how we respond to change—does it excite us so much that we struggle with stability? Or do we ignore changes until it's too late? Or fight

---

2   Butler, *Parable of the Sower*, 3.

changes that are bigger than us? It takes time and assistance to feel into and find the most strategic adaptation.

Build Communities of Care

Shift from individual transactions for self-care to collective transformation. Be in community with healers in our lives. Healers, we must make sure our gifts are available and accessible to those growing and changing our communities. Be in family with each other—offer the love and care we can, receive the love and care we need. Share your car or meals with a healer in exchange for reiki sessions. Facilitate a healing group in exchange for massages. Clean a healer's home as barter for a ritual to move through grief. Pay healing forward—buy sessions for friends. Let our lives be a practice ground where we're learning to generate the abundance of love and care we, as a species, are longing for.

This Valentine's Day, commit to developing an unflappable devotion to yourself as part of an abundant, loving whole. Make a commitment with five people to be more honest with each other, heal together, change together, and become a community of care that can grow to hold us all.

THE SWEETNESS OF SALT

Toni Cade Bambara and the Practice of Pleasure (in Five Tributes)

Alexis Pauline Gumbs

This essay of love is exactly what I expected from magical sister-doula-witch teacher Alexis Pauline Gumbs. Alexis is one of the most consistent yeses I know, her life full of rest, love, beauty and travel. She is a poet and a sower and a scholar of many things, centering around Black feminism. She has done an incredible amount of archival work on Toni Cade Bambara, the author of The Salt Eaters, *the one to tell us writing was a tool for the revolution, that our task was to make revolution irresistible.[1] Bambara is a main stream in the lineage of pleasure activism, not just because of what she put on the page and into words, but also because of the ways that she wove community, the way she supported other writers and organizers, the way she engaged healing*

---

1   Bambara, *The Salt Eaters.*

work. I get chills when I read what Bambara was dreaming and understanding, how deeply we are in the worn groove of her legacy. Alexis has pulled Bambara into the present with this essay.

Alexis's note: I have read and written about the work of Toni Cade Bambara for decades. I have sifted through her archival papers at Spelman College (which, by the way, consist of ideas written on napkins, candy wrappers, coupons, and receipts). But when I thought about what I knew about Toni Cade Bambara and pleasure, I realized I knew it best through my own lived experience, my own incredible fortune of having been loved, mentored, and taught by five Black women who create joy and clarity in the tradition of Toni Cade Bambara. So this offering is gratitude and celebration for the lessons of Toni Cade Bambara, not through her texts but through my personal witness of the impact of her self-identified students, loved ones, mentees, and collaborators: scholar Farah Jasmine Griffin, filmmaker and activist Aishah Shahidah Simmons, artist and abolitionist Kai Lumumba Barrow, healer and organizer Cara Page, and editor and intellectual activist Cheryll Y. Greene.

With love. Alexis.

The Gift
for Farah Jasmine Griffin

Those of us that have been taught by Farah Griffin have felt cherished. Not precious. Not perfect. Not without growing to do. But necessary. And dreamt of. And held.

And when she helps us. When she reads our work. When she writes us recommendations. When we turn back to thank her, she says: "Oh, it's my pleasure." And we believe her. Farah Griffin is grace. Gifted from the practiced mouths and lungs, the practiced muscles and lines of Black women who believed in freedom diligently enough to call out for it. Farah Jasmine Griffin writes about Black women, in relation, connected to generations of other Black women, connected to multi-gendered communities of possibility. Connected to her own self in a way that has space for critique but is never expendable.

For Toni Cade Bambara, Farah Jasmine Griffin is a daughter of Philadelphia, one of the several Black cities in which Bambara lived and loved. In the tradition of Toni Cade Bambara, Farah Griffin is a daydreamer and nightdreamer of Harlem. A celebrant, curator, and critical participant in the Black culture of sound, spirit, and word happening in Harlem now, documenting a legacy of generations. For Toni Cade Bambara, Farah Griffin is a disciple willing to follow her not only to Cuba but also to the dangerous and hopeful places of Black girl possibility, perspective, and precarity.

For me, Farah Jasmine Griffin is an intellectual mother. A teacher who let me take her graduate class when I was still a teenager. An example of how to be intentionally undisciplined and accountable to legacy at the same time. A person who I have looked to over and over again in order to see myself enough to be myself in a difficult moment. When I didn't know what to major in. Or where to go to graduate school. Or how to form words after my father died. Farah is the person who I drove across multiple states, accumulating multiple speeding tickets to see after I defended my dissertation and after she said, in front of a room of Black feminist scholars, "this is my first intellectual daughter."

Farah Griffin started reading Toni Cade Bambara's work as a girl-child. She often tells the story of how she was drawn to the image of the beautiful Black woman on the cover of Bambara's groundbreaking 1970 anthology *The Black Woman*, not only Black, but dark, with an afro, with her mouth shaped like she had something to say.[2] She asked her father to buy it for her, and he agreed. If she would memorize a poem from the book and present it to the family. So in a way, Farah Griffin's chosen relationship to the legacy of Toni

---

2   Toni Cade Bambara, *The Black Woman* (New York: New American Library, 1970).

Cade Bambara was a gift from her father. An opportunity to feel affirmed in her skin, a challenge to embody generations of brilliance, at home. It was not too long after this gift that Farah experienced a major loss. Her father died, while she was still a girl-child, twelve years old. And he died in a way that could have been prevented if we had the society we deserve. The police, first responders, projected their fear of Black men onto him and responded to his health emergency as if he was a threat instead of a person in dire need of medical help. And their racism, their judgment, their ineptitude cost him his life. Cost Farah and her family so much it can never be repaid.

And so Farah continued to study Toni Cade Bambara, not only because Bambara was a warrior for the world we deserve, a critic of the violence of the state, a stand for stories beyond the story racism reproduces, but also because as she has continued to write and think about and teach Bambara's work, she has extended her father's gift into her adulthood and ours, the lives and knowing of all her students. She actualizes what the police could not understand, that her father was a necessary teacher to generations, a life with the right to continue.

And as Farah Griffin reads and rereads, teaches and writes about and is taught by Toni Cade Bambara's work and her focus, in her short fiction on the perspective of Black girl-children, she also protects and celebrates her girl-child self. The self that state violence failed to take away. The person she was when she could still ask her father for a simple gift, a beautiful book. When she could still give her father a poem recitation and watch him smile and know he was proud, in a different way than she still now knows he is proud. Farah, through her following of Toni Cade Bambara, through her Instagram postings of dancing children and laughing babies, through her conferences that feature Black girls jumping double-dutch at art openings in Harlem, offers a model of protecting the Black girls that are ourselves, at any age. After everything that would attempt to take the joy and possibility we represent away from us.

And I think about this now, after the loss of my own father, who was a casualty of state policy in a different way. My father too could still be alive if not for the predictable racism of the medical-industrial complex and the systems that have left so many people without access to health insurance for decades. At this moment when my spirit feels fractured. When I am quiet I can hear myself at different ages calling out to my father, demanding his presence, refusing his absence. And I think about all the mortal knowing, the defining "afters" that shape the lives of Black girls and women. I think of the divided histories in my body. The increased difficulty of my idealism and pluck after abuse, after sexual assault, after witnessing the preventable deaths of Black people over and over again. After my father.

And I think about Farah and how she smiles, not a forced smile of polite survival but a sincere smile of joy in the moment. How she listens to jazz music in a way that allows her to find new parts of herself to grow into. How she keeps an image of a Black girl above her desk. How as a teacher, and therefore perpetual student, she honors the part of each of us that is learning, that is young and possible, that is braver than it makes sense to be, incongruently joyful in a world that targets us. The part of each of us that could embody a poem, draw out a smile, be held. You know. The gift.

Sister Is a Verb
for Aishah Shahidah Simmons

Aishah Simmons is a warrior saving her own life and bringing us all along. Aishah shares her story to break silences and make pathways to healing for multitudes. The living and the not-yet-living. The already gone ancestors who are still healing through us. And what gives Aishah's survival story so much power, or what gives Aishah so much power in relationship to her story, is that she takes the rigorous time to take a step back from her story, months of silence in order to distinguish between chosen and imposed silences, between defensive and strategic storytelling.

For Toni Cade Bambara, Aishah Shahidah Simmons is a devoted initiate. A practitioner of the intervening life-saving practice of storytelling in film and journalism that Bambara taught with her life and courses at the Scribe Video Center in Aishah's Philadelphia home. Aishah's consistent acts of radical storytelling in multiple mediums not only honor Bambara's truthteller legacy, they also honor the communities Bambara loved and the characters in her own stories. For Aishah, Toni Cade Bambara was and is infinite possibility. She was the teacher that gave Aishah permission to explore the depth of herself in her early short films (including *Breaking Silence*, an engagement with Audre Lorde's work that was also an important part of Aishah's coming out process as a person and an artist).

She was the mentor that allowed Aishah to learn to mother herself.

For me, Aishah is a cherished sister-comrade. But before that, she had already saved my life. When Aishah brought her film-in-process *NO! The Rape Documentary* to my school in 2002, I was working at the rape-crisis center and also working very hard to survive my own silence about being sexually assaulted at my school. Aishah's film, and the voices of the women organizers, scholars, poets, artists, and dancers who spoke through the film, allowed me to hear what I was not yet ready to say to myself. That I had survived. That the violence I experienced was real. That the silence I was experiencing even at that moment was a silence that other people had moved through. That though I was there at the intersection of multiple harms, shocked and bruised, I was not alone.

When Aishah decided to lend her finished world-renowned film *NO!* as a primary awareness-raising tool to UBUNTU, a women of color/survivor-led coalition to end sexual violence that I co-founded in Durham, North Carolina, in the wake of the Duke lacrosse rape scandal, authorizing multiple targeted screenings in our community, she became a sister. (In fact, I remember that one of our first one-on-one conversations in the back of someone's car on the way to an event was about how brilliant Farah Griffin is.) And it was Aishah who taught me what Toni Cade Bambara taught her: that "sister" is a verb.

The sistering technologies that Aishah has taught me can't be numbered here. But this is what I know: Sistering requires food. It requires specific intentional foods that support our spirits. Sistering meals can also last many hours. In New York, Durham, Greensboro, and Philadelphia I have sat in restaurants and at home with Aishah for so many hours that multiple mealtimes have passed. Sistering seeks speaking. Even when it is many months between our conversations, Aishah has taught me not to wait until our work brings us to the same city coincidentally but to intentionally make a phone date, even if we are sitting and eating in different rooms. Sistering begets more sisters and mothers, and fathers and brothers. The chosen and given families of sisters in practice become family across and through the sistering. My father has written praise poems in honor of Aishah's work, Aishah's father has collaborated on hosting me in Philadelphia and came to listen to me speak about Audre Lorde and Daughter Dreams when Aishah invited me to Temple University.

My relationship with Aishah has allowed me to clarify other relationships in my life. What is sistering? When is it happening? What is the freedom and accountability that accrues when "sister" is not just a static identity that you have but is something that you do or don't do, with consequences. What happens when I apply that to all of my relationships? What happens if we replace the roles patriarchy has scripted us into with actions guided by what we want to create instead?

In her essay "On the Issue of Roles," Toni Cade explains that if we want to have a revolution, we have to craft revolutionary relationships, in action, not simply in rhetoric.[3] She explains that a revolution cannot be created by conforming to existing roles in relationships already defined by the systems we want to overthrow. We have to practice creating new relationships. Aishah has taught me the joy of that practice

---

3   See "On the Issue of Roles" in Bambara, *The Black Woman*, 101–10.

and how the possibilities of our living shift directly in relationship to the rigor of our loving. Love the people. Love ourselves. Love each other. Love the possible into being.

Is Working
for Kai Lumumba Barrow

Kai Lumumba Barrow is movement. As far as I can tell, movement without rest. Which may not be what Ella Baker meant, but from all archival evidence it is what Ella Baker did. I am one of the people who tells Kai Barrow to rest. The implications of the art, activist grant cycle do not tell her to do that. Even when she sleeps, Kai is listening. Maybe Kai is our movement, our whole fragmented Black abolitionist nomadic futurist Black feminist movement. Like if earth and flesh made an installation of what it looked like, using one person's body, life on earth. Our movement aware and urgent, creative and critical and never the same and always the same and beyond understanding.

For Toni Cade Bambara, Kai was a student. An Atlanta experiment who rejected the respectability of Spelman but stayed, like Toni Cade, adjacent, compelled by the ideas of the people who would orbit the Atlanta University Center, the Institute of the Black World, Seven Stages Theater, and more. Kai was a found sculpture media-mixing memory. Remembering Toni Cade Bambara's practice of just bringing people with her to show up for women surviving abuse in Black creative community, turning. Kai remembers being at Toni Cade Bambara's Atlanta home one night and being recruited into a simple and brave intervention to come to the aid of a woman in their community. Kai turned "Let's go get her" into the bones of a Harm Free Zone framework.

For me, Kai is proof. That someone with big hair and marker ink all over her hands, paint painting her clothes, can live more than one consecutive life in one body. For me, Kai is a material mentor in the principle of revolutionary transformation in practice. Proof that change is actually change.

Unafraid of what fire does to oil, like all the other women who turn the fried chicken or banana fritters over with their fingers. Legacies of women who have been shaped and strengthened by burn. Recently, after eleven years of knowing me, Kai told me out of the window of her car that I was aging beautifully. And all I could think was, you would know.

In 2006, when we listed what we wanted as women of color survivors in response to a nationally talked-about rape case that happened blocks away, Kai was the person who said, "I want an organization." And before that, Kai was the person who invited us into her living room to have that conversation in the first place. That was the first day I met her. That organization became UBUNTU. Was she wearing overalls that day? Or just usually ever after? I didn't know, while we wrote on butcher paper in her living room, that decades earlier Kai had sat in Toni Cade Bambara's living room with brown paper from the actual butcher practicing visioning, the visual and the visceral.

As UBUNTU organized the Day of Truthtelling, Kai was the person who said that the flyers should be neon pink. Not those pastel colors from Kinko's. The T-shirts should at least be available in one baby-tee variation. The protest route should be danceable in heels. Because of Kai, at the same moment I learned to lean into my survivorship, my worst moments and scariest selves as a source of strength and leadership in community, I also learned a femme audacity of warrior adornment and creative insistence. Let's call it: you will not move through this room and not know there is a Black femme in here who loves herself at least as diligently as oppression denies her. You will not have to guess. You will not *not* see her. She is not hiding from herself.

Maybe that's as much of a reason as the other reasons people began to confuse the two of us with each other, despite decades of difference in age and a noticeable variance in complexion. In the most vulnerable places of my growth, while I was clearing out internalized oppression, I was replacing it with internalized Kai.

Kai curated our Day of Truthtelling march in a way that calibrated the need for silent reflection and mourning, with the need for poetry, with the need for dancing to Destiny's Child's "Survivor," and the need for shouting and call-and response in a way that I mimic daily in my meditation, po-em-writing, dancing, mantra-chanting practice of loving this survivor, or as Kai would say, "Me, myself, personally."

In the foreword to *This Bridge Called My Back*, Toni Cade Bambara said "the most effective way to do it is to do it."[4] Kai finds pleasure in the papercuts of creating binder after binder, resource after resource, curriculum after cur-riculum, possible project after possible project for a move-ment that sometimes moves too quick to give much back. So the pleasure in the making has to be enough. Kai finds laughter in the incisive analysis of the worst, most pervasive monsters killing us. Kai stays up all night, so many nights, making things that just weren't there the day before, visible or imaginable. She has this frenetic relationship to time and a cigarette-assisted alertness, like Toni Cade before her, that has taught me ... not to smoke or stay awake but to under-stand that the possibility of this moment, the moment with a mess of sugar and beignets, the moment laughing on the porch swing, the moment looking for moss to borrow from the trees and wondering about why exactly the trees in the park in New Orleans have cement filling their openings, the moment disagreeing about the movie that might be brilliant or just torture, the moment one of us is recording one of us painting and talking about mothering, the moment sitting on the futon with the books under and behind it and next to it on both sides and with the succulent plants creeping close when I'm asking about Toni Cade Bambara, what ex-actly do you remember, and Kai remembers who she herself was at the time. Which is different than who she is now. And she loves that former self and this self with the same

---

4   Toni Cade Bambara, foreword to *This Bridge Called My Back*, edited by Cherríe Moraga and Gloria Anzaldúa, 2nd ed. (New York: Kitchen Table: Women of Color Press, 1983), v.

awake ferocity. Meaning whatever she learned from Toni Cade worked, is working.

Dance until You Laugh until You Sing
for Cara Page

Cara Page has a laugh like a river that connects to an ocean that never ends. She did a lot to nurture that laugh, and I don't know half of it. When she speaks her vision, she lowers her tone so the people in the ground and underwater can get in and harmonize. When she points her finger, the space crackles. Have you seen it happen?

For Toni Cade Bambara, Cara Page was a student. An initiate? A person who would remember to speak her name. A person who would diligently tend the fire of the angers Toni Cade held about the fires that indeed did happen. Like the bombing of the MOVE organization on Osage Avenue, for example. For Toni Cade Bambara, Cara Page is an altar. She might arrive anytime, knowing that the message is safe. All that water. All that earth. All that intentionally breathed air. In Cara Page, Toni Cade is still on fire for freedom, still moving, burning up.

For me, Cara Page is a chosen older sister a half-step up. Bridge to the elders I will never meet but know through her knowing. Readier of the ground in Durham before I moved here. I think she trained this community to love me better. Cara Page has invited me to dream with her, to celebrate with her, to laugh. Cara Page is a co-journeyer on the mother road (we found it in Albuquerque that time). Cara Page is someone I cite at length in my dissertation. Someone whose face I saw in *The Edges of Each Other's Battles*, the Jennifer Abod film about the "I Am Your Sister" conference in honor of Audre Lorde, and squealed. For me, Cara is resonance and power. More love than one ribcage could ever hold. She is magic like that.

Cara taught me that a conference call could be church and dance class at the same time, guiding us to breathe in harmony over mute buttons and time zones, asking us to check in with our bodies. What were we holding that we could release? At Cara's fortieth birthday party, we danced until we laughed, we laughed until our laughing was also dancing, we ate things we had never eaten before, we dressed up like our queerly reclaimed ancestors so they could laugh and dance and eat and carry on too. My mom was there at some point, dressed and dreaming too. Cara taught me that the best part of this whole thing, the beautifully chosen words, the eloquently argued-for funding, the inventive structures and gatherings, is how we get to be together, how we get to enjoy each other's genius. We get to do that.

One time, we made a website about midwife storytelling in my mama's living room with reproductive justice warrior Tamika Middleton while my Auntie Arlene was visiting from Jamaica, and Auntie decided to make a website too. Another time, I learned what mung beans and mercury in retrograde meant on Southerners on New Ground organizer Kate Shapiro's deck. A completely different time, I noticed I could sing, should sing, and just sang "Spirit in the Dark," a duet between Ray Charles and Aretha Franklin, while we lit solstice candles and dissolved our fibroids at Project South.

That's how I remember it. She called it Kindred: Healing Justice. And now I understand. The healing comes from being kindred, which isn't easy to live out but is already just true. Toni Cade Bambara called it sisters of the yam and corn and rice, etc. And I know for a fact Toni Cade Bambara would have cheered to hear Cara Page explain the connection between the chopping down of the rainforest and the unethical implantation of IUDs and Norplant, in the uteruses and arms of poor women of color, in front of a thousand people at the Sistersong Conference (my mom and I were there too). Not just because of the justified rage, not just because of the recognition and brilliance, but *because what Toni Cade Bambara taught was that the cell and the creature and the circle and society and the galaxy are one thing organized by scale.* And what Cara Page learned and is teaching us now is that when you tap into that relationship, the relationship of how relationship relates, that's it. The whole body sings.

The Reaching Hands Women
for Cheryll Greene

Cheryll Greene answered her own phone on the day she died. She held her grandson while her bones betrayed her. She listened to the cars crash, in her Harlem apartment overlooking the Hudson River and the West Side Highway. She mentored Black girls like we were gold that could grow if planted. She used a red pen like a magic wand in a red sea. What I mean is that she parted the way between what you thought you were saying and what you needed to actually say. She was magic that way.

For Toni Cade Bambara, Cheryll Greene was a sister-friend and a lifelong collaborator. She was a listening ear and an honest critique. She was someone who Toni Cade could trust to love the people first and last, to believe in the people more than the divisions of genre and form, to believe in the love more than the market or the moment. In Cheryll Greene, Toni Cade Bambara recognized a kindred spirit. A Black woman willing to be anyone for the sake of the beautiful community. A Black woman who looked at other Black women and saw infinite possibility.

For me, Cheryll Greene is a chosen mother. She is tea and warm berets. She is teacher, she is truth. She is sacred vulnerability and the voice of a village of grandmothers never displaced. She is a person who taught me to look at my wildest dreams as a rough draft and dream deeper. She is neither tact nor tiptoeing. She is where I get the gall to be grown.

While executive editor at *Essence* magazine, the most widely read and longest-lasting magazine for Black women on the planet, Cheryll Y. Greene did many impossible things. With her sister-comrade Alexis De Veaux she transformed a beauty shop magazine into a transnational portal for Black feminist possibility. And in 1988 she made it physical.

In 1988, Cheryll organized a gathering called the Essence Women Writers retreat in Nassau, Bahamas, with the collaboration of Stephanie Stokes (now Stephanie Stokes-Oliver) and the full support of the then-editor-in-chief of *Essence*, Susan Taylor. All the writers you want to name were there, and the ones who didn't come were invited. Toni Cade Bambara, Sonia Sanchez, Octavia Butler, Lucille Clifton, Barbara Smith, Ntozake Shange, Thulani Davis, I can't even name them all.

What did they do? They met with editors at *Essence* to discuss what they would like to write in the magazine. They met with each other over cocktails and body-watched. They experimented with water sports. They flew and dove. They wore very bright colors. They bought sheer bathing suit wraps. They laughed so much and luxuriated in the Atlantic and the Blackness of it all. They honored their ancestors and living relatives in the Caribbean. And the food. Maybe, when some of them tried to parasail, Barbara Smith remembered the Black Feminist Retreat where she first saw aerial performance, a Black woman in silken fabrics dancing down from the ceiling, unleashing everyone's libido, relearning lust. Maybe Ntozake giggled too much for Thulani to know it wasn't just the salt air.

One day, I sat on Cheryll's living room floor and watched the video of the last night of the gathering. A Bahamian brother videotaped it the best he could while his mind was being blown. It was a circle. An old form for ceremony. And gently facilitated. Each writer would share about their work. What they wanted the other writers and editors to know. And on the video, I watched the circle become spiral. I saw some of the most outspoken women in the world say things they had never said before. I saw Toni Cade Bambara stand and reach her hands into the air proposing the people gathered make an anthology of poems and stories, and recipes and star-maps, and legal proceedings, you know, gather everything. I saw Octavia Butler demand a world where she wasn't the only Black woman science fiction author. I saw

Sonia Sanchez stand and place the writing of Black women squarely against the death of the species. I saw those who wore makeup cry it off, nodding their heads, yes.

Somewhere the saltwater of water sports and splashing in the sun became the saltwater of tears and transformation. Somehow the pleasure of treating each other well became metabolic fuel to believe in a future and demand it, to listen to each other like love would save their lives. There was a promise it would be an annual thing. It wasn't (though Cheryll did go on to co-found Yari Yari and organize writing gatherings for Black women writers in Africa and the diaspora for the rest of her life.) There was a promise from Susan Taylor that *Essence* magazine would do the work that the circle called for. I don't think it has happened yet at *Essence*. Maybe it is happening in other ways.

When Cheryll showed me the photo album, the bright snapshots of big drinks and somehow bigger smiles, Black women surrounded in purpose and recognition, Black women at play, she was teaching me something. And at the same time, she was numbering the dead. Look at Toni Cade. She said. Look at us. She numbered who in the photographs had died since then. She told me how when Toni Cade Bambara knew she was dying of cancer, a friend lent her and her daughter Karma a loft in NYC so everyone could come visit and say goodbye. Cheryll remembers them playing jazz and singing and dancing, playful up until the last moment.

And when Cheryll knew there were no more treatments for her own cancer at last, she had me over to her apartment. I wanted to conduct a long interview. I wanted to beg, give me your whole life and I will keep it. I brought a state-of-the-art audio recorder and a notebook full of questions. But she didn't feel like it. There was a beautiful sunset over the Hudson River, audacious in its purples and oranges. We chased it to every window of her apartment. We oohed and aahed and camera-phone collected it. We laughed. I really don't think I cried. The day Cheryll died I was at the beach in Anguilla, salt air and no cell phone reception. I keep the group photo of the Nassau writers' retreat from Cheryll's office in my office now. Cheryll is in the middle, smile somehow bigger than her huge glasses, watching me work. Watching me write this now. Minutes before I pack up to head to the ocean again. Toni Cade and Cheryll taught us the sweetness of salt. How the circle becomes a spiral. Reach out your hands.

WHY WE GET OFF

Moving Towards a Black Feminist
Politics of Pleasure

Joan Morgan

This, right here, is an origins tale.[1] A deliberate, black, feminist, *once upon a time* that details one of three preliminary but critical pit stops on my theory-making journey to a black feminist Politics of Pleasure. Part of my current project, "Pleasure Politics" is a multi-pronged effort that includes my dissertation, my public-intellectual work and two years of critical intellectual labor with "The Pleasure Ninjas": journalist and playwright Esther Armah and Drs. Yaba Blay, Brittney Cooper, Treva B. Lindsey and Kaila Story—a collective I founded in 2013 during my tenure as a Visiting Scholar at Stanford University. As black feminist theorists, we've made a commitment to reframe the existing narrative about black female sexuality by positioning desire, agency and black women's engagements with pleasure as a viable

---

1   This essay first appeared as Joan Morgan, "Why We Get Off: Moving Towards a Black Feminist Politics of Pleasure," *Black Scholar* 45, no. 4 (2015): 36–46.

theoretical paradigm. "Pleasure Politics" asks: What possibilities can a politics of pleasure offer for black feminist futures? Specifically, how can deepening our understanding of the multivalent ways black women produce, read and participate in pleasure complicate our understanding of black female subjectivities in ways that invigorate, inform and sharpen a contemporary black feminist agenda?

Getting to black feminist pleasure is tricky business. As my mentor historian E. Frances White said to me when I initially shared this endeavor, "You, do know that feminists are allergic to pleasure, right?" She was joking. Kind of. This is not to suggest that Black Feminist Thought (BFT) has shied away from the topic of black female sexuality. In fact, holding the United States accountable for a sordid history of legally and culturally sanctioned rape and gender violence against black women has long been a priority in BFT's agenda. Indeed, a great deal of energy has been spent disputing deeply entrenched and dehumanizing stereotypes—ranging from our uniquely mammified asexuality to our naturally animalistic, wanton and licentious ways. The corrective has been the creation of a black feminist master narrative in which black women's damaged sexuality takes center-stage as a site of reoccurring trauma—the place where intersecting oppressions can be counted on to meet and violently coalesce. The upside, of course, was a sorely needed, compassionate rendering of the difficult and compromised space black women's sexuality occupies. The downside has been a mulish inattentiveness to black women's engagements with pleasure—the complex, messy, sticky, and even joyous negotiations of agency and desire that are irrevocably twinned with our pain. From academia to the blogosphere, we've become feminist fluent in theorizing the many ways in which our sexuality has been compromised. We've been considerably less successful, however, moving past that damage to claim pleasure and a healthy erotic as fundamental rights. Echoing the sentiments of my fellow Pleasure Ninja, Brittney Cooper: "There is no justice for black women without pleasure."

This article maps the initial leg of the long feminist journey to *getting off*—the intellectual foreplay, if you will, that preceded Pleasure Politics. It focuses on one of three distinct, personal, moments that helped me to identify specific challenges BFT faces in theorizing black women's pleasure. The first takes place at a lecture at Stanford University, where a student's query forced me to confront the dearth of available language in BFT to account for the ways the erotic can potentially shape BFT or how black ethnicity and US black transnational identities complicate the master narrative of black female sexuality. The second—a recently shared bit of family history—underscores what feminist novelist Chimamanda Ngozi Adichie refers to as "the danger of the single story" by elucidating the master narrative's potential for erasure and excision in ways that foreclose possibilities of pleasure for black female subjectivities.[2] The third identifies the pedagogical challenges in teaching students to read pleasure—both in black women's visual culture and their own—when pleasure as an affective response is deemed illegitimate or uncritical. Or when black women's cultural products are read solely through a representation politic that routinely discounts *black female interiority*. While *interiority* is widely understood as the quiet composite of mental, spiritual and psychological expression, *black female interiority* is that—and then some. I use the term specifically to excavate the broad range of feelings, desires, yearning, (erotic and otherwise) that were once deemed necessarily private by the "politics of silence." Now frequently expressed in black women's cultural expressions specifically for the purpose of observance and consumption, it demands a black feminist reckoning. *Black female interiority* is the codicil to cultural dissemblance.

More than two decades ago, Evelynn M. Hammonds famously charged BFT with moving from a "politics of silence"

---

2 Chimamanda Ngozi Adichie, "The Danger of a Single Story." Lecture presented at theTedGlobal2009, July 2009, http://www.ted.com/talks/chimamanda_adichie_the_danger_of_a_single_story/transcript.

about black women's sexuality to a "politics of articulation."[3] Referencing an insular, triangulated conversation between historians, literary critics and feminist theorists, Hammonds conceded that black feminism's long-standing focus on the politics of respectability, cultural dissemblance and similar discourses of resistance—interventions that theorized black women's sexuality as an accumulation of unspeakable acts or positioned black women in "binary opposition to white women"—succeeded in identifying black women's sexuality as a site of intersecting oppressions. What they failed to do, she argued, was to produce the "politics of articulation" necessary to disrupt them.[4] Without it, Hammonds cautioned, these discourses inadvertently reified black female sexuality as pathologized, alternately invisible and hypervisible.

Particularly egregious, she argued, was black feminism's agency in reproducing those silences through its continued investments in heteronormativity. Despite a vocal and visible lesbian and bisexual presence in black feminist thought throughout much of the 1970s and 1980s, black feminist scholarship was framed in overwhelmingly heteronormative terms with even canonical texts like Angela Davis' *Women, Race and Class* and bell hooks' *Ain't I Woman: Black Women and Feminism* and *Feminist Theory: From Margin to Center* dedicating little attention to issues of pleasure, sexual agency

---

3   Evelynn M. Hammonds, "Towards a Genealogy of Black Female Sexuality and the Problematic of Silence," in *Feminist Genealogies, Colonial Legacies, Democratic Futures*, edited by Jacqui Alexander and Chandra Mohanty, (New York: Routledge, 1997), 179–80.

4   See Evelyn Brooks Higginbotham, *Righteous Discontent: The Women's Movement in the Black Baptist Church, 1880–1990* (Cambridge: Harvard University Press, 1993); Adrienne Davis, "Don't Let Nobody Bother Yo' Principle: The Sexual Economy of American Slavery," in *Sister Circle, Black Women and Work*, edited by Sharon Harley (New Brunswick, NJ: Rutgers University Press, 2002); Darlene Clark Hine, *Hine Sight: Black Women and the Re-Construction of American History* (Bloomington and Indianapolis: Indiana University Press, 1994) for more on the politics of respectability, silences and black women's sexual labor, and the theory of cultural dissemblance, respectively.

or queerness.[5] It was black lesbian and bisexual writers' deployments of sexuality in fiction, literary criticism and anthologies[6] that "often foregrounded the very aspects of black female sexuality that are submerged—namely, female desire and agency—are critical to our theorizing of black female sexualities."[7]

Reverberations of Hammonds' dissatisfaction can be found well into the twenty-first century, revealing a growing frustration by new millennium feminist thinkers whose salient critiques argue that black female sexuality in feminist scholarship remains comparatively under-theorized, stubbornly heteronormative and still too comfortably reliant on "a politics of silence." Deeply conversant with popular culture, these recent theorizations of black female sexuality engage previous black feminist historical scholarship and

---

5   Angela Y. Davis, *Women, Race and Class* (New York: Vintage Books, 1983); bell hooks, *Ain't I a Woman: Black Women and Feminism* (Cambridge: South End Press, 1981) and *Feminist Theory: From Margin to Center* (Cambridge: South End Press, 1984).

6   See Beverly Guy Sheftall, *Words of Fire: An Anthology of African-American Thought* (New York: The New Press, 1995); Gloria T. Hull, Patricia Bell Scott, and Barbara Smith, eds., *All the Women Are White, All Blacks Are Men, But Some of Us Are Brave* (New York: The Feminist Press at the City University of New York, 1982); Cherríe Moraga and Gloria Anzaldúa, *This Bridge Called My Back: Writings by Radical Women of Color* (New York: Kitchen Table Press, 1981); Barbara Smith, *Homegirls: A Black Feminist Anthology* (New York: Kitchen Table Press, 1983). Barbara Smith and others founded The Kitchen Table: Women of Color Press in 1981. In keeping with the Combahee Collective's declared commitment to collective feminist work, historical recovery, intersectionality and activism, each anthology contained a deliberate black lesbian presence offering literary criticism from queer perspectives and painstaking critiques of homophobia in both black feminist thought and the overall black community. Influential and enduring, these anthologies helped black feminist sexuality theory to make significant and early interventions into the subfields of ethnic, queer, black and women's studies. In addition, they provide a model for the more seamless models of inclusion—a given as opposed to a category—demonstrated in Sheftall's 1995 anthology, *Words of Fire: An Anthology of African-American Thought.*

7   Hammonds, "Towards a Genealogy of Black Female Sexuality," 181.

literary-criticism. They also mine film, television, music, strip clubs, pornography and visual expressive cultural work. Decidedly multi-platform, the work has a home in traditional scholarship and feminist texts but can also be found in journalism, cultural criticism, the feminist blogosphere and other forms of digital media. Jennifer Nash's *The Black Body and Ecstasy: Reading Race, Reading Pornography*, offers an encouraging example. Her analysis of "black women's feminist cultural production as a kind of theory-making"[8] demonstrates a dual commitment to rigorous, thoughtful engagement with the foundational tenets of BFT (particularly its preoccupation "with the logics of injury and recovery") and using pleasure as an interrogative lens. Similarly, Nicole Fleetwood, Jessica Marie Johnson, Shayne Lee, Treva B. Lindsey, Uri McMillan, Mireille Miller Young, L.H. Stallings and Natasha Tinsley's[9] scholarly interrogations of black women's visual and performance culture, literature and porn encourage us to imagine new erotic possibilities for black women—from the enslaved to the pop star to the sex worker.

Like Hammonds' call for a "politics of articulation," these scholars' works can be reasonably interpreted as a decisive demand for a black feminist sexuality theory that is inclusive of pleasure and the erotic. It is a call that has gone relatively unmet or countered with polarizing resistance. Iterations of *Certain black feminists need to stop talking about twerking*

---

8   Jennifer C. Nash, *The Black Body in Ecstasy: Reading Race, Reading Pornography* (Durham, NC: Duke University Press), 32.

9   See Nicole R. Fleetwood, *Troubling Vision: Performance, Visuality, and Blackness* (Chicago: University of Chicago Press, 2011); Treva B. Lindsey and Jessica Marie Johnson, "Searching for Climax: Black Erotic Lives in Slavery and Freedom," Meridians,12, no. 2 (2014): 169–95; Shayne Lee, *Erotic Revolutionaries* (Lanham, MD: Hamilton Books, 2010); Uri McMillan, *Embodied Avatars: Genealogies of Black Feminist Art and Performance* (New York: New York University Press, 2015); Omise'eke Natasha Tinsley, *Thiefing Sugar: Eroticism between Women in Caribbean Literature*. Perverse Modernities: A Series, edited by Jack Halberstam and Lisa Lowe (Durham: Duke University Press, 2010).

and pleasure and turn their attention back to structural inequalities have grown common in feminist digital terrains. But this ubiquitous reign of silence also speaks to what I've identified as a methodological sluggishness in BFT when it comes to theorizing our sexuality. We've become overly reliant on the field's most trenchant theories—specifically Kimberle Crenshaw's "intersectionality," Patricia Collins' "controlling images," Audre Lorde's deployment of the erotic, Higginbotham's "respectability politics," Hine's "cultural dissemblance."[10] Bequeathing them the sanctity of dogma and rendering them impervious to the changes of time, we've often failed to re-interrogate these venerated interventions with the temporal, cultural specificity reflected in contemporary US black women's ethnic heterogeneity, queerness and the advent of digital technologies and social media. By ignoring these changes, we've rendered BFT incapable of addressing the variegated landscape of black female sexuality or reading contemporary black women's cultural production for pleasure. Until we do, we will continue to inextricably link trauma and violence to black women's lived and historical experiences and negate pleasure as frivolous, irrelevant, or "unfeminist."

I position, quite deliberately, "Pleasure Politics" as a liberatory, black feminist project. It elevates the need for sexual autonomy and erotic agency without shame to the level of black feminist imperative. Accordingly, a politics of pleasure operates with an empirical understanding that feminist principles do not necessarily legislate desire. Black women's erotic maps exist on an expansive spectrum, which could include non-heteronormative submissiveness, hyper-masculinity, aggression, exhibitionism, and voyeurism. Finally, it

---

10   See Kimberle Crenshaw, "Mapping the Margins: Intersectionality, Identity Politics and Violence Against Women of Color," *Stanford Law Review* 43, no. 6 (1991): 1241–99; Patricia Hill Collins, "Mammies, Matriarchs and Other Controlling Images," in *Black Feminist Thought* (New York: Routledge, 2000), 53–59; Audre Lorde, "Uses of the Erotic: The Erotic as Power," in *Sister Outsider* (Orlando: Harcourt Press, 1984).

acknowledges that the hegemonic narrative of black female sexuality which dominates black feminist thought in the United States not only erases queer and transgender subjects but also ignores black multi-ethnicity and the diverse cultural influences currently operating in the world US black women occupy. Combatting racism, sexism and homophobia effectively in the midst of multiple pressures of neoliberalism, the current economic crisis, the decline of the US Empire require nuanced, careful interpretations of race, ethnicity, gender, nationhood, citizenship, and identity.

Since it is an unwritten mandate that any black feminist work that explores the erotic engage Lorde's "Uses of The Erotic: The Erotic as Power" it's important for me to distinguish the ways my usage of the terms "erotic" and "erotic agency" differs from some black feminist theorists. Like Lorde, I seek a framing of the erotic [that] is both deliberate and expansive. I am there, head nodding with my fellow feminist theorists when Lorde writes:

> The very word *erotic* comes from the Greek *eros*, the personification of love in all its aspects—born of Chaos, and personifying creative power and harmony. When I speak of the erotic, then, I speak of it as an assertion of the lifeforce of women; of that creative energy empowered, the knowledge of which we are now reclaiming in our language, our history, our dancing, our loving, our work, our lives.[11]

However, some black feminists have chosen to map a binary and heteronormative read onto Lorde's erotic that implies that the erotic can only be achieved by a transcendence of mere sex, or by eschewing sex that isn't regulated to the realms of romantic love or the spiritual. For example, in *Black Sexual Politics*, Patricia Hill Collins challenges my critique

---

11 Lorde, "Uses of the Erotic," 55 [also page 30 of this volume].

of how young women in hip-hop culture use both sex and sexuality as a type of currency that is commonly interpreted as "erotic power." Casting it as my "misread" of Lorde (whom I deliberately do not engage in the context of hip-hop and hood sexual politics), Collins goes on to contrast "erotic" with "sex/fucking." The former, she writes, requires an engagement with "the honest body."

> Rebelling against the rules and reclaiming the erotic means that Black straight and gay people alike can support one another in claiming honest bodies that are characterized by sexual autonomy. Using one's honest body engages all forms of sexual expression that bring pleasure and joy. Overall, soul, expressiveness, spirituality, sensuality, sexuality, and an expanded notion of the erotic as a life force that may include all of these ideas seem to be tightly bundled together within this notion of an honest body that is not alienated from itself and where each individual has the freedom to pursue his or her sense of the erotic.[12]

Rather than the embrace the pairing Hill Collins suggests, my hope is for a pleasure politics that actively, adamantly resists it. My interest is in a capacious casting of the erotic that includes black women's variegated sexual and non-sexual engagements with deeply internal sites of power and pleasure—among them expressions of sex and sexuality that deliberately resists binaries. Like L. H. Stallings, I am interested in erotic space that:

> looks at the constructions of Black female subjectivities cognizant of autonomous sexual

---

12   Patricia Hill Collins, *Black Sexual Politics: African Americans, Gender, and the New Racism* (New York: Routledge, 2004), 298.

desires. (And ask) how do Black women use
culture to explore sexual desire that is spiritual, intellectual, physical, emotional, and fluid
so as to avoid splits or binaries that can freeze
Black women's radical sexual subjectivities? It
is not easy.[13]

In other words, I want an erotic that demands space be made
for honest bodies that like to also *fuck*.

I share this piece as a reminder (to both the reader and
myself) that inherent in the noble search for new directions
in BFT is the diffident, exciting, uncertainty of that new-
new—that tricky, impolitic thing that positions itself precar-
iously on the firm foundation of black feminist intellectual
labor and a destabilizing, clearly crunk willingness to strip
the house down [to] it[s] structural beams, if necessary. Like
all successful renovation projects, it is driven by love, newly
identified needs and a tacit preparedness to do violence to
whatever came before it. This is not a comfortable or easily
habitable space. Like my co-contributors to this volume, I
pacify myself with hope that the ends will justify the means.

All the women are white; all the men are black … but are all the blacks are African-American?

The enquiry that catalyzed my search for a black feminist
politics of pleasure came, unwittingly, from a graduate student at Stanford. I'd been invited by the university to have
a public conversation on hip-hop and feminism with Dr.
H. Samy Alim commemorating the tenth anniversary of my
book *When Chickenheads Come Home to Roost: A Hip-Hop
Feminist Breaks it Down*. After 10 years of writing/discuss-
ing/living/breathing hip-hop and feminism, I could hardly
imagine a question I hadn't already answered in some form

---

13   L. H. Stallings, *Mutha' Is Half a Word: Intersections of Folklore,
Vernacular, Myth and Queerness in Black Female Culture* (Columbus,
OH: The Ohio State University, 2007), 1.

or another, but suddenly there it was: virginal, terrific and tongue-tying: *"Could you speak a bit about the ways your Caribbean-ness plays in shaping your theorization of hip-hop feminism, specifically your engagement with the erotic?"*

Like most terrific questions, it was one I had yet to think about—and certainly not in the context of my feminism. I knew intuitively that there was no "neat answer" to where the Caribbean-ness in my hip-hop feminist self began and ended. Any attempt would require less of an answer than a story— and one that does not easily recognize the geo-political convenience of borders, processes of citizenship or nationalities. Like the transnational imaginary that the hyphen implies, the alleged margins—Caribbean, American, hip-hop, feminist—continuously shift and do so with problematic fluidity. Rather than delineating the specifics of its stops and starts, I'd come to understand both my identity and my feminism as a *ting* that bends and leans, intersects and divides, stops *h'an* drops *h'an* bubbles and wines. I also knew that my commitment to hold the erotic front and center in hip-hop feminism was a deliberate one. But the question being asked required a specific accounting for elements routinely ignored in BFT— namely pleasure, the erotic and US black multi-ethnicity. It required mining what Caribbean rhetorician Professor Kevin A. Browne describes as the space *between* the Caribbean and the American—and when it comes to BFT there was no politics of articulation around *that*.

The reasons for this are several, not least among them propensity to conflate the racial description of "Black" with the ethnic description of "African-American." BFT, like most forms of African-American scholarship and popular discourse, tends to reduce the experience of blackness in the US to a mono-ethnic experience with a singular racial narrative—despite the fact that the number of foreign born blacks residing in the United States is currently believed to be in the millions—and growing. According to the Population Bulletin report:

> New flows of immigrants from Africa and the
> Caribbean are ... part of the racial and eth-
> nic transformation of the United States in
> the 21st century. Immigration contributed at
> least one-fifth of the growth in the U.S. black
> population between 2001 and 2006 with
> more than one-fourth of the black popula-
> tion in New York, Boston, and Miami being
> "foreign-born."[14]

But since the Hart-Cellar Act Immigration Reform Act elim-
inated national origins quotas in 1965, more than half a million Black Caribbean immigrants have migrated to the United
States. While their exact number is difficult to approximate,
the 1999 Current Population Survey estimated that there
were 600,000 Black Caribbean immigrants living in New
York City alone.[15] Despite these numbers, the scholarship
has been slow to recognize Black ethnicity, in part because it
troubles constructions of Blackness that comfortably assume
an African American essentialism. As a result, over-determinations of African-American ethnicity appear frequently in
black feminist scholarship, making little distinction between
African-American women and black women in the United
States with roots in Caribbean and other parts of the diaspora. The typical results are erroneous assignations of geo-de-
termined identities to non-African-American subjects—ones
that serve to erase their cultural specificity and render them
erotically illegible in black feminist critiques.

The question had been asked in the particular context [of]
hip-hop feminism, but it could have just as easily been asked

---

14 Mary Mederios Kent, "Immigration and America's Black Population,"
    Population Bulletin 62, no. 4 (December 2007): 3–4.
15 Sherri Ann Butterfield, "'We're Just Black': The Racial and Ethnic
    Identities of Second-Generation West Indians in New York," in
    Becoming New Yorkers: Ethnographies of the New Second Generation,
    edited by Philip Kasnitz, John H. Mollenkopf, and Mary C. Waters,
    (New York: Russell Sage Foundation, 2005), 289.

of Robyn Rihanna Fenty's oeuvre. Fenty's Caribbean-ness, typically read through the US master narrative of black female sexuality, is routinely dismissed as merely hypersexual or "othered" as foreign and therefore irrelevant. This illegibility coupled with the heightened visibility of international pop stardom often places her outside the politics of recognition that confers the citizenship inherent in belonging to what we loosely think of as "the black community." But what would be required of BFT to produce a feminist read of Rihanna's cultural products through the dual lenses of culture and pleasure? As it turns out, the very same adjustments that would be required to theorize the relationality between deployments of the erotic and Black Caribbean-American identity. The groundwork would have to be laid for a truly inclusive Pleasure Politic.

This means BFT would have to step its game up in both theoretical and methodological ways. It would require engaging a multi-disciplinary lens—one that could conceivably draw on diaspora and transnational studies, second generation West-Indian identity scholarship and Caribbean theorists like Carolyn Cooper who[se] extensive analyses of dancehall as a site of art, agency and performances of black female erotics comport in potentially fascinating ways with articulations of hip-hop feminism. Similarly, Opal Adisa Palmer's explorations of sensuality and sweetness and Carolyn Boyce Davies' discourses on Caribbean women, migrations, carnival and transnational identities elucidate the ways that nuanced attention to black ethnicity, identity and deployments of the erotic and pleasure stands to expand and fortify black feminist sexuality theory.[16]

---

16   Carolyn Cooper, *Noises in the Blood: Orality, Gender and the "Vulgar" Body in Jamaican Popular Culture* (Durham: Duke University Press, 1995); Carolyn Cooper, *Sound Clash: Jamaican Dancehall Culture At Large* (New York: Palgrave McMillan, 2004); Carolyn Cooper, "At the Crossroads—Looking for Meaning in Jamaican Dancehall Culture: A Reply," *Small Axe* 10, no. 21 (October 2006), 193–204; Opal Palmer Adisa and Donna Aza Weir-Soley, eds., *Caribbean Erotic: Poetry, Prose and Essays* (Great Britain: Pepal Tree Press, 2010).

It would also necessarily call into question the efficacy of feminist standpoint theories and interpretative practices that are over-reliant on "individual biographies and fictional narratives as entryways to understanding collective race and gender experiences"[17] at a point in our history, when black womanhood is more diverse than ever. E. Frances White staked this claim more than a decade ago, when she challenged black feminists to interrogate their positionality as middle class, African-American feminist academics—specifically their tendency to use their lived experiences as stand-ins for all black women.[18] It would require consistent engagement with what cultural theorist Stuart Hall termed the "politics of enunciation." Since the black female subject is never an essential one and incapable of speaking for the totality of black experience, it is always critical to ask, "who is this emergent subject and from where does (s)he speak?"[19]

Diaspora studies could lend a much-needed assist. Since its emergence in the 1990s, it has been a critical intervention for navigating both the scholarly and lived conundrums produced by increasingly transnational, ethnically diverse and globalized realties. The field's strong investments in the authorship of cultural identity, its continued re-imaginings of community, nation, citizenship and national belonging; its consistent challenge to the geo-determinism of nation-states and ethnic and racial essentialism, bring with it powerful potentialities for black feminist thought. In order to read both black women's pleasure and the erotic broadly, BFT would need to hold tight the tensions introduced by social constructionists Stuart Hall, James Clifford and Paul

---

17   See Melissa V. Harris-Perry, *Sister Citizen: Shame, Stereotypes and Black Women in America* (New Haven, CT: Yale University Press, 2011), 22.

18   See E. Frances White, *Dark Continent of Our Bodies: Black Feminism and the Politics of Respectability* (Philadelphia, PA: Temple University Press, 2001).

19   Stuart Hall, "Cultural Identity and Diaspora," in *Theorizing Diaspora: A Reader*, ed. Kuan-Hsing Chen and David Morley (Malden, MA: Blackwell, 2007), 225.

Gilroy who argued that identity in the post-modern world has become deterritorialized and reconstructed in situational ways.[20] These include class/cultural differences, multiple understandings of race, nation, belonging and gender that black feminist thought has not traditionally taken into account.

BFT thought could also draw heavily on Hall's canonical contributions to understandings of cultural identity, which would enable it to understand black female identity as a production that is "never complete, always in process and always constituted within, not outside representation."[21] Hall articulates two positions of cultural identity that are generative to a developing a feminist black sexuality theory and a politics of pleasure. The first is the "shared culture" that claims one true collective that is shared by a people with a common history and ancestry. It includes shared cultural codes with stable, unchanging, continuous forms of reference and meaning, and acknowledges the critical role African-American women's history has played in both the development of black feminist thought as well as other black social, political, and artistic movements. It is also true that over-determinations of the impact of shared culture can easily produce a "true black" female subject and a fundamentally essentialist identity which compromise the quest for a liberatory pleasure politics. A Pleasure Politic seeks to assuage this tension by rigorously engaging Hall's understanding of cultural identity through difference.

Using Derrida's difference as a referent, Hall deployed the term to trouble one's understanding of something by applying new meaning but without erasing original meanings. Difference is important to Hall's theorization of diaspora

---

20 See James Clifford, *Routes: Travel and Translation in the Late Twentieth Century*, (Cambridge, MA: Harvard University Press, 1997); Paul Gilroy, *The Black Atlantic: Modernity and Double Consciousness* (Cambridge, MA: Harvard University Press, 1993); Stuart Hall, "Cultural Identity and Diaspora," "New Ethnicities," in *Stuart Hall: Critical Dialogues in Cultural Studies*, edited by Jana Evans Braziel, 442–451 (London: Routledge, 1996).

21 Stuart Hall, "Cultural Identity and Diaspora," 222.

because it resists binaries, dislocates one from original interpretations and position definitions as never complete but always moving toward other supplementary meaning. Like Hall, rather than staking investments in oppositional or even dual identities, "Pleasure Politics" is invested in pushing black feminist thought to explore identity intersections—specifically how the gendered, racialized identity of "blackness" intersects with multiple, relational realities? For example: How can someone be specifically Jamaican, generally West Indian, a queer Black American citizen and claim an African motherland through reggae, a political identity vis-à-vis engagements with African-American radicalism or a cultural identity steeped in hip-hop? These generative frameworks are possible when a diaspora study is put in conversation with black feminist thought.

Utilizing this multi-disciplinary approach it is both possible and exciting to see how that student's question (similar to Rihanna), when placed simultaneously in both a US and Caribbean context, hints at a sophisticated, transnational conversation about constructions of black female sexuality that reveal fluid borrowings, cultural synergies and encourage a reconsidering of black feminist understandings of community, nation, and ethnic and racial essentialism. Furthermore, it asks, how can contextualizing both within the US racial and sexual scripts and in context of pleasure and the specific historical and culturally based logics of Caribbean erotic expression reveal useful strategies for theorizing a feminist black sexuality theory? My hope is that "Pleasure Politics" will ask those of us who work in fields other than black feminism to also consider how eliding the burgeoning identities of millions of black immigrants and their descendants compromise not only our understanding of race but inhibit our ability to develop what anthropologist David Scott refers to as the "new problem-spaces" necessary for establishing new directions in critical inquiry.[22]

---

22   See David Scott, *Conscripts of Modernity: The Tragedy of Enlightenment*

I don't remember the answer I gave to that Stanford student that day, but I do know that I've been attempting to answer his question ever since. I'm grateful for the uncertainty. The intervention I hope to make through my own scholarship is to articulate a politics of pleasure that positions pleasure not only as desirable goal and a social and political imperative, but also as an under-theorized resistance strategy for black women in the United States and the Caribbean. In doing so, I hope to make a contribution to black feminist thought that encourages recognition of black women's pleasure (sexual and otherwise) as not only an integral part of fully realized humanity, but one that understands that a politics of pleasure is capable of intersecting, challenging, and redefining dominant narratives about race, beauty, health and sex in ways that are generative and necessary.

(Durham, NC: Duke University Press, 2004).

A PLEASURE PHILOSOPHY

A Conversation with Ingrid LaFleur

Detroiter Ingrid LaFleur is the founder of Maison LaFleur and Afrotopia. Fashionista, artist, and most likely to make bank on bitcoin, she ran for mayor of Detroit in 2017 as an Afrofuturist candidate.

amb. *What do you like people to know about your pleasure activism?*

Ingrid. Fashion has definitely helped to define my pleasure activism. When my father passed away over a year ago I felt a grief I've never had before. After two months of being in a catatonic state, I began craving laughter and joy. I decided to wear the one thing that gives visual pleasure instantly no matter who is wearing it, sequins. I wore sequins every single day for about a month. Although my energy was low, my sequin jackets would make someone giggle, and then they would send me that good energy, which would soothe my wounds. It was, and still is, the best healing therapy I've experimented with. I continue to wear sequined jackets, now paired with heart-shaped red glasses, in hopes to generate more love and joy in my life and others.

amb. *What is your pleasure philosophy?*

Ingrid. I believe every moment of every day should be a pleasurable experience. If it is not, then it is time to question what is happening and why you decided to endure it.

I also believe pleasure generated through our own power should resonate as far into the future as possible. If I eat something that tastes super-delicious but makes me sluggish and tired and sends me into a spiral of body shaming, then that was not a pleasurable experience, no matter how juicy and delicious it was. However, if I eat something fresh, clean, and healthy for my body then I will feel empowered and energetic simply because I have exhibited my love for self. *Ultimately, love for the self is the deepest pleasure we deny ourselves.* I work daily to be courageous enough to indulge in the purest pleasure of self-love.

amb. *How does Detroit inform and benefit from your approach to pleasure?*

Ingrid. Detroit taught me about pleasures derived from participating in and supporting innovative ancestrally rooted loving communities. This is a soul-satisfying pleasure that is aligned with my values without compromise. The more compromise, the less soul-satisfying. It's tricky because addictions can blind us to this truth.

amb. *What are your actual daily practices of pleasure?*

Ingrid. I would love to create more rituals of pleasure. At the moment, because of my nomadic life, I have pleasure goals I try to maintain to help me keep clarity and that are necessary no matter where I am living—daily meditation for twenty minutes, keeping a clean kitchen (food is medicine), making the bed, and drinking a fresh green juice at the beginning of each day. Also, accomplishing work goals set for the day brings pure joy and gives me permission to play.

amb. *Time-travel for me: what is the most pleasurable possible future you can imagine?*

Ingrid. When our world is free from economic slavery and is prospering with joy.

SECTION TWO

THE POLITICS
OF RADICAL SEX

Forget health clinics and gyms. Sex is the
best cure. One good night of sex and your
problems are gone.
—Grace Jones

An orgasm a day keeps the doctor away.
—Mae West

PUSSY POWER WITH FAVIANNA RODRIGUEZ

Favianna Rodriguez is one of the first people I met who brought up sex in a public context with no attempt at mass seduction. She was incredibly matter-of-fact about her truth that, as an artist, as an organizer, her pleasure and her freedom are part of her larger radical creative path. These images are from her recent work around Pussy Power, liberating sexual relationships and the rights women should have over their bodies.

WHERE DID YOU LEARN STIGMA?

PUSSY POWER

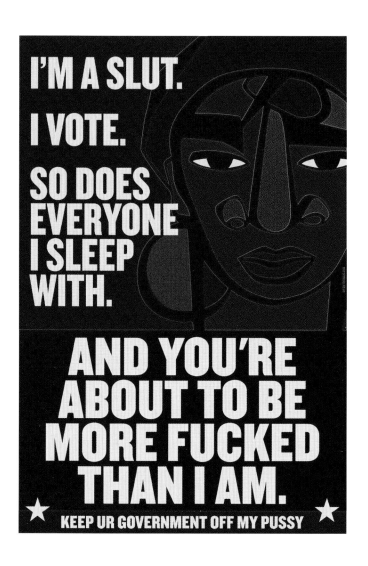

I'M A SLUT

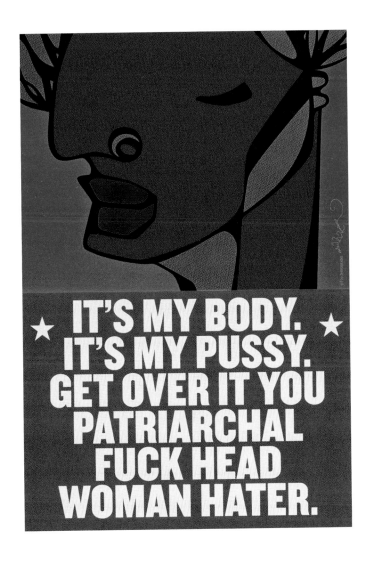

IT'S MY PUSSY

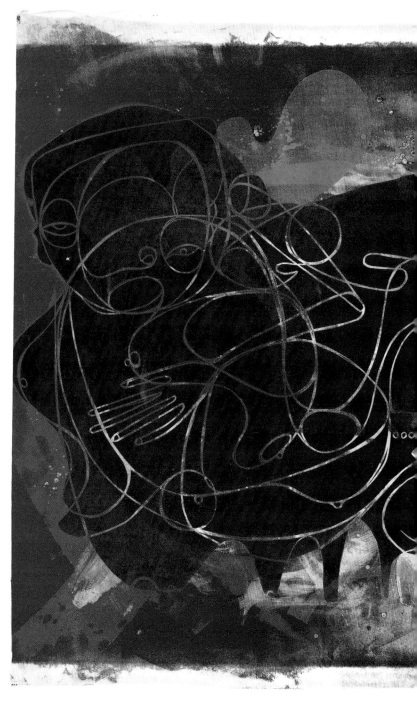

DECOLONIZE PUSSY POWER

OVER THE RAINBOW

SEX ED

A Poem:

touch yourself early and often
learn your body before you share your body
use mirrors to learn how beautiful you are
let yes come from every part of you before you
    share you
when your eggs drop, you are in heat
the risk is greater than the heat—use protection
if your pussy gets sick, feed yourself plain
    yogurt, garlic
drink primrose tea, rub her with coconut oil
when your blood comes, it's time to rest
know that you are never unclean, never
    untouchable
use a cup within, or a rag without; no trash
    needed
now you have power of life, a child is a forever
    decision
your pleasures will grow with you, never say
    never
whether voracious or sated, you are whole,
    unbroken
your orgasms are medicine and magic, use
    them well

be a lifelong lover to yourself, let others join
  you
always, always: celebrate your miraculous body[1]

---

1   I included this is for those who identify with the words/anatomy
used in this poem. It feels important for me to get to write a poem
that feels accurate and powerful for my body. I invite other poems
for those who need other words and/or have other anatomy—what
words and images bring you power? I think we need loads of experi-
ential-wisdom-sex-ed poems and classes!

WHEREIN
I WRITE ABOUT SEX

(Five Tangible Tools of a Pleasure Activist)

I started this blog the night Beyoncé's self-titled album came out.[1] I didn't know her album was coming, and Beyoncé didn't know she was unleashing a soundtrack to this moment of my life. That convergence was so special that I had to pause writing this and spend two months learning the "Flawless" dance and wondering, among other things, exactly what kind of feminism I am interested in. I decided that I am interested in a sexual, complex, whole person, imperfect feminism, one full of mothers, single people, married people, and poly people, sex workers. Women who make quality work and create systems to liberate their creativity. Women as powerful as Tina Turner and other survivors of domestic violence. Women who like to submit, talk dirty, shock even themselves. Women who like to dominate, operate outside of gender norms, women willing to disagree and sit in discomfort and

---

1   This essay first appeared as adrienne maree brown, "Wherein I Write
    about Sex (5 Tangible Tools of a Pleasure Activist)," February 12, 2014,
    http://adriennemareebrown.net/2014/02/12/wherein-i-write-about
    -sex-5-tangible-tools-of-a-pleasure-activist. *Beyoncé* was released with
    no warning on December 13, 2013.

hold their power and their ground, women willing to grow and learn in public. It is in that spirit that I return to this blog entry. Here goes:

I don't talk about sex enough here!

Anyone who knows me in real life knows that the sensual, sexual, erotic perspective is a primary lens through which I see the world. Yet I struggle with how to integrate that self with the one here who speaks about transformation, babies, grief, growth.

But the link is all in the body as a practice ground for transformation.[2]

I had a dream the other night. I boarded a train for a cross-country journey with my friend Evans, which is important only because he is a sexy beast. I was quickly recruited for a burlesque show, and I auditioned in a clear plastic belt and little else. The person running the auditions said, "To do this job you have to l.o.v.e. love your body!" And I responded, "Oh, I do. I do love my body. I love my body!" I woke up murmuring this to myself.

(Note: can you see how the lyrics "I woke up like this: flawless" struck me with joy?)

Now, that's an awesome dream outside of any analysis. But it is particularly awesome when you understand that my focus for personal transformation for the last few years (roughly thirty-plus years or so) has been learning to love my body or, more precisely, falling in love with myself through the terrain of my body. This dream made me feel that my focus is restructuring and healing me at the level of my subconscious … if I understand anything about the mysterious realm of dreams.

It is still work, daily. Thousands of choices, opposing values and longings, moments of slipping, days of feeling super active and strong, days of feeling lazy and sloth-like. I sit at

---

2   In the lineage of somatics I study, we articulate commitments that we aspire to embody. At this time of this blog entry, mine was "a commitment to my body being a practice ground for transformation."

the crux of an apparent contradiction: wanting to debunk the mythology (with my middle finger held high) that skinny = good/healthy *and* wanting to reclaim agency from the national practices of emotional eating, oversized portions, sedentary lifestyles, fast non-food, pharmaceutical concoctions over cooking, and corporate success over nutrition. Slowly, surely, I am changing habits that will liberate me from my socialization.[3]

But here's the key: it started with pleasure, not with dieting and exercise. I had to love what is before I could understand what transformations were wanted, needed. And I've been feeling so loving in my body lately that I want to be more explicit around my pleasure activist practices. Lots of them fall under the umbrella of sex. Really good sex.

Are you ready for that? If not, skip to my last blog which is probably about transformation or sci-fi. No judgment here.

For those still here—hi!

Here are five tangible tools that should work regardless of any aspect of your identity or the current state of your pleasure activism. They are in a sort of chronological order:

1. *Self-love.* Since I was a kid, I have had a penchant and passion for my touch on my body. This was sometimes shameful, sometimes wonderful, and deeply private from fairly early on, as I received messages from family and neighbors that it wasn't "right."[4] My mom gave me room for it, without words, which I appreciate. It has only been as an adult, as I

---

3   I have an incredible, vibrant, and supportive online community around this now, people in practice of shifting our relationships toward sugar and away from obsession, addiction, binging, and purging; toward moderation, balance, boundaries, and health. We lift each other up and cheer each other on.

4   Perhaps my first love was a best friend I had when I was very young. We made out, touched each other, and I thought she was the best and coolest person on earth. Her mother put a stop to our grand baby affair in a way that left a lifelong interest in me for healthy ways to engage children around their bodies and feelings without shaming them.

have witnessed every single child I have ever met come into pleasureful awareness of their bodies, that I have understood that it was a natural part of growing into my body.

In my early twenties, I learned about pleasure activism: acting from an analysis that pleasure should be a natural, safe, and liberated part of life—and that we can offer each other tools and education to make sure sex and drugs and other pleasures aren't life-threatening but life-enriching. My self-touch took on a political power. I started saying "an orgasm a day keeps the doctor away," and I was in joyful practice for my own health.[5] Toys? Yay! But I also worked to ensure that my own touch was effective. I was mostly single during this period, with lovers as they came and went. I now know that I was mostly single because I needed to reach a certain level of healing from earlier experiences of sexual trauma.

It also became clear to me that if more people were encouraged to masturbate early and often, to learn what feels good to them and that they have the right to communicate that, there would be less sexual trauma, assault, patriarchy, misogyny, and general awkwardness.

2. *Orgasmic meditation.* This was a more recent practice connected to self-love. I went to a meeting of an unrelated group in a space in San Francisco that focused on orgasmic meditation, among other things. I remember being in the space and sort of on edge. It is not unusual to end up in a room in California where people are talking openly about sex and even having it with each other, but I felt young and flustered by the idea of a room full of people bringing each other to orgasm and very glad my meeting had nothing to do with that.[6]

---

5   Quoting Mae West.
6   The location is called One Taste, and the method and location have both been raved about and have been a spot of controversy and harm in my networks, so I would say come to your own conclusions here, as with anything else. I can only testify that the method, when focused on the self, is quite effective.

But the idea stayed in my head, and a couple years ago I came across it again in my random explorations of the entire internet. I watched a few videos where folks explained the method: stroking the upper left quadrant of the clitoris to bring a person to orgasm. The focus on just that one place, following the breath patterns and emotional process of the recipient, and the power of the orgasm as a form of meditation and spiritual practice—all of it was fairly titillating to me. By this time, though, I was thousands of miles from San Francisco, with no one around I felt comfortable asking to stroke me just so without, you know, making it a whole thing. So I decided to see what happened if I just did it for myself.

I did a fifteen-minute practice every morning before anything else in my day for a few months. What I experienced was that every one of my orgasms had a different emotional flavor, like an experiential snowflake. And that I didn't always need to reach an orgasm in that fifteen minutes—sometimes not releasing yielded a more energized day. Starting my day with this practice made everything else go better, feel lighter and healthier, and generally increased my personal and interpersonal joy. I have still never attended their classes or done it with a group … we'll see. But as a solo practice, I return to this one if ever I feel I am in a funk.

3. *Self-pornography.* This is also an extension of the self-love practice but has a lot of its own specifications. I don't fit the standard for American pornography or American desire. I have traveled to other places where I have been celebrated immediately for my size and shape, my color. But not so in the U.S. Most pornography here offers the choice of brunettes, redheads, or blondes, or the "exotic" options of Asian or Black women, all having sex with white men, or, for lesbian porn, white women. Or in really freaky stuff, Black men. Perhaps you can feel the yawn in that sentence, pardon me.

But I realized that if I wanted to truly be radical in the world, truly see white and skinny as one way people are born as opposed to the physical supreme, which pours over into every other aspect of life, I had to decolonize my desire. I had to learn to desire myself, my body, my skin, my rhythms, my pleasure. I took pictures at first. The pictures weren't necessarily explicit in the beginning. They were just selfies, before Instagram.

I started with my face—how did I look smiling? Happy? Turned on? Shut down? Laughing? I took photos of every part of myself until I felt I knew more about my body, could tolerate myself, even like what I saw.

Then it was time for short videos. I would create the videos during moments of self-love, and then use them the next time I felt like touching myself. These videos were not shared, they were not for anyone else's eyes, opinions, or desires. That was radically important. The energy of them was purely self-adoration.

I dated a woman once who told me she had done sexual healing work to get to a place of screaming out her own name when she orgasmed. I let that concept be a guide. How much could I love myself, literally?

The results were life-changing. This practice changed the way I dressed, the way I walked, the way I flirted, the way I made love to others, the way I spoke—because I had seen, heard, and felt my power. I mean both my physical, earthly power, and the divine power inside of this body, this light brown, big, queer, glasses-wearing body. It wasn't ego, it was sitting with what is and finding beauty. And now no one could take that from me, however they might regard my body. I was a pleasure unto myself, I was a guaranteed delight in my own hands and my own eyes. It was, and continues to be, magnificent.

4. *Developing erotic awareness.* This section could also be called Staying Curious. It can get rote. You learn the way to release whatever is building up in your body, alone or with others, and you return and walk that path over and over, because you know it will satisfy your need. This parallels with other aspects of life—you can learn what works and keep doing it and get by.

But bringing curiosity into your sexual relationship with yourself and your lovers is related to the spiritual practice of cultivating a beginner's mind. As often as possible, I approach the experience of sex as if it is my first time feeling my flesh, feeling myself awaken. In my thirties, this led me to discover a whole new landscape of pleasure in my body and then to be able to clearly let my lover know when it feels good, how it feels good, and what adjustments to make.

I used to have lines in the sand, places of judgment. These would usually form in my mouth like, "Oh I would never (insert activity I simply hadn't tried yet here)." But I have been opening up, learning that the realm of desire is actually one of the most honest territories that can exist in the relationship with myself or anyone else. "Haven't tried yet" allows so much more eroticism than "never!" Believe me. Having curiosity, wanting to know what I desire and why and what effect it has on me to follow the desire, has led to an erotic reimagining of my life.

This curiosity in my body and my pleasure has helped me to clarify what kind of life work I enjoy and don't enjoy. Just as obligation is not a great motivator for intimacy and pleasure, I find I can't live my life doing work that feels like I am obligated to do it because of other people's expectations. I thrive when the work has elements of pleasure, titillation, total presence. That work might itself appear mundane or tedious to others—it includes housework, exercise, cooking, shoveling my car out of snow, honest conversations, facilitation, family visits. As long as I can see the glimmer of life in it. Sometimes the glimmer is so bright, and I feel utterly alive. I realize that in the present moment I am free, I am a body of sensations and memories and dreams, energies and spirits and ancestors, totally complex and utterly free. Erotic awareness, for me, is coming into an aliveness in your senses that is quite beyond the material world.

5. *Talk about sex.* Blush and fumble, ask questions, let the words fall out of my mouth. One of my favorite aspects of

the Beyoncé album is how it has led to really beautiful, powerful, nuanced, honest sex conversations with people in my life of all different ages, backgrounds, politics, and sexualities. Sex is the most common behavior among humans after birth, breathing, sleeping, and death, and too often we still feel shame or bite our tongues when it comes up.

Now some degree of secrecy increases the heat, for me at least, though I don't know if that is just the last wisp of some demure Virgo dynamic. I won't tell you of my lover then, the specific things she does with me. But I will say I am having the best sex of my life, and it isn't an accident. It is because of years of practice and hard work. It is because of friends who saw me having the most unhealthy sex of my life in my twenties and said "Honey girl, no." It is because I have been blessed with lovers who were tender and taught me things and let us explore together. It is because of periods of intentional celibacy in my life. And it is because of each practice above.

I think it is important that we hold space for each other to feel good, to be touched in whatever ways bring us pleasure. I notice the impact it has on people I care about when erotic healing, self-love, and the tender touch of a lover, or a few lovers, is needed.

I think this is yet another place to apply the wisdom of Grace Lee Boggs: "transform yourself to transform the world." I believe that if everything else in the world stayed the same, but every single person deepened their physical and spiritual practices of self-love and great sex, the domino effect would be a revolution of our understanding of our purpose here. Suffering is a massively important and absolutely true part of life, a spiritual reality. But I deeply believe we were not placed on this gorgeous, sensational planet to suffer. It is not the point.

A coach recently told me, "What is easy is sustainable." I have been thinking, what feels good is sustainable. When my body feels good, my life feels good, and I want to keep going, and fight for my right to exist and love and grow and evolve. This is true whether it is in the context of a meeting, or a relationship, or a night of lovemaking. That doesn't mean the absence of discomfort or awkwardness or hard conversations or learning. But the majority experience should be presence— being fully alive. And I think that comes from experiencing ease, pleasure, connection. As Nina sang: "Feelin' good."

So, go forth and "turn that cherry out!"

And yes, I am blushing.

SECTION THREE

A CIRCLE OF SEX

CONVERSATION WITH A SEX TOY

The Womanizer is an unfortunate name for a relatively new sex toy that gently suctions the clitoris while vibrating around it[1]. Basically wowzerpants.

amb. *Can we talk about sex and desire?*

Womanizer. I didn't know you knew how to put words into coherent sentences.

amb. *[blushing] I could say the same thing about you. You are such an incredible, miraculous toy.*

Womanizer. Thank you. I'm glad to be so effective. Sometimes I wish I knew more about pace, foreplay—me, my kind, we get such short, focused times with y'all. There's no romance.

amb. *One time I did the candle thing …*

Womanizer. I'm not upset, honey. I feel proud of my results. I think it's actually super-important to empower all humans

---

1   This essay first appeared as adrienne maree brown, "The Pleasure Dome: Conversations with My Sex Toys," May 17, 2017, *Bitch Media* (blog), https://www.bitchmedia.org/article/pleasure-dome-conversations-my-sex-toys.

to produce the healing that I give without having to negotiate it with anyone else.

amb. *I agree. I wish sex education was actually much more focused on what pleasure feels like, getting to know the sensual and sexual pleasures of our bodies before we share them with others, getting to know the distinct energy between yes and no.*

Womanizer. Yes, for so long pleasure has been controlled and vilified, which I think is because it's actually so powerful. To know that you can access, in your own body, that kind of liberation and wholeness and being fully present right here, right now—it's so much easier to dominate people who don't know how to access their own pleasure.

amb. *Within and beyond the realm of sex.*

Womanizer. Yes but—or, rather, yes and—the body is such a nonnegotiable place to learn and listen for pleasure. We toys come across people all the time who think they can't feel pleasure, can't squirt, don't have a g-spot or prostate, have no nipple sensation—don't think they deserve it. And that first time they get to control the experience, press and pace and open and design their own good feeling, with or without my help … I think it changes people, changes what feels possible. The body learns so quickly!

amb. *Testify! I feel like even when I didn't love how my body looked, and when I struggled to be seen by others, much less tell them how to make me feel good, y'all always let me know that I was a magical creature capable of something beautiful. And that truth grew from deep inside all the way up to the surface.*

Womanizer. Really glad to be of service. Have you talked to Wand yet? They love this stuff.

amb. *On it. Thanks again, for all you do.*

SEX MAJIK (NO ONE TOLD ME TO DO IT)

It was the full moon
shining in my window
I waited, a wide sea
moonlight on my thighs
heat on my fingertips
I was a wave, then a million

After, I was trembling
Writing on a page
Everything I needed
Everything I had to have
What I couldn't die without
What was in my veins

I reached into my self
Covered my fingers with yes,
My pleasure, my sea slick
Wrote my name onto the page
Mine mine mine, my pleasure
My life would be my pleasure

I buried this note in my bed
Planted it under my tongue
In my sheets
On my temples
Everywhere, my pleasure,
Everywhere, my prayer

NIPPLES ARE MAGIC

It has recently occurred to me that claiming the massive possible pleasure coming from nipples is a feminist activity.[1] This idea, unsurprisingly, occurred to me one day while under the influence of nipple pleasure, but the idea held even when my head cleared.

I must rewind.

My first conscious experience of patriarchy and boobs was in middle school. As my body went through puberty and my breasts filled in and grew heavy, it/they became objects of attention. Not the kind I wanted. Boys, generally without asking, out of the blue, wanted to smush and fondle them, to grab them with bruising pressure. They acted as if all the breasts at school belonged to them—not us, just our bodies. The boys' responses to my breasts made me feel exposed and awkward all the time. I discovered pleasure in my body early, but I came to believe that breasts were too tender for other people's hands to touch, especially rough boy hands.

Perhaps they were acting out the moves they'd seen in pornography. My first job was working at a bookstore, stocking magazines. I learned early to emulate the "naughty" magazines: No matter how I actually felt, I opened my mouth in a wet "O," furrowed my brow like I was confused, like I could

---

1 This essay first appeared as adrienne maree brown, "The Pleasure Dome: Nipples Are Magic," July 26, 2017, *Bitch Media* (blog), https://www.bitchmedia.org/article/pleasure-dome/nipples-are-magic.

not possibly understand how good it was to be so handled. My job was to just please him/him/him/and him with my existence.

The years passed, and I learned how to slap away groping hands and feel how I wanted to be touched, and I learned that I liked a spectrum of genders. There were moments of nipple pleasure with lovers here and there—most of these passed so quickly as to seem an accident. I learned through private explorations of my own body.

But that learning took a long time. The general behaviors I witnessed were to ignore and disrespect the power of my nipples. And I learned that nipples get ignored or disrespected in a number of ways.

- Nipples on those perceived as women cause much kerfuffle on social media and can get us banned or suspended.
- Nipples shock and awe people when used to breast-feed babies in public.
- Nipples, and breasts altogether, get handled more often than held, stimulated, pleasured.
- When they do get touched it's often a brief cosmetic fiddling on the way to the S.E.X.

It amazes me how often I meet people of all genders who don't understand or feel they can access the potential pleasure of our nipples. Some say they can't really feel anything there. Some say it emasculates them to feel anything there. I know that nipples work differently for everyone and that some people may not really feel much there. But I suspect that most of us could benefit from more concentrated attention on our nipples.

According to a 2011 *Journal of Sexual Medicine* study, the "sensation from the nipples travels to the same part of the brain as sensations from the vagina, clitoris and cervix."[2]

---

2   Stephanie Pappas, "Nipples 'Light Up' Brain the Way Genitals Do,"

Nipple stimulation "releases the hormone oxytocin," aka the happy juice.

I suspect our ignoring of (or under-attending to) these pleasure points is rooted in a patriarchal rejection of anything associated with women's bodies. There are a variety of laws that ban the baring of the breast, often with the explanation that the breasts are too sexual for men to witness. We live at the intersection of Hooters and Janet Jackson boob shaming. At the historical intersection of *Playboy* bunnies and bra burning. Women showing their bodies from the waist up have to fight. Sex becomes a private practice ground for that fight.

So much of sex culture is still set by straight cis men and the pornography of pounding into cis and trans women's mouths and pussies, often in whatever is the most degrading way possible.

I'd be remiss not to mention nipple hierarchy: Nipples with smaller or lighter areolas are considered more attractive than those with the darker, larger areolas—which often come with Black and Brown bodies, and with breastfeeding. Large and/or dark nipples are for fetish, not for beaches or titillating. It has to be said that disdain for the dark nipple feels connected to ancestral mammy memories.[3] What mental calisthenics it took to apply white supremacy to navigating bodies of Black and Brown people!

So it is in the face of all this complex history that I claim my/our nipples as an extension of the pleasure system in my/our bodies, directly correlating and turning up my pleasure.

It was women lovers who first slowed things down to the pace of worship at my breasts, moving past my own haste to get to business, my sense of constant scarcity as a young fat

---

Live Science, August 3, 2011, https://www.livescience.com/15380-nipples-genitals-brain-map.html.

3   The idea that Black bodies were brought to this country enslaved, and that there are practices from that time that persist in intimate space today, can still floor me. And it feels like a space to be vigilant—white supremacy is pervasive and often shows up as "preferences" we can't track from experience.

Black lover who, for a long time, thought I was lucky when someone spent any time on my body. I remember the sensation that everything was connected, the first time I asked a lover to stay at my breast a little longer, the first orgasm I had from nipple stimulation alone. I began to understand a new map of nerves threading through my system, the interconnection of desire and delight threaded through the body.

As far as I can tell from conversations with people of all genders, this pleasure is only numbed by our lack of belief in its existence! Now I want all people with nipples to have a chance at the nipple glory I regularly experience. Here are some steps:

1. Touch yourself! Slow, soft, flicker, pinch, graze. Notice what produces sensation.[4]

2. Ask lovers to spend an entire session on your breasts/chest. Same thing: approach it with curiosity and try lots of different kinds of touch. Give and receive feedback. Start soft and build up sensation, pressure, pace.

3. Use toys. I'm a fan of the Jimmy Jane form 2, which I have repurposed as a splurge of a vibrating nipple clamp. Nipple clamps are also great, just applying a consistent pressure that increases as nipples grow in arousal. Nip Pulls are also cool, using suction to increase blood flow to the nipples for heightened sensation (apply wet for best suction).

4. Constrict the rest of the body to focus only on nipples.

> ## HOT AND HEAVY HOMEWORK
> Your pleasure assignment this week is to discover or upgrade the pleasure relationship you have with your nipples.

---

4   You may need a harder pressure touch at first, to awaken awareness and sensation. As your nipples get used to being engaged, you may find you can feel a wide variety of touch.

IT'S BLOODY FANTASTIC

The only way I can even write this is to imagine I'm talking to one friend.[1] Yes, you. Just us, talking about all this weird stuff we're not supposed to discuss in polite company. Otherwise it's impossible to share things like what I'm about to tell you.

So. I'm only telling you.

I travel a lot, and I usually see lovers for a weekend or so here and there. Since forever, my bloody, messy, crampy, and moody period has landed during a visit early in the … togetherness. Suddenly I'm there, a few hundred dollars into a crush, hoping they're on Team Bloody Awesome.

I used to resent this timing, but now I'm grateful because I learned in my early twenties that anything less than Team Bloody Awesome is a red flag for me. My monthly visitor helps me gauge compatibility—weed out the unready. There is a scale, you know. It's like this:

Team Bloody Awesome!

When members of this team find out it's period time, they go tender with care. They know that blood makes us bleeders hungry for meat (or meat substitute), chocolate, and messy

1   This essay first appeared as adrienne maree brown, "It's Bloody Fantastic: Find a Lover Who Loves Period Sex," December 20, 2017, *Bitch Media* (blog), https://www.bitchmedia.org/article/the-pleasure-dome/period-sex-is-great.

multiple orgasms to help shake out the cramps. They don't have the good sheets on the bed when you arrive—or if you're away from home, they remind you that hotels bleach everything. They give you time in the bathroom to navigate your particular period situation—diva cup, tampons, pad, or panties—uninterrupted. And then? They get down.

Bonus points when they are gentle with your swollen sensitive nipples and/or enjoy rubbing your lower back while you moan and wrap your cramping body around a hot water bottle. When you're in the mood, they understand the increased sexual risk of blood and make sure all previously agreed-upon protection is lined up so you don't have to worry your period little brain. They tease and quiet you through any moments of hormonal rage, and, if everything is just feeling too blech for sex, they bring you the good ice cream in front of the TV and get under the blanket with you.

Team Bloody Fetish

These vampires can smell when it's time to bed you. They out themselves by doing extravagant things like pulling your tampon out with their teeth, or making you grind bloody poems into their thighs. They love the abundant lubrication of blood and are thrilled to meet the voracious appetite of their moon-time lovers. You may have to redirect their excitement if you aren't in a sexy mood, which happens for some of us during PMS and the first couple of bloody days. They might even be more into the bloody mess than you're comfortable with. Because the norm is so anti-blood, even if these team members seem extra, it can be healing and normalizing to experience a lover on Team Bloody Fetish.

Team Bloody Skittish

These lovers don't run away from the river of life, but there's not much enthusiasm for the swim. They might prefer a day-three or day-four period bone, when the whole thing is a bit more under control. With a sweet direct request and a quick shower, you *might* get them to kiss on your clit for a moment. It's good to be curious with these lovers, examine the reticence, and see if they have an interest in exploring Team Bloody Awesome. Best case scenario, you can negotiate a period-sex arrangement that doesn't require either of you to feel uncomfortable or undesirable.

Team Bloody Faint[2]

These lovers would prefer that God had not smote the vagina with an affliction as dire and dramatic as monthly bleeding, even in the name of fertility. They feel they need to be protected from the detritus of unused miracles, sometimes to the point of not touching their bleeding lovers or even going on dates during the week of uterine shedding. If you don't take it personally, it can be really cute when they get that deer in headlights look when your period starts mid-coitus.

They might have specific blood-related trauma or a phobia of blood. You can ask about that. If they don't, though, this team member should be invited into a learning journey around what periods are and how they work. Many of them have desires programmed by the "period = unclean" narrative that only seems to serve a male-supremacist worldview.

Now, it's important to keep in mind that this whole scale shifts relative to your own comfort with your cycle, blood, cramps, and moods. You might be Team Bloody Awesome in theory but Team Massive Cramps (if you're regularly in so much pain that period sex seems unthinkable, you might be an unknowing member of Team Fibroids, so talk to your OB-GYN) or Team PMS Hulkmonster in real life.

This piece is not to imply that you must be aroused during your monthly blessing. It's about destigmatizing this natural process, which can actually feel really good. This piece is for

---

2   This is fine if you are a gay man. You're also exempt from the homework … unless you are (or are with) a trans man who still bleeds, in which case it may or may not be interesting for you.

those who have wondered how we can live in a society that so easily embraces the blood of war (or the fake blood of the war entertainment industry) but gets faint around blood that only exists as part of a cycle of life-making. Ah, dear reader, contradictions are human, and moving through them in the name of great sex is divine.

HOT AND HEAVY HOMEWORK
As Big Freedia says, "You already know!" Have period sex with yourself (any and all penetration is easier with that natural-flowing lubrication) or another human on the first day of your/their next period.

FUCKING/HAVING SEX/ MAKING LOVE

*I have been working on a series of writings that help me recon-
ceive of the realm of sex based on my own experience, as a feminist challenge to Judeo-Christian narratives I grew up within. I
was raised to think that the only physical encounter worth having is making love, as a sexual encounter between two people of
opposite sexes who were both in love and committed to each other
in the eyes of a masculine God ... that anything else cheapens
all sacred bonds between bodies. I have learned so many other
possibilities through my embodied experiences of pleasure. I have
become committed to honoring and respecting a much wider
spectrum of ways that bodies can come together. In this piece, I
speak to the relative wonders of different levels of depth in sexual
encounters.*

Sometimes we need it to move really fast, to be about the
rush to crash into each other's bodies, to slip to the floor and
right there pull off the shirt and tug at the belt, unbuckle,
the sounds of metal and leather a cheap promise ... and are
there buttons, a zipper, is it lace, or boxers, or nothing at all?[1]

---

1   This is the urgent campaign version of intimacy, the outcome-oriented
work that is aware of the twenty-four-hour news cycle. This may include punishment, but only if you deserve it.

Is it already wet, is it hard, enter me grab me fuck me harder than you have ever fucked anyone anything fuck me and call me names slick-slit cuntfucker goddess?[2] Take my throat and scream my name until it twists and we are at the edge of pain and pleasure and release. Afterward, be dizzy, disoriented. What was that, who were those people anyway?

Sometimes it is fun, there is laughter and maybe we were drinking a minute before. We are real human bodies here, not pornography, not Hollywood, not magazines, not fantasies—we are bodies in need.[3] We kiss as we undress, we fumble out protection,[4] we have music playing that didn't know the sex was coming. The sheet tangles around your thigh when you try to roll on top of me, and we have to pause, unravel, focus. Or I am getting creative to find a way to ride you, learning to place a foot on the box spring to get leverage for my bad knee. We don't necessarily love each other, but there is desire here, I enjoy your sexual company, your body in my hands, I enjoy what you do to me, and I tell you what I need. This is the realm of imperfection, where sometimes your tongue tries to fill my mouth[5] and it makes me move away, but then you press up behind me and I open again, twerking a bit to find the angle that makes us both feel lucky. We may not come at the same time, but we come and it's wet and breathless, the body is released.[6] We don't talk a lot, or we do, but it doesn't change us much. This works, this sex between us.

Sometimes we need it to be a million increments, slower than breath,[7] a year spent with your hand moving up my

---

2   Capitalist. Patriarch. Hierarch. Monarch. Selfish. King. Daddy. Owning Class.

3   In political landscapes, this can be an alliance or coalition. We need to move together for a while—this is not our permanent home, but it does need to be satisfying.

4   Ground rules. Community agreements.

5   Microaggression.

6   We have divergent conditions of satisfaction, but both of us get closer to what we want with this work.

7   Political home, the delight of finding a place that can hold all of you, wants to.

thigh while my heart pounds. A feeling that my flesh is your favorite feeling and you want to linger in the contact. The appreciation of each layer and angle of this outfit, you unravel and undo me, open me like a cherished gift. Those times you want me to stand there while you look at my body through my clothing, reach under my skirt to ring your fingers along the top edge of my pantyhose, up higher to find the shiver of lace, the heat that waits for you, the heat you don't plunge into but hover before, worshipful. Those times when you touch my nipples with the tips of you, fingers and tongue, until my back arches. Those times when I find the tips of you, fingers, clitoris, cock, with my tongue and lips, and stay still, letting you use my mouth. How slowly can you cover this territory, how much can I need this release?[8] Sometimes I have had many releases in the erotic journey before you even see me naked, before you tell me your mouth is watering for me, before I get to feel you inside of me, slowly making me a sea.

---

8   Let's vision together. I like how you practice consensus. It is a joy to be in this life work with you.

THE HIGHS, LOWS, AND BLOWS OF CASUAL SEX

amb. *What do you count as casual sex?*[1]

Gary, thirty-eight, Black, gay cis man (name changed). One-night stands. Random hookups. Sex with a "fuck buddy." Essentially, any sexual activity with a stranger or someone with whom I'm not romantically involved.

Leah Lakshmi Piepzna-Samarasinha, forty-two, nonbinary disabled queer femme mixed Sri Lankan.[2] Sex that happens outside of an ongoing relationship *or a desire for ongoing relationship*. Certain kinds of emotional intimacy or commitment. Sex where the connection is mostly about the sex.

---

1   This essay first appeared as adrienne maree brown, "The Pleasure Dome: The Highs, Lows, and Blows of Casual Sex," July 11, 2017, *Bitch Media* (blog), https://www.bitchmedia.org/article/pleasure-dome/highs-lows-and-blows-casual-sex.

2   Check out Leah's "Care as Pleasure" in this book!, p. 313.

Holiday Simmons, thirty-nine, Black Cherokee transmasculine two-spirit person.[3] I define casual sex as sex that is either no strings attached—there's no expectation of continued contact afterward—or that there aren't necessarily feelings involved at the time or later. Or there might be appreciation/love feelings but not necessarily romance, so, like, friends with benefits can have casual sex because it's not romantic sex.

Mai'a Williams, thirty-seven, Black, queer, cis woman, mama. Really, for me, casual sex is sex I have that doesn't require other emotional labor. Like, I don't have to care about your hard day at work or your relationship with your mom or a nightmare you had last week. I might care, I might not care, but I don't have to care.

Samhita Mukhopadhyay, thirty-nine, South Asian, straight, cis woman, author of *Outdated: Why Dating Is Ruining Your Love Life*. I don't really like the term "casual" next to "sex" because sex is not casual—it's sex! Sex should be an intimate experience that relies on trust, communication, care, and honesty, which are not casual things, per se. I wish we could just call it, I don't know, something that might denote both the lack of traditional relationship structures paired with being a sexually responsible adult (not an asshole). Maybe we just call it sex.

amb. *I love that reframe. So, why do you have casual sex?*

Samhita. Sex is good and nice—that's why! I wish I was having more of it, though ...

Gary. The word "ephemeral" comes to mind, as does the acronym NSA (no strings attached). Casual sex is uncomplicated. Its singular focus is the here and now, indulging in the

---

3   Check out Holiday's "Are you there, goD? It's me, Day" in this book!, p. 153.

moment. It demands no commitment beyond the encounter itself.

Mai'a. I have a natural and crafted talent for giving and receiving pleasure. I like having sex without having all the emotional labor involved. I like practicing my craft. It feels like writing a good poem or dancing to a song you know by heart. It feels good to be good at something.

Holiday. I engage in it because I love pleasure and exploring different types and ways to please myself, be pleased, please others, and learn others. And having many different types of sexual partners and different situations that lead to those sexual partnerships is a huge learning opportunity for me as it relates to my identities, to my sense of safety, to being validated. Having casual sex is like a human experiment of desire.

Leah. I grew up in a family with two parents who had an utterly miserable, abusive relationship that both of them felt they couldn't leave. Part of my resistance was to be like, fuck that, I'm never doing that. Marriage is a prison of death. I wanted to have sex with lots of people and be in different kinds of loverships with some of them. I also am a neurodiverse hermit warrior queen who loves and needs lots of time to myself and "TOTAL SEXUAL AUTONOMY." After a childhood and young adulthood filled with parental, sexual, physical, and emotional abuse, a ton of bullying, sexual assault at school, and very little permitted autonomy (I wasn't allowed to shut the door to my room or take a shower by myself for years), having casual sex was incredibly healing because I needed some huge built-in boundaries after not being allowed any. It was a place to have intense, contained intimacy and magic.

amb. *What is the best thing about casual sex?*

Leah. The feeling of autonomy and control. The ability to explore and learn about myself. Being sexual and getting up and leaving afterward. How it was liberating to me as a brown femme survivor to be, like, I get to have wildly uncontained sexuality. Casual sex makes me feel connected to a lineage of queer sex radicalism, public sex and non-married/committed sex, which I feel is getting lost. It felt radical to articulate that sex can just be about pleasure, it doesn't have to be about Commitment, Marriage, and the Family. I loved my rituals of getting ready, adornment, going out, and walking and feeling sensual in my body. Also, small talk bores me, and I think you can learn a lot about someone by fucking them!

Samhita. With the right person, it's a sexual experience purely focused on pleasure. I know we'd like to say all sex should be focused on pleasure—it should be, but sometimes it's not, and relationship dynamics are being worked out, or you are, like, mad about the dishes so it's interrupting your flow. Casual sex is a space where you don't confuse emotional intimacy with the desire to get off. Sometimes, it gives you the freedom to really get wild, maybe experiment with things you haven't tried before.

Gary. Exploring a new body and discovering how to please it and, in turn, having it please mine.

Holiday. The best thing about casual sex is identifying a want or desire and it being finite. I want to do this with this person—and that being it. Or you can do it again. It's nice to have a finite thing that you have the power to acknowledge and go for, and it doesn't have to be tied to a larger connection, a larger dynamic. It can still be super-intimate, important, spiritual.

Mai'a. Orgasms. Getting to play with another person. Getting to feel how your body fits against another. Something new and different. Getting to try on new personas, to be different types of lovers. Getting to be awkward and having to figure things out. More than once I have met someone who was at first shy and demure. And then in bed, they are a completely different kind of person. Sex for me is about getting to see that transformation. It's about loving yourself enough to be willing to share that with another person. It's about finding out who you are when you are wild and in pleasure. It's about getting to celebrate that you have a body and that body can move and relate with another body. It's a reminder of how good it is to be human. I like getting to experience new bodies and new types of people and new styles of sex and relating.

amb. *What's the worst thing about casual sex?*

Mai'a. The worst thing is the social shame and stigma around it. You feel like you can't be honest about not wanting to have a deep emotional relationship with someone. A lot of times the sex is better, especially for women, when there isn't this whole committed relationship wrapped around it. I feel like men are allowed to have one-night stands, but women aren't because we're supposed to take care of people all the time. So, of course, we want this continuous relationship where we are emotionally invested in the other person's life. And honestly, for a lot of women that I know, casual sex is a place where we get to be served and cared for physically. Like with a one-night stand, I get to say what I want and how I want it. In some ways, I get to be more in control, and if the other person doesn't want to do that then we can just end it—right there—and I can just walk away. There is no long discussion about the emotional fallout the next morning or all this pleading for me to perform more emotional labor.

Holiday. The worst thing is, because there is an element of not knowing each other, it leaves one open to vulnerability and to being harmed, at worst. Or not being seen, validated—all the things good about casual sex, bad casual sex can do the opposite.

Gary. The anonymity promotes a lack of accountability. Casual sex, in my experience, is most frequently with strangers. The hope or assumption is that with each encounter there is mutual respect and regard for the other person involved. Sadly, this isn't always true. So, when someone is looking to "maximize" their pleasure, it may be to the detriment of their anonymous partner, such as secretly removing the condom during intercourse. Or, for example, I once had someone grab my face tightly with both hands and shout "good nigger" as he orgasmed. These violations would most likely not occur with a known partner but are always a possibility with a stranger.

Samhita. When men are terrible. Just because it's casual doesn't mean you have to be an asshole about it! If I text you after we have sex or want to make plans for the next time, I'm not actually proposing marriage—don't flatter yourself, honey. Also, sometimes I have casual sex for the wrong reasons—because I am craving closeness and I really need someone to talk to. I will have sex and realize it wasn't what I wanted or I wasn't in the right headspace for it.

Leah. I had all my casual sex before Tinder and the like (I hooked up with someone from a Craigslist ad once). While I know Tinder and other sites work for some people, for me, they also really upped the traditional desirability politics in a bad way. The thing I liked about casual sex in the nineties and 2000s was that it often really felt like a place where you could get some as a non-traditionally attractive weirdo. Now, it feels like a contest where traditionally pretty people get more ass and others don't. As I've gotten more out about being disabled, I've gotten less interested in casual sex because I only want to have sex with other people with non-normative bodyminds, and much of mainstream casual sex space (including able-bodied QTPOC) just ignores and "forgets" about disability and ableism. In most places I've encountered, there's not enough room or awareness to talk about and engage with bodyminds the way I want to. However, I believe this could change.

amb. *Thank you for raising that, I think that's also some of what holds me back. How can an app capture the needs I have related to size and ability, and even to post-gender desire? So, what do readers need to know to get the best casual sex experiences?*

Leah. Well, not everything is going to be the best sex of your life—there are going to be plenty of weird, mediocre experiences. You need to know yourself, or engage with knowing yourself as an ongoing project. Ask yourself, what are your desires? What's your motivation for doing this? What are the rituals you want to incorporate into it? What do you need to feel safe/r? It's really hard to be honest about all the things you want and in what context, but it's crucial to enjoyment. Also, there are some kinds of sex you just might not want to have casually, and that's okay. The biggest thing is figuring out what yes, no, and maybe are for you, and how they feel in your body, and knowing you can stop, leave, or change direction at any time.

amb. Repeat: any time. What else?

Samhita. Communication! Be honest about how you really feel and what you want. Don't try to be the "cool girl"—fuck chill. It's your body, demand what you want for it (or ask, I mean, whatever floats your boat). You deserve to be treated exactly how you want, so be honest about what you are bringing to the table and what you hope to get out of the experience. Also, use protection ;)

Gary.

1. Trust your instincts. If it doesn't feel right, act on that feeling. If you're worried or feel uncomfortable, then you're not enjoying the moment.

2. Be self-aware. Know your intentions and motivations. Know what you want from the encounter.
3. Communicate. Set boundaries if you need to. Ask the questions that you need to. Say "no" if you need to.
4. Be safe. For some, this means condom use, for others, it might be letting someone know where you are.
5. Indulge yourself, but not at the risk of your partner(s).
6. Don't be reckless. Never compromise yourself or lose control of a situation.

Leah. Oh, and practice saying no. Practice getting up and leaving. Practice saying, hey, I'm not feeling it, I gotta go. These are skills we're not taught and they are crucial.

amb. *Anything I didn't ask that feels important?*

Leah. You can have casual sex through meeting someone at a cafe, chance meetings through friends, grinding at a party, using online modes of connection, or going to a play party. Research play parties and be aware that many of them can be very white, abled, etc. If you don't like the sexual spaces out there, make your own! People always have, from the kind of queer male public sex Samuel Delany writes about to when queer women into BDSM started going to The Catacombs, a queer male sex club focused on fisting in San Francisco in the eighties and created a pansexual queer fisting paradise.

Gary. Get tested, regularly. Be honest with your doctor about your sexual activity. Learn your limits.

CONFESSIONS OF A QUEER SEX GODDESS

One of the most important areas of pleasure activism is to acknowledge and unlearn regressive beliefs inside our own pursuit of pleasure. I have been on my own journey of decolonization in the work of crafting these pages. It is embarrassing to name, but one key area of this kind of unlearning in my life has been around sex with partners of the same sex. It's taken me most of my life to have this particular aha, that "gay sex" is not abnormal or subpar or missing something or evil or even gay. It's just dope.

It might seem quite obvious to you, or at least obvious that I would think so, since the majority of my sex life has been with nonbinary, trans, and women lovers. That just shows the depth of internalized homophobia and how deep gender social conditioning is.

Like a lot of humans who get socialized in a religious context, I grew up believing in procreation as the primary purpose of sex. And I grew up thinking that the penis was the center of sex, the necessary component. Even when I began sleeping with people who didn't have (or want to have) a penis, we would bring the penis in. We might buy one at a store and strap it to our bodies. We might just use the language—"suck my dick, lick the shaft, kiss the tip, come inside me." Of course, I don't mind this with transmasculine lovers, but I began to wonder why, when I was with lovers who didn't identify with a penis in any way, we still felt the need for … a penis.

I started intentionally leaving the penis out, seeing how far we could go without it. It was so far! It was further, in many cases, than I'd ever gotten with a real or fake penis. I gained a new respect for the brilliant design of my hands, how I have enough fingers for simultaneous double penetration and clitoral stimulation—and a whole other hand for nipple tweaking or hair pulling and face grabbing or ass gripping. I was also amazed at how erotic and satisfying all the variations on grinding could be, especially the holy grail of tribbing.

I talked with gay cis male friends and they shared a similar experience of this phenomenon: an initial approach to the ass as if it were some alternative to a pussy, and then a recognition of the way the male body is actually structured to feel outstanding pleasure through anal stimulation. Of course, anal sex feels good to a lot of women too, even without the precious prostate.

And, of course, neither fingering nor tribbing nor anal sex (nor any other kind of sex) are actually gay sex anyway. That whole limited way of thinking is evidence of patriarchy, heteronormativity, and the moralistic effort to control what happens in our bedrooms.

All of this finally led to a breakthrough—"gay" sex isn't missing anything, and it isn't alternative, it's just been politically attacked. For a long time. Not forever, though—there is so much evidence of gay sex in all cultures from the beginning of time. We are in an era of rejecting the rigidity and lies of authoritarian systems that aim to separate us from listening to the wisdom of our bodies in order to control us. As with so many aspects of pleasure activism, we are remembering our nature and regenerating our relationships to each other in the most natural ways.

ARE YOU THERE, GOD? IT'S ME, DAY

Holiday Simmons

Holiday Simmons is a transmasculine, two-spirit, Black and Indigenous organizer and educator based in Atlanta. Holiday is someone I've watched grow and transition, someone I've known to be open in teaching others as he learns how longing, trauma and gender have shaped him.

October 2012

Still searching for that thing. Today I created a profile on Match.com. I made it under the "woman seeking man" category. I figure, you know, maybe if I just really connected with someone and he was cool enough, I could come out to him as trans later.[1]

Like after I'm pregnant.

---

1   Trans or transgender: a term used to describe people who transgress the gender assignment they were given at birth. It is often used as an umbrella term to include many other identities including but not limited to transsexual, genderqueer, gender non-conforming, or cross-dressers. People must self-identify as transgender (or trans) in order for the term to be appropriately used to describe them.

This feels like a good plan to me, since I don't know and I am not meeting any cismen who are able or want to be my donor and/or uncle or guncle. I could just pretend like I'm a ciswoman—and of course I'm still queer and just desiring at most a friends-with-benefits arrangement, some presence in the child's life, and no financial support for the intentional creation or rearing of the child.[2] This woman-passing plan feels like my last resort within the impossible options of people who produce sperm. Such people being cismen and some transwomen.

I have not yet cultivated close enough relationships with any transwomen to consider anyone as a viable sperm donor. So then the cisguys. There are cis gay men who think I'm "cute" (just like a puppy, I can only assume), who, however, claim that I don't have the body parts that excite them for sexual activity. I'm caught between that and cis straight men who either freak out if I tell them off tops that I'm a transguy, because then rolling with me would make them gay. Which is true. Or the cis straight men who say whatever you need to hear in order to get with you.

I think curating a potential donor/lover via Match.com is a good look! Also it seems like a good way to get that kind of sex. Just saying.

November 2012

Padre dios, this is harder (and more humiliating) than I thought it would be. Match.com is a trip. People really love Jesus, and everyone is a "people person." What does that even mean? I am getting a lot of messages from people but not many that I'm both interested in and attracted to.

But I did go on my first date.

Homeboy wasn't quite as cute as his picture, but he was a big Outkast fan and also fancied soccer, so I don't ask for much. But ugh. Chile, I don't know how to play these narrow ass rules of straight engagement.

---

2   Cisgender (cis, cisman, ciswoman): "Cis" is the Latin term for "same as." A cis person is someone who identifies with the gender they were assigned at birth.

We met at a restaurant, and when we were being seated at our table I friggin pulled the chair out for him. He gawked at me and said "What are you doing?," spitting out each syllable like he had a bad taste in his mouth and an inflamed canker sore. "Oh!" I snapped to his reality and tried to make a joke out of it. I pushed the chair back to the table and awkwardly stepped back to allow him to pull the chair out for me. Pray for me.

The convo was fine enough; however, it was peppered with various presumptions about me based on his assumed role as male and mine as female. Retch. At the end of the meal when we both habitually pulled out our wallets to pay, or at least offer some loot, I was caught again. Brotherman looked utterly appalled and held a momentary grimace, eyes darting between my face and my outstretched credit card. Wonk wonk.

My hypermasculine socialization was visible. I was stuck like a deer in headlights, and this was not kosher.

What did still have the potential to be halal was that ass. We messed around a bit back at my apartment, but the reality that I just wasn't very attracted to him started to catch up with me, coupled with growing tired of playing the part of a gender location that I no longer feel a part of. I made an excuse about needing to do something, and he left.

Meh.

November 2012

I met another guy on Match.com, and it was a little better. This fella is a thickums delicious. A little quirky and at times annoying but definitely sweet, and we have good chemistry. Whew lord, I hadn't kissed a man under a streetlight like that in ages.

I will give both him and Mr. Outkast another date.

December 2012

Week two on Match.com, and I can't take it anymore! I can't deal with the gross feelings of pretending and perpetually (obviously) being misgendered.[3] I changed my profile to be "man seeking man," outed myself as trans, and changed my pictures to reflect how I currently look.

In spite of these changes, I still want to give the first two guys another chance. But I couldn't bring myself to meet up with the first guy again, at least not without telling him my truth. I texted him the confession and sent him screenshots of my new profile. He cussed me a bit and said "We are done!," to which I internally thought, "Had we started anything for something to be 'done.' Boo!" Then he left me with one word:

"CATFISH!"

Mr. Outkast's response made me scared to tell Mr. Streetlamp Sugar Lips my truth. Yet I still wanted to see him and his thickness. So we met up for dinner again and had an amazing time at my place afterward. He was like a tank of flesh and curves and bald head(s) and attentive and gentle and rough and thorough. Surely I can't tell him just yet.

December 2012

Date three with Thicka-than-a-Snicka, and I definitely need to tell him. Fuck! Last night when we were going at it, at the most vulnerable moment, he said "You are such a beautiful woman."

Not only did my "O" slip away, but I also nearly projectile-vomited. "You are such a beautiful woman." The words sliced through my soul and riveted my stomach and gag reflex into a sudden convulsion. He thought it was my climax. I nearly yanked him out of me and snapped it off in one full sweep. But I breathed deep, moved from under him, and made an excuse about needing to pee. It was so tragic cuz that thing was so good. And I know he didn't intend to cause harm. Hell, he could have said, "Yea chick, whose pussy is it?"

Still, I can't pretend anymore.

---

3   Misgendered (or mispronouned): the act of referring to a person by the incorrect pronoun (e.g., she/her/hers or he/him/his) or other gender-based monikers (e.g., sir/Mr. or ma'am/Miss).

January 2013

Let me find out Sweet and Stocky also has an expansive mind. He was totally cool with my outing. Not only that I'm trans and am looking for a friends-with-benefits donor situation, but he was also understanding that I hadn't previously been honest with him. He appreciated my new profile pics as well. He said he'd try to address me with he/him/his pronouns.

But he also keeps saying "I don't judge. If you knew the life I've lived, you'd know I can't judge." But then he never tells me what that means or any stories about his past or present life at all. He deflects the conversation very well. Makes me nervous in that respect. Still … maybe he can be the one. I'll sure keep enjoying practicing what could look like baby-making until we figure out if him being a donor is in our stars. After all, he got that super D.

January 2013

Homeboy keeps saying "I accept you just as you are. I think we can really help each other."

But dammit! Without further explanation about what that means, I keep wondering if I'm about to sell my soul to the devil or something. So the whole secrecy and withholding is really becoming a turnoff.

Plus, he gets up too quickly after sex. Claims that he knows I'm tired and doesn't want to overstay his welcome. Dude, if I'm still twitching in the wet spot, I am *not* thinking that everything you own is in a box to the left. Basic-tude. Think I'm going to have to chill on him.

December 2014

Are you there goD? It's me, Day.

I haven't journaled in so long. I've been busy living and learning and successfully finding another donor (not one who I had a sexual relationship with but an old friend). I was prayed for in a sweat lodge on Shinnecock lands on Long Island and tried to get knocked up for six months, and the process ended prematurely with no fault of my own, and I'm still bitter, and now I'm deciding not to continue trying to inseminate. So there.

Because it's been eight years of planning, and conversations, and legal documents, and ovulation tracking, and fertili-teas, and inseminations, and waiting, and pregnancy tests, and frustration, and hard conversations with donors, and sadness, and steadily pushing my comfort zones, safety, and self-image as a trans person. So I'm hanging up the cleats on trying to conceive a child, and I'm going to start taking testosterone. At least for six months, and then I'll see if I want to stop and try to return to the conception process.

Also, I submitted my paperwork for top surgery![4] It will be another few weeks before I'm told if I'm even on the waiting list to choose a date for surgery. I'm feeling so excited and have really made peace with the decision to take a pause on inseminating. I'm thrilled to see the changes my body will make but scared about how my emotions may shift. I desperately fear that I'll lose my keen intuition, my empathy skills, my ability to cry, and, in general, that my range of emotion will shrink. Yikes! I need models. I need more models of gentle men, spiritual men, vulnerable men. Praying to the planet Mars!

February 2015
Man, these cats love the kid. The gay men. Literally some of the exact same ones that condescendingly tapped me on my head in response to me flirting with them are now trying to get to know a brotha. At least biblically anyway. But that's cool, cuz that's all I want right now anyway.

---

4   Top surgery: a medical procedure primarily for transmasculine people who require the removal of their breast tissue for gender-affirming and mental health reasons. While the actual procedure is a double mastectomy, the technique and results are different for transmen than they are for ciswomen with breast cancer concerns.

April 2015

It's remarkable that after only four months on T and just one month post-top surgery, I am already walking on the beach in just my trunks, being called "sir" and "he" more than 70 percent of the time.[5] I've also been getting a lot of swipes on Grindr and messages on Jack'd.[6] I even met a guy at a gay bar and went home with him afterward. That has never happened to me before!

But ... I don't feel good about appreciating the attention from guys who applaud my masculinity but also state "no fats, no femmes" in their profile. Often I feel like I'm battling between my cock and my politics. The randiness that T instills does not always help me make a respectable decision. Then I whine about wanting a moment to just be affirmed as male by other males and especially in one of the most mammalian ways that can happen, without having to think critically about the contexts in which that human-ing is happening.

I suppose it's complicated.

I am having a sexual liberation moment. I am really living the dream. I know these hookup apps are full of all kinds of the -isms, but they are allowing me to come out safely as trans and craft the experience that I want. I am able to say who I am, what I like, what I want, and what I won't tolerate. I am able to pick and choose between potential lovers. I am able to get to know them enough before meeting in person in order to decide if it's safe and worth my time.

I definitely realize that I'm able to have these rich experiences because of the privileges of my height, body composition,

---

5   Testosterone (T): a naturally occurring hormone found disproportionately higher in male-assigned people. It is the primary ingredient in Hormone Replacement Therapy (HRT) for transmasculine people. The side effects can include deepening of the voice, increase in body hair, enlarged genitalia, strong emotional shifts, and a host of other results.

6   Grindr and Jack'd: two popular hookup apps for gay men and trans people.

relatively light skin, middle-class status, being able-bodied, and my geographic location in a major queer and trans metropolis. But I still can't figure out what to do with these privileges or, rather, how to be responsible with them.

January 2016
Are you there, goD? It's me, Day.

I've been on T for a year now, and I'm feeling really good about the decision to not try anymore to carry a child. I am looking forward to looking into adoption!

I also think it's time to shift things in my dating life a bit. I've mostly had amazing, safe, and liberating experiences. But now I've learned some nuances and safety tips that have me wanting to pull back from anonymous sex for a while.

A Transmasculine Guide to Navigating Hookup Apps

1. Just because a guy is open to kicking it with a transman and isn't blatantly transphobic, doesn't mean he necessarily appreciates trans bodies. There is a boundary between being interested in someone versus holding someone as a curiosity, an item to be poked, prodded, and explored. Gross.

2. Just because a guy is open to kicking it with a transman and doesn't see the transguy as a human Rubik's Cube (as in the previous example), he may still only be committed to his own pleasure and not also that of the transman. Cis dick-centrism is so real.

3. I need to really, really, really explain that being polyamorous does not make me confused or greedy,[7] and that having a primary partner who is a woman does not in fact mean that I'm on the down-low. I can't assume that just because my profile states this or I mention it that it will necessarily be understood or believed (or even read). When speaking to these

---

7   Polyamorous: the philosophy or state of being in love or romantically involved with more than one person at the same time.

hookups about my primary partner, I've been encouraged on numerous occasions to find the courage to tell my partner the truth about my sexuality and to come out of the closet.

Girl, boo. I'm as queer as a three-dollar bill.

4. Dr. King was right; injustice anywhere is a threat to justice everywhere. The guys whose profiles read "no fats, no femmes" or compliment my lighter skin or athletic build unsolicited are the same ones that display insidious transphobic basicness. I can no longer throw my darker-skinned, more feminine, and men-of-size brothers under the bus for the temporary access of my own pleasure. I won't do it.[8]

5. One good litmus test of a hookup's gender expansiveness and potential place on the trans-safe spectrum is by asking him if he'd ever be interested in a threesome. If the answer is yes, but he's only comfortable with being with you and another transguy and not so much you and another cisguy … red flag! Fetish me not, bu.

6. For the most part, folks on the hookup apps are looking for "right now." That's fine. Except, if you don't operate in the immediate and want to plan something for another day, it can sometimes be like herding cats. Choppy communication, canceling, flaking, and ghosting are common. Like, kind of status quo.

7. Always meet a guy in a public place first (even if it's just the lobby of a hotel or the corner bodega) before being in private with him. Even if he is safe, you just may not be as attracted to him in person as you thought you'd be and you'll need a safer environment to cancel or make alternative plans.

8. Designate a safety support person who you send a photo and any contact information for the hookup

---

8   amb: "We will not have it!" —MBaku, Black Panther

to before y'all together, then text that person again to check-in as safe once you and the hookup have parted ways.

9. White boys are dangerous. White boys are unpredictable. If you must, be careful with white boys.

10. Request a recent photo. Somewhere between age shame and stupidity lies an eight-year-old profile picture just waiting to surprise you when the real person shows up. I can't.

January 2017

Are you there, goD? It's me, Day.

Two years on testosterone now and the intersections between this medical transition and my path of sexual liberation feel unexpectedly whole. Never was the Native adage "our culture is the cure" more true. I feel righteously spared from the narrow Western notions of being a "gay male" and even of being "trans."

While there is a growing visibility of non-binary people, and they are creating beautiful safe spaces in the world, I never quite identified as non-binary. I feel closer to the male and masculine pole than not.

I mean, I do have flair, though. I'm not a femme, I just flame a lot.

Still, that's where being two-spirit and getting entrenched in two-spirit communities around the country has given me such confidence and so many resilience strategies.[9] Not being very hairy, having long hair, singing, sewing, and crying are all traditional traits of many Native men. Some of these same

---

9   Two-spirit: a modern term used to refer to past roles in Native American cultures that believed these special people embodied both male and female spirits. Traditionally, these people were highly revered and played vital roles as healers, counselors, and negotiators. Contemporarily, the term refers to lesbian, gay, bisexual and transgender Native Americans who also play a significant cultural role in honoring their indigenous traditions while decolonizing harmful aspects of Western culture.

traits and behaviors I do/have, and I've previously felt shame around these things in the Western transmasculine world.[10] Even recognizing that I have two (likely more) spirits within me has helped me be less upset and more gracious when people make mistakes on my pronouns.

But perhaps the most surprising and amazing aspect of my two-spirit identity within the mainstream trans world is that the more I am comfortable in my own body and history and culture, the more my lovers expand themselves. There were several men that I hooked up with who had never been with a trans person or any female-assigned person, and afterward, they would exclaim, "Wow! I never knew things could be so amazing. I'm actually rethinking my own gender now."[11]

I guess it's true that the more we are brave, take risks, and try to bring our full selves to the table (or the bed, countertop, etc.) the more it encourages others to do the same. I know hurt people hurt people … but healing people heal people!

And as much as it's important to keep pushing forward for our liberation, we must also pause and reflect and not forget about getting back on D.[12] ;)

---

10   Transmasculine/Transfeminine: a trans person who is more binary and identifies closer to the poles on the masculine and feminine spectrum.

11   Assigned at birth (female/male assigned at birth): the process wherein medical personnel decide which gender a baby is based on genitalia when that baby is born. This process is known as an "assignment" because a person's sex is different than their gender, as trans people illustrate when they transgress this genitalia-based designation.

12   In case you were wondering, the D in "Are you there, goD" stands for Dick <3.

FEELMORE

A Conversation with Nenna Joiner

Nenna Joiner greets you when you come through the door, down past the rainbow of dildos, vibrators, floggers, and pornography, smiling and at ease, sexy and friendly. Since she opened her store the Feelmore Adult Gallery on Telegraph Avenue in Oakland, I have been a patron and a fan.

amb. *Tell me all the things you do to bring more pleasure into the world.*

Nenna. I have done many things, but what I am most focused on is continuing to cultivate a unique space called Feelmore Adult Gallery. The idea of opening an adult store came to me in a dream. Feelmore gives me a unique platform to stand upon in order to be a verified source when I point out opportunities in my community.

No one really listens unless you have a stake in the game. Being the founder has given me compassion, understanding, and a responsibility to inform so many others in so many ways that help my community. Feelmore's motto, "It's More Than Just Sex," is honest and real. There are so many issues that come up because of sex and intimacy in the world that I wanted to create a place that just lets others reset and educate themselves on their own desires.

It was a challenge to have a unique sex shop, aka sacred space, in Oakland that is truly welcoming to all.

Second, I am just myself. I had to work on loving all that I am in order to encourage and empower others.

amb. *Can you tell us how you came to be on this path?*

Nenna. Life is truly an adventure. The path came to me by simply looking at the industry and viewing it through a gap analysis lens. It was missing me … my ideas, my freshness. For now, this is what I have desired to put my everything into. It isn't easy, and days are long, but I am grateful.

But I want more.

amb. *You say the idea came to you in a dream—were you already in the practice of pleasure or adult films? When did you know this was a calling?*

Nenna. When I had the dream, that was day zero for me. I had never been "in the practice of pleasure or adult films." My producing adult films came after. It isn't a calling, per se. I am just maximizing my time and doing good things with my gifts and talents while in this industry.

amb. *What are some of the challenges you have run into on this path? (Family, financial, societal opinion, gentrification, homophobia?)*

Nenna. Most of the challenges have been financial. Given that I am Black and female, there is already a great deal that America can help you unpack given its historical policies on financial lending. Other than financial challenges, another has been zoning, as adult stores have to be in certain areas. I have always wanted Feelmore to be a part of a community, and am grateful that so many are believing in Oakland and helping to bring new customers to our area.

amb. *Why is it important that you are specifically creating erotic material?*

Nenna. Material of any kind is what people can hold onto … what they can interpret … what they can critique. If it doesn't exist, it isn't real.

The content I've had the honor of creating includes two adult films (*Tight Places: A Drop of Color*, *Hella Brown: Real Sex in the City*), countless erotic art pieces, and a book (*Never Let the Odds Stop You*), as well as being the keeper of the Feelmore trademark, which make the legacy of the erotic much more necessary and sacred. As the content will always live, past my point on earth, I am honored to leave the world a fresh perspective that no one else should own, my body [of work].

amb. *Something I love about you that I've witnessed as your success has grown is that you really hold the sacred in the center of your life, often thanking God for things that happen, holding Feelmore as a sacred space. Can you speak about the role of the sacred, and of faith, in your pursuit of pleasure?*

Nenna. Faith is important. I would venture to say that all who are self-employed are tapping into some kind of faith or spiritual practice. When I first moved into Feelmore, I cleaned out the entire place. The previous business had been there more than twenty years.

Everyone believes something even if it's in themselves. I am grateful that I get to talk, within, to something I believe is greater than me. Ego doesn't serve my business or me … why give it power? I look to give power to that which empowers me at all times.

amb. *Tell me about a moment of power that has happened in the store (I know I've had a few).*

Nenna. Opening the door is a true moment of power. Tracing my pockets to find the key that holds the door to my life captive. Ever so gently, I place the tip of the key, guided by my index finder, into the hole. Turning the key gently and hearing the sound that it makes when it frees the door lets me know that the idea I had of Feelmore has been proved. Power comes in many forms, but this daily ritual gives me a moment of pleasure. Ownership of the body is something that many are familiar with, but to own one's own body … be it mind, work, ideas. But truly the body is a power point.

BODYMINDS REIMAGINED

A Conversation with Sami Schalk

Sami is the author of Bodyminds Reimagined: Disability, Race, and Gender in Black Women's Speculative Fiction.[1] *She also teaches at the University of Wisconsin, where three floor-to-ceiling bookshelves of Black feminism and science fiction have her back.*

amb. *Tell me how you became who you are, so interested in bodies.*

Sami. I grew up as the mixed-race child of a white single mother in a small, Catholic town in Kentucky. I went to twelve years of Catholic school. This shaped a lot of who I am today, growing up around no people of color, no out queer people, no women of color with bodies shaped like mine—I struggled with my racial and sexual identities as well as with eating disorders growing up, but I was blessed to have a mother who knew I was different and wanted to support my interests in reading and writing. One summer, she signed me up for a creative writing camp at a nonprofit

---

1   Sami Schalk, *Bodyminds Reimagined: Disability, Race, and Gender in Black Women's Speculative Fiction* (Durham, NC: Duke University Press, 2018).

in Cincinnati called Young Women Writing for (a) Change. In some ways, the origins of who I am today started there. I was already a writer, but there I discovered feminism, deep listening, safe space, and authentic voice. I attended camps throughout high school and assisted with the girls' camps. Later, in college, I continued to teach there, and I led writing circles inspired by that work during graduate school as well.

Growing up, though, I always had this sense that some other way of living was possible, so even though I tried to envision a life like those around me, I was pretty sure I was going to leave. I came out in college, developed my relationship to Blackness, engaged in activism, and encountered disability studies. This next stage shaped my academic path to an MFA in poetry and a PhD in gender studies with a focus on Black feminism and disability studies. But the most current version of me has been vastly shaped by my graduate school experiences with queer community, BDSM, and polyamory. Through these spaces I have come to embrace myself as a fat Black queer sexual being whose desires and politics can exist happily alongside one another.

amb. *We're gonna get to the BDSM and polyamory, but I am curious about what made you tune into the realm of disability? You mention encountering disability studies, and I am curious about why it particularly sparked your interest.*

Sami. I first got invested in disability studies and disability rights in college. I was a women's studies major, and I took an elective course called Women and Disability. At the time I was nineteen and embracing my Black queer womanhood, so I thought I knew all there was to know about oppression. Then that class made me really think about disability as a vector of oppression and a marginalized identity. For the first time in my life, I really had to examine privilege I never knew I had. I remember distinctly thinking, "is this what white people feel like when they find out about white privilege?" I was horrified at how little I knew and how much I benefited from non-disabled privilege. I decided then that if I was going to continue to ask other people to be allies to me and my communities, then I needed to be a non-disabled ally. The more I learned about how ableism often intersects with and undergirds manifestations of other oppressions (like calling women hysterical to discount their competency for voting rights), the more I realized that understanding disability and ability as a major ideology and social system was key to understanding how power functions in the western social and political world.

amb. *What is most commonly misunderstood about disability? Set us straight.*

Sami. People think disability means inherent deficit rather than difference, that disability is automatically bad, painful, a worse life. People assume disabled people don't have lives, especially not sex lives. Part of this stems from disabled people being segregated and isolated for so much of our history—institutions and segregated educational spaces for disabled people existed (and in some ways continue to exist) well into the 1970s. Only now are we beginning to see disabled people who grew up with the American Disabilities Association (ADA) in place, who have had significantly more opportunities and political/social support. People with disabilities are different—from non-disabled people and from each other—and those differences shape how they live in the world, but this different way of living, even as it may negate doing some things, opens up new ways of being and existing that are valuable and important as well.

amb. *Thank you. And where does BDSM enter your analysis, life, play, work?*

Sami. I don't do research on BDSM, though I do enjoy reading some of the work that is coming out right now (like the book *The Color of Kink*),[2] but it's an important part of my life. I am a fat Black queer woman in the academy, a place where I have to fight for voice and power, where I am not recognized as an authority, where I have to project confidence at all times, where I cannot let go or be vulnerable. I enjoy BDSM play for how it allows me to turn off my brain in certain ways (hard to do as a person who is paid to think critically), to just be in my body, to experience pleasure in an uncomplicated way and give myself over to that, to my partner. BDSM also is a major reason why I claim queer rather than bisexual or other sexuality terms. For me, my sexuality has space for all gender identities and presentations, but my attraction to BDSM, my polyamory, and my political stance against marriage are just as central to my sexuality and relationships.

amb. *I am so excited to hear that you're playing in all these realms, Sami! I feel like polyamory and nonmonogamy are finally getting more room to be explored outside patriarchal models (like sister wives). Are there any particular guidelines you have found that make polyamory a liberatory practice?*

Sami. Polyamory has been legitimately life-changing for me. It has allowed me to embrace truths about myself (like, I love kids but don't want to have them. Or, I want local, committed partners, but I don't want to cohabit) without feeling guilt or shame. Polyamory offers me new models of being in the world and being in relationships. I am not just a better partner because I talk about my desires and needs openly when establishing and growing a relationship, I am also a better friend, colleague, and person. I listen better, to others and to myself, and I am more honest too. For me, poly is a set of communication tools to build any kind of relationship at all, romantic, sexual, intimate, et cetera. None of my relationships follow a blueprint, they develop organically from

---

2   Ariane Cruz, *The Color of Kink: Black Women, BDSM, and Pornography* (New York: New York University Press, 2016).

the needs and the desires of the people in the relationship at that time—and they shift as needed.

For example, when I first moved to Albany, New York, for my first job, the first woman I went on a date with was amazing; I liked her a lot. But at the time, she was totally saturated, dating like four other people. So we were casual friends for a long time, seeing each other at gay bar trivia and for the occasional dinner. But as circumstances in her life shifted, we became much closer. We aren't girlfriends, we've never dated, but we spent a lot of time together, sometimes eating or drinking or dancing, but sometimes having sex or just cuddling naked after a night out. I spent Thanksgiving with her last year. We spent a lot of time processing issues in our other relationships together as we sat around eating and drinking all day. Then, when we went to bed, we both pulled out our Hitachi magic wands and cheered them together like toasting glasses for pre-sleep orgasms. That moment for me is peak poly perfection, having a friend who is loving, supportive, gives advice, and is also comfortable masturbating in the same bed before falling asleep. That level of comfort with a person that is intimate and even sexual, but isn't some official dating romantic thing, is amazing to me, and I value it so much.

amb. *That does sound dreamy. You are expanding me with each answer. A couple more questions—what can people with disabilities teach all humans about pleasure?*

Sami. Disabled people's sexual and intimate lives teach us that sex and pleasure are not merely about penetrative, goal-oriented sex. Disabled people have sex and receive pleasure in many ways and spaces that general society does not recognize or approve, like sexualizing caretaking, sex in hospitals or rehabilitative spaces, sex without orgasms, sex with/around medical equipment. Sex for disabled people often means throwing out the norms and working with a partner to discover what their body can and cannot do, what they do and do not enjoy. Often for able-bodied people, there is an assumption that there are certain things everyone wants or enjoys, but when you have an atypical body or mind, it makes potential partners pause, ask more questions, take a little more time. We would all benefit from such an approach that takes each partner's body, each sexual interaction, as new, figuring out what is best with this person in this moment, given how their body feels, what's on their mind, etc.

amb. *I deeply agree. It has been so powerful to recognize my body's abilities and disabilities and start to ask for what I need instead of silently engaging in activities that exacerbate pain. Unless pain is what you're seeking, which brings us back to BDSM. Can BDSM help all humans increase their pleasure?*

Sami. I don't think BDSM is for everyone. But I do think the communication skills, the self-reflection, the after-care practices, and the play elements of BDSM are useful for everyone. Maybe you never want to be tied up or never want to tie someone up, but talking to your partner about your desires, identifying things you might want to do once you build trust with a person, having safe words or code words to quickly communicate to your partner how you're feeling, checking in with someone after a sexual interaction, these are things all relationships would benefit from, I believe. Power play is central to BDSM, but all the techniques folks have developed to ensure power play can occur safely and consensually are valuable in all sexual and intimate interactions.

amb. *Thank you for that insight. Last question—would you share with us one of the most pleasurable experiences you have had at the intersections of disability, BDSM, and Black queer bodies?*

Sami. The intersection of all of these things is a rare feat! In terms of personal experiences, I once attended a women/female-only kinky sex party that was so good about inclusion and access that I want it modeled everywhere. They asked people about access needs in advance, so we had a wheel-chair-accessible room, no scented products, and a variety of snack options for different dietary needs. Prior to starting, everyone introduced themselves with name, identities we wanted to share, how we were feeling, any triggers we had, and what we wanted out of that night. As a fat Black queer person, I felt very safe in that space, which is not my experience in all BDSM spaces. The night was so fun and sexy and sweet all at once. There was a literal buffet of dicks—a table just covered in dildos and vibrators people brought to share (along with lots of safer sex equipment like gloves and condoms). Outside of my own experience, though, I also really like the work of Sins Invalid, a performance group in the Bay Area run by mostly disabled queer people and disabled people of color. Their films and performances often really embrace sexuality and occasionally kink among disabled queers and POCs as well.

FUCK YOU, PAY ME

The Pleasures of Sex Work

Chanelle Gallant

Chanelle Gallant has been a delight, comrade and teacher of mine in the realm of sex trade. She is currently working on a book—a theory of sexual labor.

"What can I do to please you?" he asks as she stands before him, slowly unbuttoning his shirt. She opens the next button, gives him her slow, practiced smile, and says with a wink, "You can leave your money on the table, sweetie."

Sex work takes what women and feminine people of all genders are expected to do for free and monetizes it: be sexualized by cisgender men, validate their masculinity, give them attention, smile, flirt, make them feel important and wanted even if they're tedious, create intimacy and hold vulnerability, pour time and money into white middle-class beauty standards, and have sex that's mostly focused on men's pleasure.[1] Sex workers do all of those things—just not for free.

---

1   For the purposes of this essay, I will be using this definition of "femme" from Leah Lakshmi Piepzna-Samarasinha:

There is nothing natural or effortless about this labor. Sexual pleasure is valuable and life-giving—and it takes work, *real* work. To acknowledge the work of sexual pleasure doesn't diminish it; it just honors sexual pleasure as involving skills—valuable, worthy-of-being-paid skills. The difference between sex workers and non-sex-working women and femmes is just that sex workers get to admit that sex is work and get paid for it. Since it's too late to worry about being called a whore, they also get to enjoy the pleasures of getting paid for it.

People are always asking sex workers, "Do you feel pleasure at work?" Do you ask your nail tech that? Your barista? People obsess about how sex workers feel about sex—not how they feel about *work*. But the pleasure of sex work is the pleasure of surviving, thriving, and having food on the table and an apartment that's all your own. I've been a sex work activist for over a decade and have organized with badasses in the biz from Bangkok, Thailand to Sydney, Australia. And from street-based trans women of color to European migrants working under the table at strip clubs to bi guys hustling on Rentboy, what I've seen is that sex workers aren't all that much different from other workers—many workers are expected to make someone happy, be pleasing, and look

---

Femme: A person who has one of a million kinds of queer femme or feminine genders. Part of a multiverse of femme gendered people who have histories and communities in every culture since the dawn of time. A queer gender that often breaks away from white, able bodied, upper middle class, cis ideas of femininity, remixing it to harken to fat or working class or Black or brown or trans or non-binary or disabled or sex worker or other genders of femme to grant strength, vulnerability and power to the person embodying them. A revolutionary gender universe.

See Leah Lakshmi Piepzna-Samarasinha, "A Modest Proposal for a Fair Trade Emotional Labour Economy," *Bitch*, July 13, 2017, https://www.bitchmedia.org/article/modest-proposal-fair-trade-emotional-labor-economy/centered-disabled-femme-color-working.

good while doing it. Inside and outside of the sex industry, sex is a tool for economic survival and mobility.

Paid and unpaid sex have a lot in common, but you'd never know that when you look at the media's overheated fantasies about the sex industry. Instead, we see the same lurid, sensationalistic images of cisgender women in peril, waiting to be rescued into the "safety" of domesticity. Meanwhile, unpaid sex, especially unpaid heterosexual sex? Oh, *that* apparently happens in a paradise of mutual pleasure, "healthy sexualities," and individual choice. The truth is more complicated.

Smile for Me, Baby

We are sexualized our entire lives: assessed for our desirability according to men and masculine people's shitty (racist, ableist, classist, fatphobic, sexist) standards, then penalized when we fall short. And we have so little control over how and when nonconsensual sexualization will happen: at work, while meeting our kid's teacher, or walking down the street to the corner store. At any time, we can be turned into someone's sex object. We are sexualized as early as infancy, when girls are told to close their legs and be "decent" and some start experiencing sexual abuse. We are sexualized when our employers require that we look good at work so they can sell a product to customers (but not pay *us* for the extra time, money, and work we put into beauty). Trans femmes are sexualized constantly, shut out of every single employment sector except for the sex industry.[2] At home, at work, at school, just walking down the street: all women and femmes can get

---

2   Trans women of color in the US have an unemployment rate of four times the average, and about half of TWOC in the US have worked in the sex industry. See Human Rights Campaign and Trans People of Color Coalition, "Addressing Anti-Transgender Violence: Exploring Realities, Challenges and Solutions for Policymakers and Community Advocates," November 2015, https://assets2.hrc.org/files/assets/resources/HRC-AntiTransgenderViolence-0519.pdf?_ga=2.37418594.399382019.1536798503-1304962530.1536798503.

turned into sexual entertainment for men with or without our consent.

> People try to shame me for being fat. When I am walking down the street, men lean out of their car windows and shout vulgar things at me about my body, how they see it and how it upsets them that I am not catering to their gaze and their preferences and desires. I try not to take these men seriously because what they are really saying is, "I am not attracted to you. I do not want to fuck you and this confuses my understanding of masculinity, entitlement, and place in this world." It is not my job to please them with my body.[3]

We don't get all that much choice about men's sexual domination. Even if we defy it, we still have to respond to it. Men—in particular white, moneyed, cisgender men and the institutions they control—have the resources we need to survive. So if we are never sexual with men (or anyone), we are still forced to be *in relation* with their sexual desires and expectations. With our safety, social status, and economic survival on the line, our own desires, our own sense of beauty, and our pleasures can become secondary. And if we are poor, working-class, trans feminine, fat, disabled, crazy, or racial-ized women, our sexualities are subject to even more intense control and violence. Our glorious, complex sexualities get typecast into narrow fantasies like the trailer park slut, the fun fatty, the Jezebel, the "shemale," the Geisha.

Wifely Duty

The most likely place we'll be sexualized, though, is in our part-nerships. Consider this quip from the comedy *Bridesmaids*:

---

3   Roxane Gay, *Hunger* (New York: Harper Collins, 2017), 188–89.

Becca. What are you doing when you're having sex then?

Rita. Thinking about other things and wishing it would stop. You know, sometimes I just wanna watch *The Daily Show* without him entering me.[4]

That's supposed to be funny because our society thinks that women having unwanted sex is just one of the "inconveniences of marriage." For centuries, the marriage vow has functioned as an irrevocable, blanket sexual consent—by women, for men. So why aren't we talking about how one in ten women will be raped by their husbands? Another 13 percent of women say they've had sex because they were "bullied or humiliated" into it by their current husbands. About a third of married women have complied with their husbands' demands for sex because it was expected after he spent money on her, even though the sexual act was unwanted. The majority of married women report that they experience coercion to have sex from their current husband. Marriage remains the site of the most widespread rape and sexual exploitation in our society.[5]

---

4 Kristen Wiig and Annie Mumolo, *Bridesmaids*, directed by Paul Feig (Universal City, CA: Universal Films, 2011).

5 Based on British legal tradition, marital rape was explicitly exempted from sexual assault legislation in the US until the 1980s. Some laws remained on the books until the 1990s. Data drawn from Kathleen Basile, "Prevalence of Wife Rape and Other Intimate Partner Sexual Coercion in a Nationally Representative Sample of Women," *Violence Victims* 17, no. 5 (2002): 511–24; Elaine K. Martin, Casey T. Taft, and Patricia A. Resick, "A Review of Marital Rape," *Aggression and Violent Behavior* 12, no. 3 (2007): 329–47; Patricia Mahoney and Linda M. Williams, "Sexual Assault in Marriage: Prevalence, Consequences and Treatment of Wife Rape," in *Partner Violence: A Comprehensive Review of 20 Years of Research*, ed. J. L. Jasinski and L. M. Williams (Thousand Oaks, CA: Sage Publications, 1998), 113–62; and Kathleen Basile, "Rape by Acquiescence: The Ways in Which Women 'Give in' to Unwanted Sex with Their Husbands," *Violence against Women* 5, no. 9 (1999): 1036–58.

Who's Afraid of the Big Bad Whore?

In a sense, women and femmes are all forced to be sexual laborers—to please men and masculine people with our bodies. But we are never allowed to admit that this giving of pleasure is real work and that sometimes it is forced work. We are certainly never allowed to take control of this work and negotiate to receive something in exchange for it. Because asking for money makes a woman or femme a whore. And—surprise!—our culture tells us this is the very worst thing we can be. Whores are degraded! Unlovable! Rape-able! Better off dead! We use the term "whore" to refer to the feminine sin of demanding too much. "Attention whore," "fame whore," "money whore": a whore commits the sin of wanting—whether it's money, sex, or attention. Instead, women and femmes are supposed to treat sexual pleasure like good wives doing the housework: do it for straight men, mostly at home, invisibly, with a smile and, of course, for free. Make him happy. Don't ask for too much. Wouldn't want to see women and femmes actually *get something* in return, would we?

Much of our culture's fear about selling sex is exaggerated and misunderstood. This is because the imaginary sex industry is used as a mirror of our larger problems with sex and with work. Tell me what you fear about sex work, and I'll tell you what makes you anxious about your own sex life—and your own working life. The stories we tell about sex work are about our culture's hidden realities—that, even in the "safety" of love and marriage, sex can be a lot of work; sometimes we don't have much choice about it; nonconsensual domination and violence are common (including among queers); sex is still tied to economic survival and class mobility for many people (especially women); and under capitalism, all of us "sell our bodies" in one way or another.[6]

---

6   That is, all labor is "embodied" labor. Or as Marx put it, labor power is the collection of "mental and physical capabilities existing in the physical form, the living personality, of a human being." Karl Marx, *Capital*, vol. 1 (Toronto: Penguin Books, 1990), 270.

Selling Our Bodies

When people ask me if sex workers really choose it, I say, "That's a trick question." Yes, absolutely sex workers have agency and make smart choices all the time, including the choice to do sex work, thank you very much. But the deeper question is: who really gets to choose to work? What about the force and exploitation of regular, everyday capitalism? Unless you have a trust fund or make all your money in the stock exchange, you are also forced to work.

And don't be fooled—we are all selling our bodies. If you sell your work, you're selling the body that performs that work. And that body matters. If you have a body that's not white, if you get too sick to stand for forty hours a week, if you have a body that's fat, that's femme, that's trans, your body is considered less valuable. If that body of yours stops being well-suited to making somebody else a profit, it can be locked into low-wage, precarious, and dangerous work or disposed of in prisons, institutions, and detention centers. Why aren't we so mad about that? It's not right, the way our bodies are assessed by the marketplace and assigned a value (called a wage) at rates we have almost no control over until we are too old or sick to keep selling them. Instead of "ending the demand" for sex work, how about we "end the demand" for profit?

Is paid sex so different from other work? The garment industry is the single largest employer of women on earth. One in every six women doing paid work is in the garment trade, mostly in manufacturing in the Global South. This work is notoriously exploitative, dangerous, and does not provide a living wage. Workers in the garment trade are excluded from labor protections, barred from organizing, and face regular sexual violence from bosses.[7]

In the Global North, garment work is more likely to be in retail. It is still underpaid and non-unionized. Workers face

---

7   Anne Elizabeth Moore, *Threadbare: Clothes, Sex and Trafficking* (Portland: Microcosm Publishing, 2015).

high rates of sexual harassment by bosses and customers, with little power to prevent or stop the harassment.[8] Meanwhile, being pretty, pleasing, smiling, flattering and flirting with customers is an unspoken requirement of the job—for women. Wherever we work, women are sexualized and, for the most part, not paid an extra dime for it, often with little right to refuse the work. Check out the dress codes for waitresses, nurses, airline stewards, on-air reporters: requirements for hairstyles, make-up, nails, the cut, color, even the fabric texture of their clothing are crafted according to aesthetics that please elite white men.[9] *We might not understand the value of our sexuality—but capitalism sure as hell does.*

Everyone from evangelicals to feminists clutch their pearls about how "it's so sad to commodify something as intimate and sacred as sexual pleasure!" Never mind that people get paid for intimate labor all the time taking care of children, our emotions, our bodies. People sell their sperm, ovum, and breastmilk, folks. Where's *their* rescue squad? Blaming the sex industry for commercializing sex misses the point. The problem isn't sex work: the problem is that there is no escape for women and femmes from the expectation that we will perform sexual labor for men on demand. The problem is that we have so little control over the ways we are expected to provide sexual pleasure *for free.*

The Pleasures of Getting Paid

Is it really so awful to get money for sexual labor? Our legal system has tried to make the sex industry as dangerous

---

8   Ritu Mahajan, "The Naked Truth: Appearance Discrimination, Employment, and the Law," *Asian American Law Journal* 14 (2007): 165–203.

9   Sexual harassment of women retail workers ranges from 25 percent to nearly 70 percent. See Laura Good and Rae Cooper, "'But It's Your Job to Be Friendly': Employees Coping with and Contesting Sexual Harassment from Customers in the Service Sector," *Gender, Work and Organization* 23 no. 5 (2016): 447–69.

as it can be (though still designed to serve cisgender men, naturally). As a result, the sex industry can be really rough for some, yet it *still* manages to be the best economic option for many. Sex work can offer poor and working-class women and femmes more financial and personal independence, better working conditions, including more control over how they are sexualized, more flexibility, and more pay in a single day than they might earn during a week in other jobs like in the garment trade. This fact about sex work is treated like a side note compared to all the dumb questions about "why'd you get into this?" So let me repeat: sex workers can earn *more pay in a single fucking day than in a week in other industries.* That matters, and it matters *a lot* to people who are confined to shitty, low-paid work. Pluma Sumaq writes, "For many women of color in my position, prostitution is not what you do when you hit rock bottom. Prostitution is what you do to stay afloat, to swim rather than sink, to defy rather than disappear. For me, this was 'financial strategy' and not 'easy money.'"[10]

When poor, working-class, and racialized women and femmes get paid well for sexual labor, it is a victory. We all win: every woman or femme who's been ordered to smile, to be sexy, to make him feel good, to give him an orgasm—in exchange for what? Being a "good woman"? Being picked by a man? The pleasure of sex work is in the power to take control over our work, our bodies, and what the world tells us we are worth.

There is also pleasure in money itself. Women and femmes aren't supposed to enjoy money, to luxuriate in it, to demand it. In some social justice circles, loving money is a sign of capitalist greed and selfishness. But feeling good about having enough money to put food on the table isn't the same as hoarding wealth or supporting capitalism, and it isn't "lean-in" feminism. Getting good wages is the harm reduction of

---

10   Pulma Sumac, "A Disgrace Reserved for Prostitutes: Complicity and the Beloved Community," *Lies: A Journal of Materialist Feminism* 2 (2015): 13.

capitalism, and poor/working-class women and femmes are entitled to demand money and take joy in their cash.

We can learn from how sex workers revel in their money. Watch how they celebrate that night's haul at the club (sometimes taking pics with their cats: a meme called "cats and stacks"), how bruja sex workers perform money-attracting rituals, get dollar signs tattooed on their wedding ring finger, organize their own workshops and online groups to troubleshoot business problems, concoct schemes for opening up men's wallets in every avenue of life, celebrate financial successes, and commiserate with downturns. More than anyone else, sex workers teach us that our sexuality is our property (not his), that it is valuable (not priceless, the opposite of priceless actually), and that we have a right to unbridled joy about getting something for it. All of us doing undervalued feminized work (in the service industry, child care, personal support, teaching, counseling, secretaries, artists) can benefit from the gleeful sex worker mantra: "fuck you, pay me."

About 80 percent of sex workers are women. That's about the same proportion of secretaries, nurses, and teachers. But when was the last time you saw a kindergarten teacher cracking jokes about being "a dope-ass cunt who loves money" or nurse hyping herself up by blasting "Bitch Betta Have My Money" as she prepares to go ask for a raise?[11] Women and femmes who love money are free to be demanding. The world has tried to fool them into thinking that getting paid for care or sex "cheapens" it. *Please.* You know what's "cheap"? When men think they're entitled to free and unlimited care, attention, and sex. That's cheap.

But "money can't buy you happiness," right? Like fuck it can't. Try telling that to the twenty-year-old single mother who, after six months of stripping, can stack presents under the Christmas tree for her three-year-old. Or to the forty-year-old escort who can send her son to university, the first

---

11 Jacqueline Frances, *Striptastic! A Celebration of Dope-ass Cunts Who Love Money* (self-published, 2017).

one in their family to go to college. Or to the fifty-something grandmother missing a front tooth who gets to enjoy a yearly trip somewhere warm with her sugar daddy.

Money buys protection. It buys time off and privacy. And it buys nice, pretty shit. Money also buys food, housing, and health care. Getting paid enough to meet our needs—*and more*—feels good. I'm not romanticizing the sex industry, I know it has risks; I'm just not going to romanticize economic deprivation in the name of being a "good girl," either.

So do sex workers feel pleasure at work? Yeah. Because you know what feels *amazing*? Surviving capitalism.

Reclaiming the Gold Digger

> Is that wrong? For wanting more for
> myself? Wanting people to treat me with
> respect? But you know what? Next time
> they know better.
> —Nicki Minaj, "Pickle Juice," 2010

A good girl stays grateful with crumbs. She may be broke, but damn she's a good girl! *Fuck that.* Gold-digging whores hack the system and ask for too much—all the money, pleasure, and attention they damn well want. They recognize the value of their body and beauty, but also maybe more than anything else, the value of their time and attention. They know these are gold. Whores ask: Is this worth it? What's in this for me?

It isn't always about money. Respecting and protecting our work and our bodies doesn't always mean getting paid. But consider that women and femmes will always be under pressure to give up their sexuality and care for free. Under capitalism, putting a price on something is the best way to make work visible.

Things change when we recognize our own worth, even just for ourselves. Women and femmes—all of us—deserve enough money to buy delicious food, a comfortable roof over our heads, and health care when we need it. We deserve enough money to take care of our families and friends. We deserve the money for ease, leisure, and luxuries in our lives. We deserve the pleasure of having enough. And we have the right to use our sexuality to get it.

Thank you to M'Kali Hashiki, Pluma Sumaq, Clare Bayard, Karen Pittelman, Isaac Lev Szmonko, and the members of the Lambda Literary Retreat Non-Fiction "ho-hort" of 2017 for their invaluable feedback on this essay.

A TIMELINE/TUTORIAL ON SQUIRTING

This is another piece that my feminist heart says should be a common conversation. I am tired of old narratives that don't acknowledge that the majority of the human species, regardless of gender, ejaculate.

The first time was an accident, being fucked from behind I suddenly felt I would come apart and then something was loose in me, something was on my thighs, something covered the bed beneath me, tears with the intensity of grief or joy on my cheeks. I hoped he wouldn't notice, but he did, and he seemed confused and pleased. No one had told us this could happen.

The second time, it was a lover who knew where the water was inside me and didn't say a word but reached into me with busy fingers, tireless, finding me, bringing me to the surface, inviting my breath with hers, bringing me out. I trusted her touch. I relaxed, I opened.

I thought squirting was only possible on my later orgasms in a multi-orgasmic sexual session, that the third orgasm was the gate, after which the water might come. I became voracious, wanting my lovers to continue and continue and continue, insatiable until the water came. Each orgasm brought down defenses, opened me up, brought breadth and width between my thighs. But the pressure of ejaculation, of feeling incomplete without it, began to distort my connection to my lovers, my presence in the moment. Perhaps this was what men feel?

With time I realized it wasn't about orgasmic marathons but about my presence, about my detachment from outcome, about my ability to bring my whole self to the point of contact with a lover or a finger or a toy. About letting my lover know when they are at the mouth of the river, of saying yes (and stay, and harder).

I change the bedding, I prepare for oceans, I learn to respect the sea within.

SUB-SECTION

SKILLS FOR SEX IN THE #METOO ERA

Most of the following pieces emerged in the wake of the latest wave of #metoo storytelling. I wrote these columns to address pleasure in this context and learn how we can begin to deconstruct rape culture through both a pleasure politic and pleasure practices.

I feel very underwhelmed by strategies to eliminate sexual attraction, connection, or energy between humans as a way of ending rape culture, because it feels like asking everyone to be less honest about their feelings and complexity, asking everyone to repress some aspect of nature that wants to flow and actually needs healthy boundaries and transparency. The level of harm that still exists after several decades of trying to eliminate sexual tension from professional spaces would suggest that desexualization leads to repression and then toxic outbursts of harm, rather than actually decreasing harm.

Part of transformative justice is getting to the root of harm, and so much sexual harm is rooted in sexual shame and repression. Increasing this with punitive frameworks around human connection seems bound to continue or increase resentment and harm. The following pieces acknowledge that many of us, at least during certain phases of our lives, are navigating an ever-shifting landscape of desire. They suggest that we can shift from a rape/punishment culture to a culture of enthusiastic consent and clear, respected boundaries. This series explores the skills all genders need in this navigation—clear conversations, boundaries, flirtation skills, liberated fantasies, and more.

FROM #METOO TO #WECONSENT

In 2004, Tarana Burke started a Me Too movement, centered around Black women and girls telling their stories of sexual harassment and assault at the hands of men.[1] With the recent exposure of Hollywood mogul Harvey Weinstein's predatory behaviors and the infrastructure that supported him, #metoo became a hashtag used by Alyssa Milano and other actors and people in the Hollywood realm who have been hurt by Weinstein.

Then millions of other people from other walks of life began to come forward. For months now, I have been reading the stories of childhood sexual abuse, molestation, sexual harassment, disrespect, sexual assault, rape. Stories where boundaries were transgressed, where power was abused, where secrecy was demanded, where protection was given to the perpetrators of harm.

On the heels of this hashtag have come other angles on rape culture, including that while it is rooted in toxic masculinity it is not limited by gender, it's not just men hurting

1   This essay first appeared as adrienne maree brown, "The Pleasure Dome: From #Metoo to #Weconsented: Reclaiming the Pleasure of Consent," October 25, 2017, *Bitch Media* (blog), https://www.bitchmedia .org/article/the-pleasure-dome/me-too-reclaiming-consent.

women. People of all genders have been harmed and have caused harm. Men are assaulted and raped in astounding numbers, which get swallowed by the shame and homophobia of masculine culture. The dynamics repeat in same-sex relationships and communities.

Sexual aggression is a malfunction of masculinity that is not bound by genitalia.

Some have questioned why we are sharing survivor stories when the people who need to step forward and take responsibility are those who have caused harm. I'm sure fear and shame are major factors here, but I also think we are still in such early stages of learning to practice transformative justice.[2] I am not interested in exposing names, in exposing the most harmful moments of people's lives. I am interested in how we transform the underlying conditions that generated the harm in the first place. I think the truth will continue to shake loose in these kind of waves, stories that map our pain and show where we are as a species in terms of being able and ready to face rape culture and end it.

It is humbling to realize that the majority of us are trying to reach pleasure through the complex trauma of transgression. In the onslaught of unveiling, I thought it would be useful to take a step back and address something crucial: the pleasure of consent.

Consent means saying yes on your own terms. Giving permission or agreement for something to happen.

Many of us have/had our boundaries crossed before we learned anything about saying yes and no. Crossed when we are young, by adults we trust. Crossed when we are coming into the realm of desire. Many of us are truncated in our sexual liberation by these transgressions. We are taught to act cool, even when others were doing things to us that

---

2   Transformative justice goes beyond calling for punishment or even restoring the original conditions, which were often imbalanced and unhealthy in the first place. Transformative justice asks us to dive deep to understand and transform the underlying conditions that allowed the harm to happen.

diminished our power and safety. We were taught in sex education programs that sex is scary, that sex means babies and disease.

I want to uplift another way. If we focused on teaching consent and boundaries instead of trying to scare people away from the most common and natural activity of our species, I think we could make major headway in the effort to turn our collective story from #metoo and #itwasme into #notme, and even #weconsentedanditwasdelicious.

The pleasures of consent are multitudinous. Here are some keys to consent-based pleasure.

Self-Awareness

It is a gift to be in touch with your own desire, to know when you do and don't want something. For survivors of molestation and assault, it can be really difficult to get in touch with our own desires. We can go along with things because we don't believe we have a choice, because we want to seem normal, because the depression of survival is isolating and touch can temporarily ease the loneliness, or because we have been misdirected into deep insecurity and think we should be lucky for sexual attention.

The first step of consent is tuning into your own desire, being able to feel a distinct yes or no in your system. For me, I had to engage in a period of intentional celibacy, get really still and clear of other people's attention, in order to hear my own longings. You might be able to get there without that celibacy, but the key is that you can identify and point to three different physical and emotional signals that you are feeling a yes for a potential lover. Signs like quickening breath, flushed face, pressure in the groin, sweat on the palms, tingling up the spine, weakening of the knees, and so much more.

This self-awareness will help you navigate giving and receiving consent.

Consent Has Levels

Consent can cover a lot of ground. It isn't just about the consent of a certain touch or sexual act. Consent can cover the ground of boundaries and communication: Can we flirt?[3] Are you actually available for us to build an intimate connection? Can I send you pictures? Can I take pictures of you? Can I share our connection with others, in public, on social media? Can we fuck? Are you open to ass play? Disclosing sexual history and risk is a part of a consent conversation. For some people, disclosing relationship and parental status can be part of a consent conversation. As I have gotten more in touch with my shifting abilities, I also bring into consent conversations things like, "Can you be careful with my knees? I tore my meniscus a while back, so don't just throw me around."

Asking for these things helps build a space of trust. Eventually you may get past needing to ask for consent on each of these things because you will have developed a space of trust, where you know consent matters and can be navigated as needed.

Asking for Consent

This one takes so much practice. Many of us are taught anti-consent practices as children, to hug and kiss whatever adult comes around asking for affection, that it's rude if we don't make the demanded contact. This culture of access based on power grows with us. Power gives an assumed total access of older people to younger people's bodies, white people to people of color's bodies, men to women's bodies, cis to trans bodies, those with resources to those with less, those with more physical strength to those with less. It's the way

---

3   One thing to add here is that consent changes. I recently had an experience of grinding up on a friend at a party, a friend who I have often ground on before. She said "not right now." Later, sober, we checked in about what had shifted in terms of her needs. It reminded me that consent is a present moment offering.

systems of hierarchy, domination, patriarchy, misogyny, and capitalism converge in the realm of flesh.

Self-awareness helps us begin to see that everyone has sovereignty over their own bodies, their time, attention, boundaries, and desires. But practice makes this awareness transformative—asking if someone is open to physical contact, to a hug, to intimate touch, to sex begins to create a foundation of consent, a path to grow beyond the sick system we've been shaped by.

The pleasure that comes from knowing that you are offering someone something that they wholeheartedly say yes to is sacred. It acknowledges that we are each a walking miracle, we each have power, and we each have the responsibility to share and grow power in ourselves and others.

No Is a Complete Sentence

Your strong and solid no makes way for your deep, authentic yes. I was taught this late in life: "No is a complete sentence." You don't have to say no apologetically, and you don't have to explain your no. By practicing your no, you will cultivate a yes that is rooted in having agency, having power, and having respect for your own boundaries.

Giving Consent

Even if every single thing you have been told and shown has taught you that you do not have the right to give consent, to navigate the boundaries of your body, you do. The culture of access that says someone can exert power over your body for any reason other than you saying yes is a lie.

When you want to say yes, when you choose to give consent, you are in your power.

Your consent isn't made of stone. You might feel a yes for attention or a kiss but then feel a boundary that says slow down or stop when it comes to the next steps—touching, sex, etc. You get to be in touch with that consent.

Consent that is shored up by the real option of a strong no, by respected boundaries, and by a visceral yes that floods the entire body, is a pre-orgasmic experience. It lays a foundation for thrilling intimate connections that are clear of the shadows of manipulation and abuse.

HOT AND HEAVY HOMEWORK

Choose one physical activity that you might take for granted right now—hugs, handshakes, flirtatious touch, blow jobs, or sex, and track your consent in this activity for a week. You can keep doing what you normally do, but start to really pay attention to the signals in your body—are you a total yes to this contact? If not, why are you doing it? If yes, give yourself an internal high five. Learn your own landscape of consent.

IT'S ABOUT YOUR GAME

Beloveds, I'm observing a pattern in the flood of #metoo and #itwasme stories: a lot of us don't know how to articulate what we really want and don't want in real time.[1] The pressure of desire unexpressed can blow out a system and lead to harmful behaviors such as abuse of power, harassment, molestation, assault, and rape. It also shows up in misogyny on the internet.

Repression is at the root of so much sexual transgression. It's a story—that desire is to be fully contained as an indication of purity, moral supremacy, or maturity. The story gets upheld in very old social, political, and religious norms that aim to control us. The story gets upheld by those who have survived harm and want to regenerate safety with impenetrable boundaries, who go so far that any desire shocks the system.

Last year, I went to a hot spring with a loved one who wasn't raised in the United States. It was a naked space, and there was a big sign on the wall in the changing room that said bathers were not to extend any sexual attention toward others. I nodded, not really noticing it. My friend pointed at the sign and laughed at how unnatural and American it was:

---

1   This essay first appeared as adrienne maree brown, "It's About Your Game: Flirting to Find Your Authentic Self," November 9, 2017, *Bitch Media* (blog), https://www.bitchmedia.org/article/Its-about-your-game/flirting-to-find-your-authentic-self.

come be naked and wet and sweating, but make sure you don't see each other at all.

I got the laughter. And, as a survivor of multiple experiences of discomfort, danger and harm, I appreciate what the signs attend to. But it made me think about what is encouraged, what is allowed, what is safe, what is forbidden—and how rarely what we *really* want is encouraged. We're expected more and more often to find sexual and love connection through a screen, ceding the territory of real-life connections to those who transgress the rules of ignoring each other's bodies, chemistry, and desire when face to face.

Transgression has a whole industry—dark clubs with no windows, anonymous hotel rooms and phone lines, internet porn, apps for cheaters, et cetera. It's hard to know how to balance between the absolute need for practicing consent and the unspeakable or forbidden energy that, for many of us, turns up the heat in pleasure land.

Is it possible for the world to be as sexy if there's consent and permission and openness about our deepest desires, if we truly bring our nakedness into the light?

I don't know. I still love touching into the forbidden places—partially because they are forbidden. I know for sure that part of this is conditioning, being raised in a culture of repression, sex shaming, patriarchy, and danger. But it's also how my desire is wired, even after decades of therapy and somatics.

We all need to be able to ask for what we want, say no to what we don't want, and understand each other's desires and forbidden places with as little judgment as possible. We develop this skill by practicing over and over, by being uncomfortable and honest, by taking the risk in real time to say what we really feel and want, by saying no when we feel no, by remembering that our way of doing things was learned, and that it isn't right (or wrong).

Perhaps the forbidden is even sexier when it's an informed choice.

This means we need to increase our attention on, and skill

in, the things that happen before we get physical, the dynamics that continue to be important as we build trust and figure out relationships of love and/or sex. One of the largely uncharted boundaries in the world is between those with game and those without it. Those who can engage in flirtation or banter versus those who freeze or go quiet under the pressure of their desires.

I have friends with game and friends without it, and friends who have it but think they don't, and those who think they have it but actually don't. Lately I have been asked to help a few friends out with basic flirtation skills. In trying to understand the art of flirtation enough to be of use, I've noticed some things. All game is not created equal, and it's largely misunderstood. The quality of game is much more about being honest and being yourself than being smooth. It's not about small talk, filling the space, or easing the awkwardness. It's letting true desire and curiosity come to the forefront of an interaction.

Flirtation, or game, is a great way to map out the visible and invisible landscape of another, with your titillation intact. I became aware that I had game in my late twenties. Something clicked between my body and me after years of depression and therapy. I began to believe that my desires mattered. Before I believed that my desires mattered, it was nearly impossible for me to tell if attraction was mutual, because when I was sober I couldn't believe anyone would really be attracted to me. Now I'm only into people who are worshipful with my body and my heart and who inspire that in me. And I can assess that mutual quality of worship after a few moments of good flirtation.

I define game as the ability to engage potential mutual attraction in ways that grow the chemistry. There's not necessarily a sexual end goal, but the territory of sex is the thinly veiled landscape of good game: the pace and power dynamics of sex are part of the process, the nonverbal cues are weighted to deepen the sensual connection.

I used to blurt out my desire and then crash into my lovers like a wave, often knocking them over with my uninhibited commitment to pleasure. Now I still do this, but I've learned to be more clear with myself and others about how powerful my desire is and what I want. I'm still learning to enjoy communicating those things.

In the spirit of creating safer, braver sexual space for all of us, here are a few quick tips for getting your game up:

Notice the nonverbal cues before starting a conversation.
We are all unlearning coy—if someone is avoiding your eyes, it's intentional. Lingering eye contact is a great way to begin a flirtation. And if you feel a little smile coming, let it show, that's real.

Be yourself.
They're going to meet your real self eventually. Might as well lead with it and save yourself the whole relationship phase where you're both actually obsessed with each other's projections. Let yourself show, and the right people will be compelled by you.

Release the end goal.
Let yourself really be present with the person in front of you, really see them, attend to them, compliment them. Learn from the journey. The play.

The framework of game is not about catching the other person but connecting with the other person while being yourself.
Instead of trying to impress the other person, pay attention to your own interest (is it growing? where do you feel it in your body?) and how good you feel being yourself.

Even in flirtation, value the differences between yourself and this other human.

Don't compromise on your core values, don't giggle at something you find ignorant or offensive. But don't hang up because this human with a different life than you has reached different conclusions.

Take risks!

When you feel something come up that you want to say but you're scared to say, you're on the precipice between the lie of omission and the bravery of honesty. You want what's on the other side of that precipice. Say what you want, so you'll either get it or know you can't get it in this connection.

Have fun!

HOT AND HEAVY HOMEWORK

Flirt! With your partner(s) or with someone really cute to you. Be curious, laugh, and keep feeling for your genuine yes, your genuine desire to be in the conversation. And take a risk.

IT'S TIME TO RECLAIM OUR SKIN

This is a time where everyone needs to bring their best selves.[1] We are actively making a case for our species to exist on this beautiful planet. Can we be just? Can we practice freedom together? Can we rediscover right relations with each other, including between humans and the earth? Can we remember what it is to be alive with each other, beyond suffering and survival?

I believe yes, against all evidence to the contrary. I believe yes because I have had so many experiences of vulnerability, moments where I saw that we all struggle with belonging, with finding home, with being honest, with adapting, with getting our needs met, with cultivating safety. With being unapologetically ourselves, not in a defensive way, not in a performative way, just … us.

My late comrade Charity Hicks called this "getting naked." She said that when we come into meetings and movement spaces with each other we need to drop the pretense and manipulation and salesperson-ing, and get naked. When

---

1   This essay first appeared as adrienne maree brown, "It's Time to Reclaim Our Skin: How Getting Naked Restores Our Dignity," January 10, 2018, *Bitch Media* (blog), https://www.bitchmedia.org/article/its-time-reclaim-our-skin/how-getting-naked-restores-our-dignity.

she'd say it, some of us would blush and others would say "Ase!" Others still would find a way to escape the space altogether.

There are so many reasons why people are scared to get naked. We are told over and over again by capitalism that our true selves are not good enough. We are told that only the wealthy deserve to be well and receive care. That our bodies are not beautiful because we are disabled or fat or not white or not pleasing to a man or…

I want to offer that the same practices we use for getting naked in the realm of sex and intimacy—the unveiling of skin—can teach us to bring our unapologetic selves into any space where we need to get naked.

Know Your Own Nakedness

In my early years of hooking up, I never looked at myself naked. I would get my outfit on, and once things were sucked in and lifted up and shaped into a stiff mannequin version of my body I would look in the mirror and approve. Later, if the night went well, as the clothes were coming off I would turn off or move away from bright light and hope the other person didn't notice the difference between presentation and reality.

I am grateful for formative experiences where I got to practice being naked around others in relationship, at hot springs and bathhouses. I am grateful for children who love my soft enveloping hugs. And for lovers who said, "You're beautiful."

But the most meaningful work was a year of personal practice: looking in mirrors at my naked body and finding something I liked. It's tender to remember that at first I could only say "my left pinky," but it was a beginning: "Left pinky, you are smooth and unbitten. You look delicate, and your nail is beautiful."

My standard was that I couldn't repeat a body part. Eventually I got to the stretch marks, scars, and dimples of cellulite. Eventually I got to a place of seeing myself whole, in motion, decompartmentalized. Eventually I realized it was a sacred and beautiful body.

I have been through a similar process for my emotions, for my spirit, and for my movement worker self.

Knowing this nakedness allows me to have more than gumption when it is time to show myself to others; it allows me to have dignity. I keep up the practice, and these days I sometimes find it hard to keep any clothes on at all.

Be Good to Your Body

Moisturize. Eat your greens. Stretch. Say nice things in the mirror like "damn god/dess, you look delectable today."

Be Sure You Want to Be Naked

If you're in a situation where keeping clothes on *feels* right, listen to that feeling without judgment; be curious. What is the data inside that feeling that can help you understand yourself and the situation? There's a lot of fun and sexy sex to be had in various states of partial dress, and I support all of that. Or there might be a question of safety or comfort that needs attending to that hasn't been articulated or agreed on yet.

And while there's nothing that compares to the experience of skin on skin, it has to be in the right setting with the right person or people. Nakedness is vulnerability. Vulnerability is something we offer where it is earned; as it is held well, we can offer more. So ask yourself, has this moment earned my nakedness?

If you find yourself naked with someone who doesn't look at you with the love, care, and worship with which you see yourself, reclaim your skin—there are always more lovers in the sea or the app. Someone wants your body whole. Wait for that.

Get Consent

While it's amazing that this needs to be said, don't get naked in front of others without consent. Don't show up and just whip off your raincoat or expose yourself on someone's lawn as a romantic gesture. You don't know how your nakedness will impact another. Permission and boundaries—those powerful acts of saying maybe or no—allow for real freedom within a connection.

Get Naked

Your miraculous body is a gift to you and a gift to those who get to see it and be with it. Undress in that manner, as if you are untying a bow around a precious and well thought-out gift. Make eye contact and see your power and desirability in your lover's eyes. This is your living body; this is what aliveness feels like.

HOT AND HEAVY HOMEWORK

Assess your comfort in your nakedness: If you don't feel fully comfortable dancing (it can just be a head bop) naked in your bathroom mirror, begin a practice of looking and finding your sexy, whole, and sacred self.

One of my practices this past year has been to take pictures of my whole body and post them with the hashtag #sexyfat—to will myself and others to understand that the thickness truly is a delight. I feel like it has been a reprogramming that has made my nakedness, my movement, my sex, and my life feel much more powerful. It's also been helpful to engage others. At first people would say "that's sexy, not fat," like they thought I didn't know how to choose words to describe myself. Slowly, though, I think folks have caught on to the intention. Perhaps even been a bit reprogrammed themselves.

I WANT YOU, BUT I'M TRIGGERED

We don't see it coming.[1]

We are having a moment of intimacy: a moment we've been desiring and have been moving toward. And here it is, clothing is coming off, and the connection is good and new and hot, and then *boom*—a flashback comes at the tip of a lover's fingers, the thrust of a tongue, a hand at the throat—suddenly we are pulled back to a moment of terror, violation, or confusion.

Our bodies feel caught up in that memory state and cannot register the present moment, can't tell if we are, in fact, safe here. Our hearts pound, sweat comes to the palms and upper lip, and perhaps we gasp for air, pull into balls of ourselves, lose our ability to explain coherently what is happening. We break the connection with our lover.

Or perhaps we are the lover, and we are moving forward with consent and connection and suddenly see fear and withdrawal in place of arousal and excitement.

1   This essay first appeared as adrienne maree brown, "I Want You, but I'm Triggered: Finding Pleasure When Trauma and Memory Collide," January 24, 2018, *Bitch Media* (blog), https://www.bitchmedia.org/article/i-want-you-im-triggered/finding-pleasure-when-trauma-and-memory-collide.

I use "we" intentionally here, because so many of us have experienced trauma related to intimacy, and so many of us have experienced moments of getting triggered by that trauma when we are in situations where we want to be present and healed and connected. And we feel super-isolated in these moments of being triggered or triggering.

I have been put off for a while at the overuse of the word "trigger"—I think too often people use it when they mean annoyed or offended or something less visceral than triggered. Inside that sense of overuse, I am simultaneously glad that people are finding ways to say, in real time, "something happening right now isn't right for me."

For this article, I am using the word "trigger" to mean a visceral reaction of sensations and emotions in the body that we can't control, an experience that brings past trauma to the present. There are so many reasons why these triggers happen. Childhood sexual trauma, abuse, sexual assault—triggers can include times when we are made to feel scared or powerless, even if there was no physical harm.

And as I write this, it's been a week of news about an encounter between a woman called Grace and *Master of None* creator Aziz Ansari. I have felt within me every possible response to the story, wondering why she didn't say no, why I didn't learn to say no, when men aren't taught to feel and hear no, swinging on a pendulum that keeps landing on "this iceberg of rape culture is the entire planet." There was so much detail in the story, but I didn't see anything about either player's background of trauma and what dynamics and socialization might have been playing out in that room.

What I do know is that triggers can look like extreme and overt responses, but they can also make us freeze, keep us very quiet, steal no from our mouths, keep us from being clear about what we want and don't want, and cause confusion afterward. We are socialized to swallow extreme reactions, to be pleasant instead of present. So here are a few tips for what to do if you find yourself triggered, or suspect your partner is triggered, in a consensual sexual experience.[2]

Stop

Pause what you are doing.

If you can speak, say, "Wait, stop, I need a moment."

If you can't speak, remove your partner's hands from your body and step away, holding your hands up.

If that is too much, just fully withdraw your body from contact.

If you know from past experiences that you have some triggers, it can help to name this up front and let your person know what they can do if you get triggered. This is also a good thing to ask a new lover: "Is there anything I might do that could trigger you?" Or, "If anything I'm doing doesn't work for you, please say 'stop' or hold up your hands."

Take Time to Recover

Let your breath return to normal, however long that takes. Notice if you are caught in a memory or if you are actually feeling unsafe in the present moment. Again, if you can speak, say "Something is coming up from my past, I need a moment."

If you can't speak, closing your eyes can help you to establish a boundary around your attention and keep it on your own well-being and breath.

Decide What to Share

You are not obligated to disclose your past trauma. At this point, I generally assume that anyone I am beginning a situationship with has some sexual or other trauma in their

---

2   If it's nonconsensual, there are options: https://www.wikihow.com/Prevent-a-Potential-Rape.

history, and I try to be forthcoming about the fact that I do as well. But actually sharing the details of it in or right after the moment of trigger may not be appropriate for the connection or the moment or your healing. Or it might be exactly right.

Some options:

"I want to share more about my history of trauma with you but not right now." Intimacy, yes, but I need time. This might include, "I'd like to continue—but can you avoid [if the trigger is a physical place or activity, name it as an emerging boundary]?"

"Are you open to hearing about what's coming up for me right now?" Hearing about other people's trauma can be hard, even re-traumatizing for people. It can also be a swift transition from heavy petting to deep sharing. The connection may not be about that kind of depth, even if something is coming up in that moment.

"I am feeling like myself again. I don't want to talk about it. I would like to keep making out, if you're down." Sometimes the trigger is familiar, and once it passes I just want to keep going, not move into a big process moment.

"Something is coming up for me, I'm not ready to share it, I think I [you] need to head home."

Let Your Body Follow Your Words/Desires

If you want to leave or want your lover to go—make those moves.

If you have a friend who can come and get you, call them up. You don't need to drive when your system is taken over by trauma.

If you want to continue the encounter and your lover is still game, start slow. Move within the boundaries you need. But it's really important to know that you deserve pleasure. Experiences where you can be triggered and recover, which usually come after doing healing work at a somatic and/or therapeutic level, help to reset your system to know that you can enjoy the connections you choose to and reclaim your freedom and pleasure inside of spaces absent of harm.

HOT AND HEAVY HOMEWORK

Make an intimate trigger map. This map is just for you. Draw a mug-sized circle in the center with two to three concentric circles around it. The center circle represents a full trigger, and as you move out from the center, there can be things that are painful to remember but have less of a full body impact.

Fill it in: Are there certain touches or experiences that you know can completely hijack your system? Those go in the center. You can leave it empty if you don't actually get triggered in that way. Experiences that make you extremely uncomfortable can go in the middle ring, and so on.

The more clarity you have on what pushes your buttons, the more informed and empowered you can be in navigating pleasurable sexual experiences with others.

STRATEGIC
CELIBACY

Recently there's been a lot of back and forth about the line between bad sex and rape.[1] For some people, this public dialogue has made us look back at our own intimate lives with new eyes.[2]

What did we want to happen? What actually happened? Why did it happen? Was it harmful? Were we harmed? Did we ever discuss it? Why or why not?

There's a world of work to be done—people with any sort of privilege in intimate situations have to stop denying what they know, stop pushing past no, stop waiting for mouths to say no when bodies have already expressed it, stop getting off on power expressed as sexual access and harm.

But I think we all need to ask ourselves: Have I been complicit in continuing harmful patterns of sex that blur the line?

---

1   This essay first appeared as adrienne maree brown, "Strategic Celibacy: Liberating Your Desire, Part 1," February 7, 2018, *Bitch Media* (blog), https://www.bitchmedia.org/article/strategic-celibacy/liberating-your-desire-part-1.

2   See Lili Loofbourow's article examining the Aziz Ansari scandal: Lili Loofbourow, "The Female Price of Male Pleasure," *The Week,* January 25, 2018, https://theweek.com/articles/749978/female-price-male-pleasure.

I've been getting really interested inside this inquiry about a slightly different question: how many of us are trapped in a politically regressive loop of desire?

How many of us, even as we hone a feminist or womanist or post-gender or otherwise radical politics around who we are relative to power, regress in bed into submission practices we are taught are biological, primal, even spiritual? To say it plainly, I suspect many of the most powerful women in the species are still convinced that in bed we need to be dragged by our hair into a cave and ravaged by a lover who plays a traditionally patriarchal role of dominance.

I suspect a key aspect of succeeding in the work of #metoo and smashing the patriarchy will be examining not just true rape culture but our culture of desire. Not with shame or with righteousness but with deep curiosity: What turns us on, and can we change it if it doesn't align with what we believe? How many of us can even imagine desire that is liberated from patriarchy?

The next few sections are going to focus on how we can grow our desires to align more closely with our dignity, using celibacy, fantasy, pornography, and communication to cultivate new possibilities for desire within ourselves and between us and others.

Celibacy is intentionally refraining from sexual relations. This means not having sex with other people. It can include not cultivating sexual energy with others. Some people also limit their masturbation practices during celibacy.

I've intentionally practiced celibacy a few times in my life and find it to be a glorious way to reconnect with what matters in my body, to slow and deepen my pace and relationships outside the paradigm of desire, to decolonize my longings and remember my sacred sensual self.

We are still learning all the strategies we will need to truly dismantle patriarchy. Strategy is just a plan of action toward a goal. To use celibacy as part of our strategy to dismantle patriarchy, we must have a clear goal, a clear intention, a clear process. Here are a few steps for a strategic celibacy.

Why

Get clear on why you might need an intentional period of celibacy. Do you suspect you are in patterns of sexual relationship that sustain patriarchy? Are you regularly engaging in sex that hurts, that is confusing, that your body isn't saying an ecstatic yes to? Maybe you've never even considered it and you are just curious to learn more about your desire. Know your own reasons. Generate questions on the front end that you would like to understand better by the end of your celibacy.

How Long

Set a time period. How long do you want to be in this practice? You are ideally practicing long enough to let your body take a break from any harmful or unclear erotic behavior. The time period should feel doable but long enough to really observe yourself.

Put it on your calendar.

Get Curious and Reflective

What are you focused on? What do you see, hear, or otherwise sense that makes you feel flushed and quick? What produces a physical response of desire? Keep a desire journal, write down what you feel, and if you notice a of lack of desire, track that as well.

It's all data.

Once you've started tuning into what you desire, check it against your values. Again, this is a time for curiosity, not judgment. Be tender with yourself, tender with your history.

See Yourself

Get honest with yourself. You may learn that you're right where you want to be sexually! You may find that you're engaging in practices that compromise your values. Noticing and knowing are the first steps.

HOT AND HEAVY HOMEWORK

What's your next step? A period of celibacy? A shift in your sensual focus? There may be healing work to do. Or it may be that in the next phase of your sexual life it's time to turn to fantasy and erotica and pornography to awaken new threads of desire in your system.

LIBERATING YOUR FANTASIES

What are your go-to fantasies?[1] What do you imagine that arouses you? Have you shared it with anyone?

The brain, home of the sensual imagination, is such a private place. There's a ton of mystery, controversy, scholarship, and questions about how the brain works, what lights it up, what generates desire.

Somewhere along the journey, through attraction we feel for others, media images, and healthy and/or unhealthy interactions with those older than us, visuals and story lines groove a pathway for desire in our brains. We begin to have certain scenarios that turn us on, fantasies of what we want to do or have done to us or witness.

Fantasy is defined by the *Oxford Living Dictionary* as "the faculty or activity of imagining things, especially things that

---

1   This essay first appeared as adrienne maree brown, "Liberating Desire: It's Time to Shift Your Fantasies," February 21, 2018, *Bitch Media* (blog), https://www.bitchmedia.org/article/liberating-desire/its-time-shift-your-fantasies.

There were a few people who felt that this piece was about policing the realm of fantasy and that it was not feminist. I include this piece here because it feels important to examine what we are training our bodies to find pleasurable and to be as intentional as possible about it—that feels very feminist to me. And I hope to stay in complex conversations around it.

are impossible or improbable."[2] Fantasy, then, becomes a safe space to desire things that we might never do or allow in real life.

But because the realm of imagination is also where culture begins—we imagine things that in turn shape our real life desires and practices. Where did capitalism, white supremacy, and patriarchy come from? Some imagining of scarcity and power that isn't true.

This is where things can get tricky, because, for most of us, this desire-setting happens early, and if we aren't both careful and creative we can get stuck in fantasies that don't mature and politicize with us. We can get caught in fantasies that perpetuate things so counter to our beliefs and values that we feel ashamed of what we want, even as we find ways to get it.

I had a babysitter when I was quite young who watched the *Porky's* movies, which can best be described as rape culture time capsules from the eighties. My family's military-issue apartment was small, and I easily snuck out of bed and found a spot from which I took in sexually disempowering images I didn't understand. I also loved musicals—*Grease* and *Seven Brides for Seven Brothers* were favorites. As a result of this kind of media, my early fantasy life was often about men taking advantage of skinny women, secretly watching them, trapping them, or women having to change for the desires of men. I thought this was how sex happens, that it centers men, and that we as women should be in a constant state of seducing, playing hard to get, and getting caught by men.

Hence, my twenties. But I learned! To see differently, to imagine differently.

I once got to swim in a body of water where saltwater met freshwater. With goggles on, I could see the subtle horizontal line between the freshwater on top and the heavier, denser seawater below. That visual comes to mind as I think of the cultures in which we swim in the United States. The heavier

---

2   *Oxford Living Dictionary*, s.v. "fantasy," 2018, https://en.oxforddiction aries.com/definition/fantasy.

seawater is our much-defended rape culture, which is fed by fantasies of incest, rape, coercion, boundary transgression, force, transaction, and scenarios where the masculine wields power over the feminine. Floating above that is the culture of repression, often rooted in religious spaces. Repression fantasies focus on purity, innocence, virginity, monogamy, and youth.

These fantasies are one of the ways we get trained in the gender-normative behaviors that sustain our layered culture. We learn from parents, teachers, extended family, media, religious leaders, and basically all adults we encounter. And, of course, our early lovers, who are often fumbling in their own confusion and learning.

Men learn to be dominant, initiating penetrators: they learn that it's in their nature to ravish women. Women learn to be coy, dishonest receptacles: we're taught to say no until the last moment—and then say nothing but yes. Or say nothing and mean yes. Those who don't fit into this binary construction, or who shift within it in their lifetimes, are often expected to still don these roles in sexual encounters. The lessons are sometimes very direct, other times implied: cross your legs like a lady, save that for your husband, take her like a man, it hurts a little at first, it's just nature, who's your Daddy.

Layer into this our intersecting systems of hierarchy—racism, ableism, classism, etc.—and you have a plethora of fantasies that perpetuate and sustain a janky reality.

Note: I'm not saying there aren't people in the United States whose early fantasies are generated outside of a mainstream paradigm stretched between rape culture and a culture of repression, I just have yet to meet such a person.

These gendered fantasies shape our very sense of self. How do I fit in this world? Am I desirable? How do I become desirable? What role must I play? Do I take or give?

So few people make it to this question: what do I really want?

From our first moments, we should be encouraged to focus on how our bodies feel, what sensations and interactions awaken us, what feels wrong, what kind of touch feels right, and how to communicate a spectrum of boundaries and consent. Instead, many of us spend our formative years in our heads, learning to be something we are not, unlearning the skills of truth we're all born with. Eventually our desires are woven so thoroughly with these social norm fantasies that we think that we desire our own disempowerment or someone else's.

I have been intentionally working on developing new fantasies. Fantasy is where I first explored the impossible idea that I am desirable. The improbable idea that fat bodies, brown and Black bodies, scarred and dimpled bodies, bodies that hurt and lurch and roll, bodies with hair and acne, bodies that sweat and make sounds and messes—that all of our bodies are desirable. This work has shifted my reality of lovers and my reality of how I see myself and let myself be treated.

And, and, and … even as I write this, I won't tell you all of my fantasies. Some of them are rooted so deeply in my system that I'm not sure I'll ever let them go—I'm not even sure I want to. But I do want to be able to recognize what is mine and what isn't, what should stay in fantasy and what is aligned with the world I'm generating—one in which gender is not an indication of power in or out of the bedroom.

HOT AND HEAVY HOMEWORK

Examine your fantasies!
What initiates your desire?
What sustains and builds your desire?
What makes you cum?
Are you, or people who look like you, included in your fantasies?
Do your fantasies primarily focus on having unjust power over another person? If yes, does this show up in your life?
Do your fantasies primarily focus on having someone else have unjust power over you? If yes, does this show up in your life?
What do you want to be turned on by? Can you even imagine it? Try. Again. Again. Keep trying until you feel something.

PORNOGRAPHY AND ACCOUNTABILITY

In 2016, among the top pornography searches for men were "stepmom," "stepsister," "mom," "teen," and "stepmom and son." Men also liked videos in the categories of "Japanese," "Ebony," and "Asian," in that order.[1] Women were searching for "stepdad and daughter," as well as "gangbang" and "extreme gangbang." They wanted to see "big Black dick" or just "Black sex" in general and sometimes "Japanese." (That appears to heavily overlap with specific kinks like foot worship, breast worship, and sexual games.) And everyone wanted to see "lesbians." These aren't the only things people were searching for, but they were the top searches for millions of people the world over, according to Pornhub, the top porn site in the world.[2]

Pornography, like sex work, is an industry that exists to meet a need that the needy generally prefer to deny. In the case of porn, the need is having content outside our own

---

1   This essay first appeared as adrienne maree brown, "The Pleasure Dome: You Can Say Yes to Pornography and Accountability," March 7, 2018, *Bitch Media* (blog), https://www.bitchmedia.org/article/pleasure-dome/saying-yes-pornography-and-accountability.

2   Sarah Rense, "The Human Race Really Outdid Itself with Porn Searches in 2017," *Esquire*, May 29, 2018, https://www.esquire.com/lifestyle/sex/news/a52061/most-popular-porn-searches.

imaginations and memories to feed into the steam engine of our desire. It includes ideas that turn us on, things we want to do or feel but think we can't have, things that feel forbidden, and things that are habitual. It is primarily created for the male gaze, especially the free or cheap content.

Pornography is generally pursued in private these days, now that the internet can bring you all the sex you can imagine, and lots you can't, through free sites and, for some, paid sites with higher quality, longer content, and more specificity (meaning you can get higher-definition porn in areas you find arousing versus whatever free content has to offer).

There are a lot of articles and books about the ways that porn can become an addiction—a lot of Christians are particularly concerned with this phenomenon. I am not going to spend much time exploring that here except to say that if you can't masturbate and/or orgasm without pornography, it would be worth reading up on signs of porn addiction and just getting clear on your situation.

I am more concerned with what we watch when we watch pornography and how it interacts with desire pathways in our brains and bodies. What are we programming ourselves to desire?

On this journey of liberating our desire, we have to look at our relationship to pornography. And as with all things in this column, we want to use a harm reduction approach, to learn to look at our practices without judgment, without shaming, but with curiosity and agency. What shapes us as we turn to pornography? How does porn, in turn, shape our real-life desires? And can we use pornography to shape our real-world desires?

I am particularly interested in what our pornographic practices do to our imaginations.

There are several museums of sex in the world, and I have been to many of them.[3] What always strikes me is that back

---

3 I actually visited my first, the Museum of Sex in Amsterdam, with my mom. Thanks for being cool, Mom!

in the day, meaning before I was born, pornography was mostly in the form of still images. You looked at a Polaroid of people having sex, a black-and-white still of a woman splayed on a chaise lounge, or a *Kama Sutra* drawing, and your mind did the rest of the work.

Your imagination animated the scene, imagining your fingers moving across the flesh that you never actually saw in motion, building erotic charge. Perhaps that imagined sex was pretty vanilla, especially in the pre-Hentai era. On your own, you may or may not have added tentacle porn, bukkake, or an anal gangbang to your fantasy playlist. But the desires were mostly created within you.

Now, everything is POV, high-definition porn or amateur porn shot on peoples' phones. You can watch badly acted porn or skip to pounding porn without any story line. You can tune into live people who will respond to your text requests to touch themselves while you watch. The instant your mind begins to move in any direction of desire, you can type your longing into a search bar and watch your fantasy or something close to it.

Your imagination isn't really needed.

And perhaps that would be fine if the top searches were "woman on top of someone she could never identify as a family member," "strapped women taking tender tushes," "grown up legal-aged professionals of all genders in hot consensual antiracist role play." But if pornography is another space in which we practice exploring our fantasies, I have questions.

How do we face the national truth that our trending fantasy sexual experiences center around incest, underage lovers, racialized power dynamics, or sexual encounters in which women are objects?

How do we face ourselves and what we've been programmed to desire, especially if it works against our sense of agency and connection and integrity in our real-life sex?

How do we move beyond the things we have accidentally come to want and need in order to get off, toward the desires we want and need to cultivate to break the intersecting cycles of harm we are in?

And how do we face the deeply embedded shame around what we desire? Because while we didn't create the water we're swimming in, it's still poisoning us.

How do we take responsibility for the ways in which we are programming ourselves to participate in rape culture in the deepest recesses of our minds? And that our imaginations are being discarded in the process?

And what is the consequence of discarded erotic imagination?

It concerns me. I believe our imaginations—particularly the parts of our imaginations that hold what we most desire, what brings us pleasure, what makes us scream yes—are where we must seed the future, turn toward justice and liberation, and reprogram ourselves to desire sexually and erotically empowered lives.

Ideally, porn is a spark for, and an extension of, a vibrant sexual imagination. And just like with fantasy, we may choose to continue watching stuff beyond our politics, stuff we never plan to practice—but this should be an intentional, informed sexual choice.

This begins by examining our search bars, finding our collective dignity. It could also include writing ourselves into original erotica and porn scripts or trying out some new pornographic narratives that are fully feminist, so that we can experience sexy content without some built-in cost of collaborating in our own oppression.

> ### HOT AND HEAVY HOMEWORK
> Choose your own adventure. Either take a
> two-week break from pornography and see
> what kind of fantasies get generated in absence
> of provided content or watch feminist porn.

USE YOUR VOICE

As the incredible unveiling of #metoo has progressed, I've been in a community of people who are also unveiling new realms of sexual confusion and trauma.[1] A pattern has emerged around a lack of communication—this usually happens in moments of sexual harm, but it also shows up in moments of desired intimacy, when a socialization of silence keeps lovers from saying what they really want and need. To address this pattern, I want to share examples that are rooted in true stories from my own life and people I've spoken with in the last few months.

Example One: They'd been flirting the whole conference, and she thought he liked her. Her radar was all messed up by racism and fatphobia, so she never considered that he just wanted to have sex, because … no one would ever want that? He called and asked to come see her. She said yes, hung up, swirled around thinking they were going to *connect* and maybe even *make out*. He showed up and immediately started to tongue her down (that move where the tongue is just thrusting into another's mouth and no one can feel anything). After maybe two minutes of this, he pulled out a condom. She wasn't ready, she wasn't feeling sexy, and she wasn't saying anything.

---

1   This essay first appeared as adrienne maree brown, "The Pleasure Dome: Use Your Words," March 21, 2018, *Bitch Media* (blog) https://www.bitchmedia.org/article/the-pleasure-dome/use-your-words.

Afterward she thought about all the things she wanted to say, wished she had said. They were all variations of no.

Example Two: She got really great at giving handjobs. You can do a lot with a handjob. She learned to give the impression that she really wanted to escalate to a blowjob or sex but the handjob was just so sexy to her. This performance was easier to her than saying that she wanted to leave or that she wanted to stay and not be pressured for sex.

Afterward she often wondered what kind of magical thinking men had to engage in to believe her performance. She was a theater kid. Fear shows in a live performance. How could they miss it? Did she really have to say it?

Example Three: It was a massive fight, but then every fight was. And now, instead of understanding that the fight meant they shouldn't be together, her abuser was kissing her again. And her body was responding but confused. "Doesn't he hate me? Shouldn't we break up? Why does this feel good but so guilt-ridden?" Their bodies were trying to hold together what their minds and power dynamics were destroying. Surely it was worth a conversation, but she didn't say anything.

Afterward she thought about all the things she wanted to say, wished she could have said in real time. They were all variations on "wait."

Example Four: They met, felt instant connection and heat, and hooked up quickly. They stayed in touch at a distance for months, during which A realized that they weren't compatible at the level of conversation. A often found herself drifting away inside as B spoke. When they next saw each other, A tried to make herself feel something physically, but it was gone. And for the first time in A's life, she said so. "I'm not feeling sexual. I don't want to have sex."

Afterward, A felt some guilt for being honest, hurting their feelings, and lacking desire for them. But she also felt increased agency over her body.

Example Five: The sex was pretty good, but sometimes they didn't seem to be listening to her body. The moment when she needed things to slow down, they would start pounding away at her, or just be a little to the right when her orgasm was a little to the left. One day, with the sun shining on them, her heart drumming with fear of hurting them or disconnecting, her body longing to communicate what she knew she needed, she whispered: "Softer." They paused. This was new. Then they continued sexing her, but softer. Later they thanked her for saying what she needed.

Afterward, she became a lover who speaks. She realized that using her voice as guidance, invitation, and boundary actually allows her to be present, to exercise control over her body and her pleasure, and sometimes to build the kind of trust that lets her relinquish control, which is a big deal for her and for most sexual harm survivors.

I have to honor all the silence in these examples—honor my own silence. Our silence is a survival strategy. Our silence has protected us against potential violence, an unfortunately common response of patriarchy and/or other kinds of power when met with rejection. Our silence protects us from being rejected. Our silence upholds social norms that teach us that it's more important to be polite than to be honest, even when discussing our own flesh.

Silence played some role in helping us survive to get to this moment.[2] But silence will not get us to a place of power over our bodies. And it will not get us the pleasure we want.

We need to learn to say some very basic things:

No.
It has been said before but it's always relevant: no is a complete sentence. It can be an incredibly uncomfortable complete sentence but be all that needs to be said.

---

2   Check out the work of Generative Somatics: Somatic Transformation and Social Justice (www.generativesomatics.org) or Generation Five (www.generationfive.org) for more on survival.

We must remember that our socialized aversion to no, particularly in capitalist countries, is strategic for those who aim to hold power over us. If we are made to feel uncomfortable saying no, then we will say yes to anyone and anything that tries to sell us shit.

We must remember that we are learning to say no as we recover from patriarchy, capitalism, racism.

Practice it: No.

Not Now.

This is not the right time. It's too soon or too late. We're fighting, and this will confuse things. We're breaking up, and this will regenerate connection in an unhealthy way. I'm not feeling sexual right now. I really have a headache or backache. Or I'm cramping. Or I just had chemo. Or I just helped a friend through grief. I just want to be held. Maybe I'll want sex in the future, but not right now.

I'm not sure why, but not now.

Practice it: Not now.

I Want [Insert Desire].

I want it slower. Faster. Softer. Harder.

Right there.

I want more fingers. I want one finger. I want your tongue on me. I want to role play. I want to be tied to the bed. I want a blindfold.

I know what I want, my body is responding to you. Yes that. Don't stop. Don't stop.

Practice it: I want.

Part of liberating our desires from the rape culture and patriarchy we're swimming in is reclaiming our right to communicate. We must learn to say, sign, or type the truth in real time about what our bodies actually want and need and what we don't want. We must become verbose lovers, especially in the realm of consent, feedback, and direction. We must recognize that we were taught silence with threats of physical and emotional violence (beatings, rape, withdrawal, abandonment, gaslighting, etc.), and we will no longer tolerate violence in the decision-making processes of our sensual lives.

HOT AND HEAVY HOMEWORK

However you communicate, practice saying "no," "not now," and "I want." Practice with friends who are committed to liberating desire. Practice with your lover/s, so you know for sure that you can both/all survive anything that gets said in truth. Practice in the mirror, learn what faces accompany your honesty, learn to respect your true face. Practice, practice, practice liberating the language of your desire.

SECTION FOUR

THE POLITICS OF RADICAL DRUG USE

I got high last night and took my man to his
wife's front door.
—Dinah Washington, *Me and My Gin*,
1958

I am so grateful for the many drugs I have had the chance to try out in my lifetime and for coming across harm reduction early in my life. In this section I will touch on my personal experiences with weed and ecstasy, and include an interview with the director of the Harm Reduction Coalition. I could have also included a long piece on the wonders of mushrooms, which I recommend as a detox for the spirit, much the way they can detox the earth. But with mushrooms, with all drugs, the most important thing is taking the substance seriously and reducing potential harms so that you can access the magic, so really tune in to the interview with Monique Tula, and apply it to your next mushroom adventure.

In general, I want to encourage people to be safe and adventurous and open about drug use. Repression and the myth of control around drug use leads to overuse, overdose, and incarceration. May we all be honest about the substances we need and use and educated about how to interact with substances in healthy, connected ways.

WEED ON, WEED OFF

I'm high, and I just decided: Why not write from this place?[1]

One instant reason not to do it is because I can't tell if there should be a question mark on that first line or something different, because I'm quoting my mind.

But it's not deterring me.

I'm persisting.

I don't want to write too much because I'm trying to feel the absence of responsibility for a minute … so I'm just going to leave some questions or prompts for my not-high self to reflect on:

Is weed de debbil?

Harm reduction.

Why is it the ultimate sign of relaxation to fall asleep on the couch?

Legalize it?

***

Can't remember what to write in here. Time to solo dance party.

***

---

1   This essay first appeared as adrienne maree brown, "The Pleasure Dome: Weed on, Weed Off," June 1, 2017, *Bitch Media* (blog), https://www.bitchmedia.org/article/pleasure-dome-weed-weed.

It's the morning after, and I've awakened to prompts.

First, obviously, weed is not the devil.

I grew up during the war on drugs, in a country that has used drugs and criminalization to advance hierarchy rooted in racism. My first memory of this was the alarmist educational setting of D.A.R.E., where I learned that weed makes people lazy and untrustworthy and would kill my brain cells while also serving as a gateway drug to addiction to heroin or crack.

Now marijuana is used as legal medicine in several states and being legalized from coast to coast.

Where was the lie?

Frank Ocean has written a lyric that I love: "Rolling marijuana, that's a cheap vacation."[2] For me, getting high can be a cheap way to slow down, a way to focus on the immediate. It can be medicine for my physical and emotional pain, give me spiritual experiences of awakening and connectedness, soften the impact of a wounded world in long tantrum. It can make me funny when I'm sad, calm when I'm anxious, sweet when I'm bitter, sensual when I'm in a prickly mood.

But, like almost all substances or experiences associated with pleasure, weed can be used in ways that help or harm people and relationships. I smoke, vape, and/or eat edibles to help me relax but try to be careful about numbing myself—using weed to put a fog over life. Not feeling the hard stuff means sacrificing the lessons that come with pain and heartache. And the good stuff can get numbed alongside the hard stuff.

When I sense that I'm numbing myself, I'll go months without getting high.[3] I also step back from weed when I'm

---

2   Frank Ocean, "Nights," on *Blond* (XL Recordings, 2016).

3   As a point of vulnerability, I want to share that writing this piece actually made me realize that I had been high in some way since the 2016 election—at least it felt that way. As I wrote these words about taking a break from weed, my body was like "YES LIKE RIGHT NOW." I took a break, another dip, and have rediscovered a good balance at the time of writing this book.

writing first drafts of most nonfiction writing, in which I want to be precise and reality-based. But I often get high for brainstorming fiction writing, when I want access to my imagination, dreams, and magic.

I was raised on military bases and rarely came across the ganja—not that it wasn't there, but I was still aiming to be a good girl, to please my parents. It wasn't until halfway through college that I *really* got high, rolling a gifted bud in a dollar bill in a horrible mash-up of movie drug-use behaviors.[4] I was also politicized in college, where I learned about the legacies of colonization, racism, capitalism, patriarchy. Early on, weed was a quick way to soften the blunt edge of learning, to feel ease in spite of the horrors.

I believe the worst harm that comes from smoking weed is prison. There are so many practices more harmful than weed that are legal. I'm a fan of legalization but also really concerned with who profits from that legalization. It blows my mind that privileged people, largely white folk, are getting wealthy selling a substance that poor, Black and Brown people are still imprisoned for smoking and selling. Yes, legalize, but also liberate and invest in those street entrepreneurs who have kept this medicine accessible through a prohibition.

Trying to make things better through organizing and social change was another way for me to believe in the potential of our species rather than to accept and be complicit in the destruction we reap. So my first nonprofit job was with the Harm Reduction Coalition. I had a history of some trauma, a couple of years of drinking and weed use under my belt, and a growing personal interest in the role of pleasure in the liberation of humans from suffering.

The principles of harm reduction shaped my own substance use in ways I believe have kept me functional, moderate, and intentional in spite of my inherited legacy of, and tendency toward, addiction. They've also shaped the way I

---

4   I want to emphasize that no one should ever, ever smoke a dollar bill. I am still recovering, twenty years later.

think of inviting other people into change and transformation. Here are some of the key principles of harm reduction from the Harm Reduction Coalition, which shaped my thinking:

- Accepts for better and or worse, that licit and illicit drug use is part of our world and chooses to work to minimize its harmful effects rather than simply ignore or condemn them....
- Calls for the non-judgmental, non-coercive provision of services and resources to people who use drugs and the communities in which they live in order to assist them in reducing attendant harm....
- Affirms drugs users themselves as the primary agents of reducing the harms of their drug use, and seeks to empower users to share information and support each other in strategies which meet their actual conditions of use.
- Recognizes that the realities of poverty, class, racism, social isolation, past trauma, sex-based discrimination and other social inequalities affect both people's vulnerability to and capacity for effectively dealing with drug-related harm.[5]

I want to acknowledge early and often that pleasure is that "I'm alive" feeling that can intersect with addiction, control, coping, escape, trauma, and so many other experiences of harm. In my twenties, I lived in the grip of a stealthy depression that hid itself well. I did too much of everything and hid my true intake of drugs, alcohol, sugar, and tobacco. Even when I couldn't find the right *Alice in Wonderland* cocktail, even when I was paranoid or lonely in my high, I was grateful for the options.[6]

---

5   Harm Reduction Coalition, "Principles of Harm Reduction," Accessed July 23, 2018, http://harmreduction.org/about-us/principles -of-harm-reduction/.

6   Ah, let's not play games here like this was just one decade. Perhaps that

I was and am so deeply moved by the Harm Reduction Coalition's approach of nonjudgement, of dignifying humans responding to the harmful choices of our species, and the understanding that each person has to determine their own power and choose their own harm-reduction practices. Harm reduction is personal and can include active use or twelve-step abstinence.

One time when I was high, as a young pothead, a new friend noticed the terror in my face and helped me break with the paranoia I used to experience by reciting this quote popularly attributed to Mark Twain: "I've lived through some terrible things in my life, some of which actually happened." They told me to put my thoughts on what *I* wanted to happen.

Since then, most of my high experiences have been amazing. If I notice paranoia or anxiety creeping in, I remind myself that my mind is not the world and the future hasn't happened yet. I notice if I need to step away from others and recalibrate. I smoke much-higher-quality weed. And if all of that doesn't work, I turn and ask the paranoia what it needs me to attend to.

Our world inspires a certain level of paranoia. Perhaps it is a measure of intelligence—after all, everyone *is* being watched and controlled within borders they didn't determine, exchanging paper someone else told us is valuable for things of actual value, living under a dangerous government since forever. These truths, along with the constant violence and death and ego-based conflict, can make it hard to relax, to rest and sustain ourselves in the longer arc of justice and transformation.

---

was the low point; only time will tell. In general, I am a high-functioning depressive person. I get extremely hopeless in cycles, I feel restless for the end of everything, and I feel like I need help to see the good, to feel joy. I have come to believe that this is a part of my magic, that I dance with darkness and respect it. I know what it is to need therapy, medicate myself, not be able to get out of bed, and not want to live. And while it isn't easy, it makes me feel like I can see things whole, and whatever joy I have is grounded in the miraculous and tragic dual nature of the real world.

So … smoke up.

HOT AND HEAVY HOMEWORK

Reflect on the pleasures you intentionally
practice to soften the physical, emotional,
and political pain of modern life.
Now. Let me get off this couch.

CONDITIONS OF POSSIBILITY

A Conversation with Monique Tula

After years of local level harm reduction work, Monique Tula became the first woman-of-color executive director of the national Harm Reduction Coalition (HRC), working to reduce the harms that come from drug use. I have been honored to facilitate the HRC in this transition, a full-circle moment, as this was my first paid social justice work. Monique and harm reduction are crucial parts of pleasure activism.

amb. *First of all, can you tell the readers what harm reduction is?*

Monique. Harm reduction is a social justice movement built on the belief in, and respect for, the rights of people who use drugs. Harm reduction combines two key strategies: 1) public health strategies to reduce harms associated with substance use; and 2) advocacy and drug policy reform to address harms caused to communities by the war on drugs. Our bottom line is that *everyone* has the right to health and well-being. And *everyone* has the right to participate in the public policy dialogue.

Our mandate is to create the conditions of possibility where both of those things can occur by keeping people safe and making sure they have the tools necessary to advocate for themselves.

Fueled by the collision of the HIV/AIDS crisis and the war on drugs thirty years ago, a small group of visionary people made the bold decision to care and advocate for drug users who were dying from AIDS. That decision gave rise to an entire community whose anarchistic vision was to keep ourselves safe while disrupting the prevailing criminal "justice" regime that dominated drug policy. The founders of the harm reduction movement were predominantly people who were active or former drug users, people of color, LGBTQ+ activists, and veterans of social justice movements. And together they changed the world.

amb. *I have been shaped by the principles of harm reduction—the idea that the users of drugs are the primary agents of any harm reduction, any change, in their own lives ... this is still such a radical and foundational aspect of my politics for any change work. Can you share some of the principles that center and guide you?*

Monique. First and foremost: no one should be punished for what they put in their own body if it doesn't cause harm to other people. The Foundation for a Drug-Free World estimates that more than 200 million people around the world consume "illegal drugs." The 2016 National Survey on Drug Use and Health reports nearly 25 million Americans use "illegal drugs." What happens to those figures when you include "legal" drugs?

Perhaps more importantly: what is it about drugs that makes so many people want to use them?

Sometimes we just want to feel differently than we do every day. It feels good, causing pleasure and excitement. Sometimes we need to find a way to escape from the harsh realities of our lives. Why is this a criminal act?

People who use drugs become "other" based on behaviors that aren't culturally acceptable. People who use drugs are among the most stigmatized and criminalized groups in society. We cast moral judgment for not saying "no." We say it's your own fault for getting HIV or hepatitis C. We're quick to point out their lack of willpower and selfishness. We stereotype and pathologize people who use drugs. We make them "other."

Stigmatization involves severe social disapproval of a person's characteristics or their beliefs, which are considered to be unacceptable to dominant cultural norms.

The cycle of drug-related stigma reinforces stereotypes and labels, which in turn reinforce stigma, which sets expectations about roles. These expectations lead to limited opportunities based on what people think a drug user is capable of doing, which in turn leads to internalized/reinforced expectations. It's a series of diminishing returns that make it difficult for drug users—or really any marginalized community—to break free.

It's become easier to judge people who use drugs instead of seeing them as human beings who deserve love. For many, it's easier to impose simplistic, moralistic expectations instead of asking ourselves, what if?

What if someone is using as an attempt to mitigate the stress and impact of previous or concomitant trauma or mental health issues?

What if someone comes from a community of people who use, and thus drug use is a cultural "norm?"

What if drug use is part of a spiritual practice?

What if drug use is a way to tap into an inner, creative self?

What if a person uses drugs because they get great pleasure in doing so?

What if people who use drugs are people first—people who are more than the sum total of their drug use?

In most cultures, we judge a person who "loses control" over their substance use. They become "other," a scourge reflecting the worst of humanity. We revile and even terrorize people who use drugs. Harm reduction is a way to change that narrative.

The late Don McVinney, one of the "first wave" of harm reductionists in the States, often spoke about the American moral perspective on drug use, which at its core locates the problem in the person.[1] According to Don, harm reduction "locates the problem [if there is one] in the relationship between the person and drug, because lots of people use substances and don't do so problematically."

There are six basic principles of harm reduction—all centered around people who use drugs:

- Health and dignity—the right to be well and seen as a whole person
- Participant-centered services—meeting people where they are rather than where we want them to be
- Meaningful involvement of people who use drugs—both in the design of services and the ability to participate in the public policy dialogue
- Autonomy—the right and ability to make your own choices
- Socio-cultural competency—interacting with people in a way that values their customs, beliefs, practices, and experiences
- Pragmatism—not ignoring or minimizing the very real and potentially tragic harms associated with some behaviors

These sensible and humane principles ground our work and are based in the realities of what people who use drugs experience on a daily basis: stigma, trauma, poverty, classism, race- sex- and gender-based discrimination, social isolation, and other social inequities that affect people's vulnerability to, and capacity for, effectively dealing with harm.

---

1   amb: Don was my first supervisor in the harm reduction world and an incredible sweet, smart man. With gorgeous hair. See Monique Tula, "Remembering Don McVinney: A Harm Reduction Pioneer," Harm Reduction Coalition, http://harmreduction.org/blog/remembering-don-mcvinney.

The principles of harm reduction also acknowledge that some drug use isn't all tied up in full on addiction. In practice, harm reduction is comprised of a continuum of strategies that range from working with people to maintain abstinence from substances if that's what they choose, to reducing risks around controlled or even chaotic use. Regardless of where a person is on that continuum, they deserve to be treated respectfully and seen as an equal.

amb. *Before you became the executive director of the Harm Reduction Coalition, what was your journey/experience with harm reduction?*

Monique. I come from at least four generations of people who use drugs. In the 1930s, my grandfather on my mother's side started using heroin—something he did intermittently for forty years. My grandmother Mary Ellen gave birth to my father, Darrell Lee, when she was just sixteen years old. It was her second pregnancy; her first aborted against her will. Before she left the operating table, her tubes were tied. Wondering why she could never bear more children, Mary Ellen drank every day until she died from breast cancer at the age of 51. That's a year younger than I am now …

Darrell Lee lived with his aunt Mabel in Chillicothe, Ohio, until he was about sixteen. He never knew his daddy and wondered why his mother didn't raise him. He experienced depression and anxiety at a young age but had no words to describe it. And besides, he came from a culture where you didn't put your business out on the street, so he kept whatever he was feeling to himself.

My father's untreated mental health issues continued to grow as he made his way to Los Angeles in the mid-sixties. Like most of his generation, he loved and drugged freely, and it wasn't long before he tried heroin. And when he did, he said it was like finding his purpose.

amb. *That is intense. How did that impact his life?*

Monique. The hustle for enough money to cop dope overtook other priorities like putting food on the table and paying rent. Hustling for money led to arrests and a couple of bids in the penitentiary. Each time he was released, he vowed to stop shooting dope, and eventually he quit it for good. But by then crack had flooded the streets of Los Angeles. I've often said that Daddy probably didn't contract HIV because he put down the needle and picked up the pipe.

I don't think my father ever completely forgave himself for what he saw as his failings and what I eventually came to see as inevitabilities caused by a system designed to keep "haves" divided from the "you will never have."

I gotta say, though, that life with my family wasn't always doom and gloom. I remember coming home after school and walking into our rundown Hollywood apartment that was filled with the rich scent of weed being rolled into fat spliffs. Our home was often filled with laughter, with Black fathers and white mothers kekein' it up for hours.[2] My sister and I used to love to watch them dance and sing along to Stevie, The O'Jays, and Earth, Wind, and Fire. It was magical sometimes. My parents and their friends dabbled in a bit of everything, but what began for them as recreational drug use gave way to harder times. Poverty and untreated mental health issues fueled by chaotic substance use took their toll on our little family, and life grew grim.

As I reflect on my own family's story, I realize it isn't much different than the generations of families caught in the web of chaos created by extreme poverty; generational, societal, and institutional trauma; cycling in and out of prisons; exposure to stigmatizing and potentially deadly diseases like HIV and hepatitis C; untreated mental health; homelessness—the list goes on and on. Every single one of these issues touched my family. Every. Single. One.

It is no mystery to me why many people turn to drugs to

---

2   To keke (or kiki) is to gather together, gossip, and laugh. Gay culture, gay men are often the ones doing the kekeing.

cope. British author Johann Hari once said that eventually people can "no longer bear to be present in their lives." I get it.

I had my son Christian when I was twenty and raised him while working at a retail pharmacy. Ten years later, in 1995, I left LA and moved to Massachusetts, where I studied art and philosophy at community college. I wrote queer erotica and read at a few shows with people like Tristan Taormino. I found work in a nonprofit organization serving people living with HIV and people who used drugs at a needle exchange program, and it was there that I learned about harm reduction, and it changed my life for good. I met my partner of twenty years there too.

I'm clear that my views on drug user health and drug user rights are informed by my own experience, my own biases, my own perspectives. I'm not an academic, an organizer, or a politician. I am a product of an imperfect world filled with people struggling to survive. When I was a child in the middle of my family's chaos, I didn't have words to describe what we were experiencing. But thanks to harm reduction I do now.

amb. *What is your long-term vision for harm reduction's impact in the world?*

Monique. There's an exclusive, until recently, men-only club near Sonoma, California, called the Bohemian Club. Their motto used to be "spiders, weave not thy web here." The spiders they're referring to are women. Members of this club include politicians, university presidents, oil tycoons—basically rich white men who believe they own the world. I envision a world full of spiders, weaving interconnected webs that resist patriarchal forms of supremacy that work so well at keeping us distraught, distracted, and divided.

The harm reduction movement is composed of such spiders, the likes of which the founders of the original Bohemian Club never imagined. We are a collective of trans- and cisgender people. We are LGBTQIA+ and straight folks. We are people of all races and all ethnicities. We are pacifists and warriors, anarchists and mainstream-ists, socialists and liber-tarians—all working toward a more just world. One that is powered by people who have been historically pushed toward society's margins.

The rise of the twenty-first-century social justice warrior isn't simply a trope created by the alt-right or others desper-ately clinging to the status quo. We're working to dismantle the very structures designed to keep us divided—and collec-tively we are legion.

I think about the web of mycelium fungi growing under-ground that you describe in *Emergent Strategy*. It can kill a forest several times over, but, in doing so, it builds deeper, richer layers of soil that allow larger trees to grow. Harm re-ductionists, along with our racial, social, and environmen-tal justice warriors, are both mycelium and tree—interde-pendent and deeply rooted, paving the way for those who come after us.

amb. *I deeply believe harm reduction is a crucial concept for pleasure activism … in a nutshell, pleasure activism is learning from what pleases us about how to make justice and liberation the most pleasurable experiences we can have. Can you break down how you see harm reduction practices potentially increas-ing our capacity for pleasure?*

Monique. We take pleasure in treating people kindly. At the core of harm reduction is unconditional love for people who sometimes have very little love in their lives. For years now, harm reduction practitioners have served as role models for people searching for ways to work with drug users. We use community-centered and people-centered approaches to re-mind them they are worth more than what the rest of the world tells them, that they are valued, and they don't have to hide themselves from us. We're here to help in whatever healthy ways they want us to. We won't push, but we will support.

To get more technical: drug use is a complex phenome-non. Using safely requires not only an understanding of the drug itself but also the circumstances under which you're using. We call this DRUG, SET, and SETTING, a model of looking at the complexities of drug use, but it can also be used to think about other contexts, like having sex. It's essentially looking at the type of drug or sex a person is having, their mind-set and health at that moment, and the environment in which the event is taking place.

Harm reduction also aims to reduce stigmatization experienced by people who use drugs. Stigmatization is a process that involves severe social disapproval of a person's characteristics or their beliefs considered to be unacceptable to dominant cultural norms. The outcomes of the process of stigmatization result in a series of diminishing returns that keep people on the outside. People who use drugs are among the most marginalized and criminalized people in society. But we reject stigmatization, we restore dignity and agency to people who use drugs, and effective harm reduction programs provide a sense of place, purpose, and participation.

amb. *What do you do for pleasure?*

Monique. My current favorite pleasure-receiving activity is to put my hands in the earth. I garden. I love to feel soil under my bare feet. It gives me immense pleasure to watch something grow that I planted. Our place in Oakland has the perfect little backyard where I'm cultivating a xeriscape full of succulents and other drought-tolerant plant life. I built a bamboo arbor and sit under it as often as I can, soaking in the sun and watching bees drift from flower to flower. It's hypnotic.

I have about three different books I'm reading now on Black feminism and the spirituality of Black women. I binge on shows like *Black Mirror* while waiting for the Queen of Dragons to return. I listen to podcasts like *How to Survive the End of the World* on Sunday mornings while I'm making miniatures—like Freamon in *The Wire*. I watch nail art videos ('cause: miniature art!).

I love taking road trips with my partner—we're exceptionally good travel companions. I get to spend time with people I love all around the country. I just came back from New Orleans, where I got to see people I deeply respect and am inspired by.

I laugh from the gut often. Deep, belly-aching, loud-ass guffaws. My son and I like to text each other using memes only—those moments are often the highlight of my day—making me bust out laughing in the middle of my shared office space. And my partner is easily the funniest person I know. Laughing with him is like singing in a Baptist church choir. For real.

amb. *That sounds like a true abundance of pleasure, Monique. Is there anything else you want the readers to know?*

Monique. It's almost inconceivable that what began as a small, ragtag group of angry activists managed to set the pace for the rest of the world when it comes to working with and loving drug users. We are change-makers and risk-takers and rabble rousers. We are people who've made the decision to continue to love those among us that society casts out. And I am proud to be part of this tribe.

The people who comprise the harm reduction movement are far from perfect—this may be one of the reasons I love them so much. The harm reduction movement reflects the dogged perseverance, outsider politics, and gnarly attitudes of all the imperfect people who make up this bad-ass community. I can't believe most of us still like each other after more than thirty years together! This is deeply pleasing to note—that we still love each other. We've built a community and figured out how to support each other in times of hardship and pain.

This sentiment—that we still love each other—can be seen when we come together after long periods of time apart. And nowhere is that more obvious than the national harm reduction conference. People travel from all over the world every couple of years to build, laugh, cry, and learn together. The high people get at our conference is unmistakable—it's filled with positive energy, love, and inspiration. It's truly a magical space that embraces people who use drugs and those of us who love them. We create the space to love ourselves. And if that isn't pleasure activism, I don't know what is.

EXPERIMENTS IN CANNABIS FOR THE COLLECTIVE

by Malachi Garza

Malachi Garza bounces into a room, so full of boyish energy that you might forget just how experienced he is as a leader and organizer. Then he busts out some incredible strategic vision with a multi-year plan for execution and your jaw drops. Here, see for yourself.

The less one has, the less one has to do to get incarcerated. I have watched this engagement, by specific design, destroy the future for most everyone in its path. Growing up in the 1980s, all I knew of policing was the "war on drugs," which targeted communities of color and poor people across generations. I could see in my neighborhoods and then in cities, counties, states, regions across the whole country systematic forced economic isolation en masse—an outcome of criminalization that shapes the fabric of our communities and nation.

I have spent the last decade on the road working in jurisdiction after jurisdiction to confront criminalization and economic disenfranchisement. We are all responsible to find a way, a moment, an opening, or a set of relationships that allow us to grow as interrupters of despair. For years I have been looking for ways to experiment in reparations, to think about building wealth—real, stabilizing, intergenerational wealth. But how, as a person with a working-class community and a nonprofit salary? How can we begin to lift all boats? Reparations from the war on drugs must lift up the Black community and folks directly impacted by criminalization. The moment is upon us to figure out how.

For years I have known the therapeutic qualities of cannabis. I have seen it bring freedom to folks who suffer from anxiety, those who are trying to quit other medications, and those who have relief from the intensity of their pain. I watched, for years, folks in the underground economy, who were in and out of prison for using and/or selling this medicine. Then the tide started to shift. "Legalization" echoed in halls of power. As the fight gain traction, I thought this might be one of those special times when one sees the tide coming before it crashes upon the shore.

As marijuana legalization spreads across the United States, the accompanying marijuana industry is projected to grow to $44 billion by the year 2020, with California as the largest cannabis market in the country. As legalization looked inevitable, I saw white straight men quitting their Silicon Valley tech jobs and moving to Oakland in droves, bragging that they were finally "free" to make a boatload of money in the cannabis business. They talked of operating in a "legal gray area" because they had the money to do so. "It's not legal yet, *but* I have my warehouse up and running! I have my delivery service driving a Tesla! I have two houses in the Hills growing. Who's gonna arrest *me*?" Lighting up a joint, those with money, power, and privilege were unabashedly gobbling up any competitive advantage of early entry, benefiting from a lack of competition in the space and not thinking *ever*. Not once did I hear them talk about the war on drugs or its effects on people of color or poor people. I began to see what turned into a white ownership tsunami. Limited social indicator research in the cannabis business has found there is only 1 percent African American ownership across the entire industry. This led me to explore the structural barriers put into place that restrict people out of ownership and jobs in the industry.

So

- criminalization of drug use destroys Black and Brown futures
- criminalization for drug use has fueled the money made to reinforce the carceral state
- legalization of drugs has locked Black and Brown people out of ownership, jobs, and profits
- 80 percent of public monies generated from cannabis goes to funding the carceral state

My stomach turns as I try to dream up justice schemes that can interrupt this.

I recently visited members of a home-grown queer feminist POC business collective who imagine equity frameworks that support local business in giving back to their communities. There some typical standards for this—hiring formerly incarcerated people (especially those with drug offenses) with good pay and benefits—but what else can we do? How do we deepen and broaden that work?

We thought about sending a percentage of profits into a fund that supports formerly incarcerated people's organizations. What if dispensaries fund these organizations in the same geography of the dispensaries? That, in and of itself, people were tripping on. Especially in an economic sector so saturated with white tech bros proudly declaring they are only looking out for themselves. Folks already thought we were onto something. They looked at us like Robin Hood. After all, who would dare to think about sharing profits with ordinary people in the community? But the cannabis industry is excited and ready for it—if you approach the right people.

So, I kept at it. Using my relationships to connect the progressive Left with people who are creating business models and funding projects that build up real wealth opportunities at scale. After I saw the potential for decriminalization and the opportunity to realize major wealth, I couldn't stop talking about it. What are we going to do in this moment? Are we ready to stand in active solidarity while also trying something new? Let's stop begging for crumbs of money and get dollars into people's hands.

We can create opportunities for communities of color, people directly impacted by criminalization, to *own* these companies. Of course, to become a legal investor in a cannabis company, one must have hundreds of thousands of dollars lying around available to invest. Yet, as organizers know, barriers are for overcoming. There are ways to have those with wealth enter this market and then give over ownership to those with fewer resources. There are ways to create opportunities for "micro-investors" to get in the game. These strategies are moving forward, here and now. This is some lifting-all-boats type of ish.

This is the time to ask more of the private sector. Individuals of wealth must become co-conspirators. There is about to be the largest intergenerational wealth transference (to young folks with family money) in history, and wealthy, young, progressive folks are looking for ways to support projects like reparations, wealth redistribution, and other forms of self-determined community power building. They are interested in helping to build and sustain self-determination. This is the time for investment, to create regulations and rules that prioritize and steer profits toward people who are most directly impacted by criminalization.

I have seen some of these projects grow beyond what I imagined. Already millions of dollars have moved, and cannabis can help transform communities that have been harmed by its historical criminalization. From dispensaries (which earn 60 to 80 cents on every dollar made in the industry) to legislators (writing the rules around who can play); from impact investors (who can invest, seed and turn over percentages of ownership and profits) to cannabis businesses (that can hire and direct portions of profits)—we all have a responsibility and ability to proactively vest these opportunities into communities of color, particularly Back and Brown communities.

With a more than $44 billion projected net profit in the United States by 2020, this work must be a part of the foundation of this industry. These models are key to realizing the opportunities alive at this moment, which we will not see again in our lifetime. Let us be bold and brave and work across all levels of power and privilege to create the world all of our people deserve.

ECSTASY SAVED MY LIFE

I want to tell you about my relationship with ecstasy. Rolling, what we call the high of ecstasy, is how I danced as close to the edge as I ever have and felt the most alive I had felt at that point in my life.

It was my senior year of college when I swallowed MDMA for the first time with a friend who showed up with a bag of like one hundred pills. I took one. He took seven over the course of the evening, some of them crushed and snorted up his nose. Within an hour, it felt like the world was made of pleasure, that my bones were shivering with miracles. I understood that my beating heart shared a rhythm with the wind and the dirt—that I was not separate from anything. It was more true than anything else I'd ever felt. I remember thinking in the moment that maybe sex was *supposed* to feel like this, but I hadn't met that level of lover yet.

I had met a pill, though. I had met a medicine.

My friendships in my early twenties were shaped in part around finding other people who were interested in rolling, going to a club or three where the low lights would keep changing, and someone would give us glow sticks, and we would dance until we couldn't anymore, pile into cabs, come home and sit on a Brooklyn rooftop watching the sunrise, chain-smoking through the come-down.

Or we would be in my little apartment, taking turns as the DJ of the *best* music *ever* made, telling each other *all* of our secrets, telling each other *what we were gonna do* with our lives, trying not to mess everything up with sex, but … you live and learn. These were brilliant people, my fellow adventurers. We had jobs, we had oppressions, but the center of our lives was pleasure, celebration, dancing, music, cooking together, sharing a critique of our country, seeking freedom in the here and now.

I have distinct memories—a club with glowing pink walls and Janet Jackson's "All for You" playing, and I knew it was for me. A warehouse with endless rooms where my high came on while I was in the bathroom line, and I forgot to pee because I started making out with the hottest man I'd ever seen. A New Year's party where I sang Rihanna's "Shine Bright Like a Diamond" with two famous musicians.[1] Rolling in my little studio apartment with a friend who took my face in her hands and told me I was beautiful and kept saying it until I believed her. Ecstasy is a hyperbolic, hypnotic drug.

Here's the only downside: I was depressed. You may have guessed that, but in case you didn't—that's one of the things you can call it when someone needs pills in order to access their natural magic, interconnectedness, and pleasure. There was unnamed sexual trauma, unspoken abuse, fatphobia, depressive tendencies, and perfectionism challenged by having failed to graduate college. I felt like a fraud all the time. I had anxiety, I had paranoia, I was scared of everything and everyone. And although it was beautiful to flood my brain with serotonin, my weekday struggles were sometimes intensified by the crash that would come after these blissful weekends.

But … looking back, I was going to be depressed either way. I was down in the gray place, the nothing. Most of the activists around me were also depressed and finding ways to cope. This once-illicit path is getting therapists' attention

---

1   I often think about how fun it would be to be high with Rihanna. She gives me the impression that her head is on straight, that she prioritizes pleasure and fun and knowing her body, loving up her body. I also like how she stays in dignity, in her independence, in her hard work. Basically, I love Rihanna. #fentyforever #neverafailurealwaysalesson

now, but, at the time, I felt I had to hide my use from those who I worked with, that I would be judged. These brushes with joy were promises that there was some brightness, some delight, that was also me.

There was a major ecstasy drug bust in the city, after which other things were packaged and sold as ecstasy, but it was speedy miserable stuff, so that was the end of that era. But by then I had found an amazing therapist who was ready to catch me when I jumped, and I began to talk. Later, I found somatics, authentic relationships, bodywork—I began to shake off the demons that trauma had left on me, in me. And the more I felt, the more I could see the numbness I had been living in, the majority of myself dormant, with just patches of bright. And I am so grateful for those patches, when I look back and see how they lit the way to this moment, this functional self, this growing sense of agency, this high that can be boosted with pills or drugs but exists outside of any alteration in my state: this pleasure.

SECTION FIVE

PLEASURE AS POLITICAL PRACTICE

We are what we practice. We become what we do over and over again.

In this chapter, we will look at practices beyond the realm of sex and drugs that are crucial for living into a pleasure politic.

First we look at a series of practices for healing toward pleasure, how we practice intentional resilience and recover access to pleasure once harm has happened, or during illness.

Then we will look at wholeness in movement spaces—how we bring to our justice work all of our fullness, our pleasures, our bodies, humor, fashion, music, everything we are.

Finally we will look at how we craft liberated relationships. We can learn to fight for freedom and transformation with and for our romantic partners, our friends, our families. And we can bring that intention, and those practices, to everyone we meet, to every relationship, political, organizational, and intergenerational.

SUB-SECTION

THE POLITICS OF HEALING TOWARD PLEASURE

For oppressed people to intentionally
cultivate pleasure is an act of resistance.
—Ingrid LaFleur

FEELING FROM WITHIN

A Life of Somatics

For the past nine years, I have been learning to feel, to connect with others while feeling, and to begin to understand what is possible when a collective of humans is not afraid to feel life together.

I have always felt strong emotions, but I have never known what to do with them. When they were sad or hard emotions, I would try to contain them. For years, I would experience a shaking in my belly when I was locking my jaw tight to keep from crying or showing that I was scared or hurt. I could tell that there was tension in a room through quivering in my belly and knees. Good feelings didn't go much better. I would use biting humor to move through intimacy with family and friends, not aware of how sharp my teeth were, how powerful my mood could be. With lovers, I would often be in my head trying to think my way to happiness or to orgasm instead of breathing into the actual sensations of my body, especially in my heart and below the waist.

In 2009, my beloved movement comrade Malkia Cyril invited me to a course called Somatics and Social Justice being offered by a group called Generative Somatics.

The word Somatics comes from the Greek
root soma which means "the living organism
in its wholeness." It is the best word we have
in English to understand human beings as an
integrated mind/body/spirit, and as social,
relational beings. In somatic speak, we call
this embodiment, "shape," and the collective
"body" or collective psycho-biology. Somatics
is a path, a methodology, a change theory, by
which we can embody transformation, individually and collectively. Embodied transformation is foundational change that shows in
our actions, ways of being, relating, and perceiving. It is transformation that sustains over
time. Somatics pragmatically supports our values and actions becoming aligned. It helps us
to develop depth and the capacity to feel ourselves, each other and life around us. Somatics
builds in us the ability to act from strategy and
empathy, and teaches us to be able to assess
conditions and "what is" clearly. Somatics is a
practice-able theory of change that can move
us toward individual, community and collective liberation. Somatics works through the
body, engaging us in our thinking, emotions,
commitments, vision and action.[1]

Sounded good to me, even though I was scared of what
I might discover in the process. I knew there was trauma in
my life that I hadn't dealt with, and I knew there were big,
suspicious gaps in my memory. But I felt ready for something
to move in me. I went through the course with equal parts
enthusiasm and trepidation. It was a learning year for the
organization, but enough of what was offered stuck with me

---

1   "What Is Somatics?," Generative Somatics, http://www.generative
somatics.org/content/what-somatics.

that I said yes to another course a couple years later, Somatics and Trauma.

In each course, I was learning the basic building blocks of the methodology, learning to drop in and feel myself from within, to begin to understand how I had been shaped by the circumstances of my birth, the structures of my generation. For a long time, I was still in my head, kind of imagining myself as a little ball of energy dropping down into my mysterious body. And then, slowly, I started to feel sensations below my head, below my neck. A lot of what I initially felt was pain—sensations in my back, hips, and legs that I had been overriding in order to keep up an overactive travel and work life. My knees hurt immensely—turns out I had early onset arthritis.

I also began to feel my true center, my center of gravity, the center of my being. It was a place inside myself that was as vast as the ocean, that gave me the resources I needed to feel all of my feelings and still be in my dignity, to make mistakes and still be in my dignity, still be connected to other people, to stay open and present.

I learned new things about pain. My pain was holding onto my past for me. In an individual, pain can be a reminder of what we have not turned to face. For me, that included memories I had seemingly displaced with my survival behavior of dissociation. I felt distinct moments of release, as I would let a memory surface in class or while being held in the hands of a somatic bodyworker.

One of the reasons the Generative Somatics approach works for me is that it is concerned about somatics as a collective way of understanding trauma and pain. It isn't about going away from the community to heal, which was the main way I had experienced healing work prior to somatics. It isn't about being a special "healer" who is apart from community. Generative Somatics feels into how, in a collective or group, patterns of pain can indicate the mass, or intergenerational, trauma people are surviving. And how each of us has the power to help each other feel more, heal, and move toward our longings for liberation and justice together.

I recall a session with Black Organizing for Leadership and Dignity (BOLD), a Generative Somatics movement partner, where one man's honesty about facing constant racist fear of his Black body every day opened up a floodgate of shared grief, pain, anger, and shame in the room. Afterward we were able to have political conversations that were so authentic and joyful, because we had gotten to the root of a shared pain together.

It is still a rare thing for most of us to sit with what we feel, how we feel, the reality that we carry memories and feelings from what our ancestors experienced, and that we carry our current continuous collective trauma together. The pain can open to other feelings, more nuanced and clear. It can begin to make authentic connection and collectivity more possible.

Every mass movement, every collective effort, is made up of relationships that exist between members of the larger group. Around friends old and new, somatics helped me begin to gauge what I truly wanted and needed from connections, from political space. I got clearer on what I could offer. I got in touch with a feeling of restlessness and wandering that let me know when I didn't want to be somewhere or with someone or with a political project. I could also feel the distinct energy of moving toward, or forward, that let me know when I did want to be around someone, did want to join in an effort from a place of authentic alignment, rather than obligation.

This awareness extended until I could begin to feel when I wanted to be in a certain place, job, political project, or even city. And when it was time to go. Yes is an embodiment. Yes is a future.

In physical connections, I was able to stay more present.[2] I learned that I had a no, a visceral, clear "hell no." If I listened

---

2   It was much later that I read the book *Healing Sex*, written by one of my somatics teachers, Staci Haines. It's really helpful and has all this homework for the reader to do, to learn your landscape of sexual trauma, to move toward healing. I highly recommend it. See Staci Haines, *Healing Sex: A Mind-Body Approach to Healing Sexual Trauma* (San Francisco: Cleis Press, 2007).

to the no, if I honored it and set boundaries, it made more room for my yes.

And the beautiful, miraculous new possibility is: I am able to stay present in my yes. I can feel the yes in person, I can feel it at a distance. I can feel my face flush, my heart pound, a smile I can't swallow. I can feel my body get wet and warm, open. I can feel myself move toward an idea, a longing, a vision. I am a whole system; we are whole systems. We are not just our pains, not just our fears, and not just our thoughts. We are entire systems wired for pleasure, and we can learn how to say yes from the inside out.

For me, from that yes, I am learning to communicate in real time, both what I want and what I don't want. To be with the twisting gut and pounding heart that don't want to speak uncomfortable truths, the burrowing, masking tucked chin of shame, the circular, overthinking busyness of my brain, and with the deep breath and interconnected dignity that allow me to be more honest every day. To be with the tingling spine and warm solar plexus that hint that I am feeling love. To pull in my energy when I am in a situation where I need better boundaries. And to keep bringing my attention back to center, back to the present moment, to show up where I am.

It turns out, being present is the most important part of every single experience in my life.

It turns out, every other human being is also wired in these ways, entire systems shaped by pain and pleasure. And I can grant others the same autonomy I am learning to wield on my own behalf—how I spend my life is my decision, based on all kinds of data coming from my body. And I can grant others the same level of complexity and contradiction as I am learning to embody—we are all multitudes in process. We get to have boundaries. We get to have longings and articulate them. We can begin to imagine a society coordinated around honest, clearly articulated longings.

At the end of the Somatics and Trauma course, I was invited into teacher training, to become part of the community that brings embodiment to new students, new geographies, and social movements. I have been learning and teaching for eight years as of the writing of this book. Last year we brought the course to Detroit for the first time, and it was an incredible experience to share this liberation technology with a place that has given me so much, with people I love and am growing with. It was also thrilling to grow skills with Detroit and midwestern and southern organizers who often get overlooked by efforts based in New York City or the Bay. I can already feel the impact in the community of having more organizers who can feel themselves, who have been practicing returning to center and moving toward longing, all of us organizing ourselves around what we long for rather than what we are against.

I believe somatics, in coursework and/or bodywork, is one of the most effective ways to get a group of complex, contradictory humans into alignment with a liberated collective future. Seeing, feeling ourselves, as we are, with agency to shape the future ... that's the miracle.

BLACK WOMAN WILDNESS

A Spell

Junauda Petrus

Junauda Petrus is a soul sweetener, filmmaker, writer, runaway witch, cosmic bag lady, and cofounder at Free Black Dirt.

Some summers ago, I was going through a hard and breathtaking breakup. The kind where I was carrying on crying, listening to Bilal on repeat, puffing all the trees. The fatigue of sadness left me an emo hermit in fetal position in my bed. It was my first relationship with a woman after coming out to myself fully in my early thirties, and my nose may have been a little wide open. Just a little.

My deep and wild friend Keegan had called me one afternoon and, in the midst of this hurt, gave me some sister-girl-witchy wisdom: "Go put on a long and flowy skirt with no underwear, and go find somewhere in nature to sit your coochie on the earth. Let the earth hold the ache for you. Just cry and let it all out."

I had stopped mid-sob at the suggestion. The advice was unexpected and profound as an actual act, something I could do with myself and not just a thought to obsess over. And later that day, I swung my skirt off my ass in a swirl and lowered my pum pum onto the sweet, green grass in the park by my house.

I felt soothed and understood by the depth and weight of the earth, that nobody's words or my mental pondering could provide my heart. I was going through a heartache existing on the energetic and physical level, and getting to feel the breeze on my pussy reminded me of a part of me that was essential and limitless. I really did feel a relief and release as I melted into all the layers of earth beneath me.

This experience taught me to ask nature to hold and ground me in my immensity, and I have brought that to my work as an organizing artist. Because it is so intense being a human, descended from legacies of trauma and triumph and all kinds of things that we carry within us as Black folks (and all folks), invisible yet influential on a soul level. So much of our healing will include sweetening on, rubbing on, and laying open in the expanses of nature and letting it wrap our bodies in remembering and pampering. The ancestors in our bodies, known and unknown, need these rituals of healing and softness, as do we. In the wilderness of ancient, marrow-deep trauma, I'm figuring it out. And despite any of the delusions of oppression, I'm allowed to luxuriate, for me and all of those in my blood.

I have learned to rely on nature, desire and creative inspiration to be a compass and a place of solace for my heart in the persistent struggle for justice and transformation that I'm committed to. In this lifetime, I was born a warrior, healer, and sweetener, and nature was my first mentor on how to be erotic, wild, free, generative, intelligent, rhythmic, sexual, sensual, and shameless. When I create and work in the community, in the presence and meditation of nature's wildness, it becomes a practice of sweetness I offer myself within the beautiful struggle.

It gives me permission like nothing else to accept myself in all of my own wildness and growth. Nature puts the struggle in perspective, and I am filled with my own power. Whether I am sitting coochie directly to the earth or am looking at a waterfall pour from its source, abundant, orgasmic, and confident of its origins or am floating in the ocean letting the rage and grief in my ovaries be rocked out of me with each wave. Nature loves on me and helps me realign. Being in my wildness has allowed me to know divine consciousness in a real way. I pray to be like nature, to unfurl without permission or fear.

A Prayer for Pussies, by Junauda Petrus

Grown women know that feeling.
You a little girl under all that skin.
All of that life and holding back.
All of that gray coochie hair
And planted placentas under the tree the kids climb,
when hiding from spankings.
Under piles of unpaid bills and expired lottery tickets.
In your shadow sits that girl within.
Wise and wild.
Quiet and unforgiving.
Indignant and quick.
Clitoris driven.
An emotional wreck with soulful perfection.
Plotting on wildness
You start thinking:
Remember when I was all one hot heat?
One red ferocious flash?
One smooth sweet licorice?
One free flying unknown?

About Prayers for Pussies

In 2016, I was commissioned with three other poets to write poetry to be made into sculptured steel lanterns for a downtown Minneapolis public art project. These would be around for thirty-plus years to reflect the moment and place in time. Prince had passed away that year, a bigot and misogynist had been elected as forty-five, and, as writers, we were observers and alchemists to transformation. When I submitted the poem "Prayers for Pussies" to the City of Minneapolis, it was refused due to them feeling the language was inappropriate.

The piece had an intention beyond instigation. The practice of prayer is witness and devotion. The term "pussy" for me was no longer just a juicy and provocative euphemism for a vulva or a perceived derogatory term for people who live in the power of femmeness and queerness. It became symbolic of all things that our society has gotten sweetness and limitlessness from and figured out ways to grab and use with no reverence for the sacred.

BEYOND TRANS DESIRE

micha cárdenas

Micha Cardenas is often blowing my mind, taking the stage in bright red lipstick, a gorgeous dress, and stomping boots, talking about art and technology in ways that reshape the future. She is working on tech to support refugees finding water in the desert, and bulletproof vests for Black people made from recycled tires. And she is working, always, on herself.

Author's note: Transformative justice, as I understand it, is rooted in an understanding that we have all been harmed and all caused harm. It requires a process of rigorous self-examination, honesty, and accountability. To those ends, I offer this reflection on my previous writing about pleasure in activism.

I was that girl, in the camo miniskirt with the tight pink Jem and the Holograms T-shirt and no bra, short hair in a Spanish anarchist mullet and big boots. Something like Cameron Howe in season one of *Halt and Catch Fire*, I was that trans hacker activist girl in early transition, and when I realized it was a big deal if I took my clothes off, I did. As I was finishing my MFA in visual art, focusing on networked mixed-reality performance, around 2009, I was committed to becoming an internationally known performance artist. I was fascinated by art movements like cyberfeminism, post-porn, and netporn. With my partner, I created erotic performances online and onscreen, hacking our own electronic devices and coding our avatars to imagine new possibilities for pleasure, sexuality, and gender.

I recall reading Audre Lorde's essay "Uses of the Erotic: The Erotic as Power" for the first time, years ago, and rejecting her claim that "to refuse to be conscious of what we are feeling at any time, however comfortable that might seem, is to deny a large part of the experience, and to allow ourselves to be re-duced to the pornographic, the abused, and the absurd." I re-fused to see the pornographic as negative. I was deep in denial. Now I feel the depth and truth of her claims in my own life. Lorde describes the power of erotic not only in the connection between any two people but also in so many more experiences, saying "the erotic connection … is the open and fearless under-lining of my capacity for joy. In the way my body stretches to music and opens into response."[1] Her description of the erotic as a source of power, which can be distorted or misused, reso-nates with my experience.

In my 2010 essay "Trans Desire," published with Barbara Fornssler's essay "Affective Cyborgs" in the book *Trans Desire/ Affective Cyborgs*, I made an argument that I no longer agree with.[2] I argued that do-it-yourself (DIY) queer porn could be a form of liberatory, biopolitical world-building. I argued that desire could be a central guide for political struggle, par-ticularly for trans politics, in which there is no logical way to decide to transition one's gender, given the danger of doing so and the unknowability of the outcomes.

After going through medical, emotional, and spiritual transition, I feel differently now. My gender transition took

---

1   See Lorde, "Uses of the Erotic," this volume, p. 27.
2   micha cárdenas, ed. *Trans Desires/Affective Cyborgs* (New York: Atropos Press, 2010), esp. "Trans Desire" and "Affective Cyborgs."

almost ten years, and I understand my art practice as an important process of experimentation that led me to where I am today. Still, now I see how much of the erotic art that I did in the beginning of my career was a way to unconsciously re-create traumatic experiences I had as a young child and primarily about seeking approval and validation. The behavior was reinforced by being rewarded with attention as a performance artist.

In response to the daily physical and emotional violence I was experiencing in the beginning of my gender transition, living in the conservative militarized city of San Diego and being outwardly non-binary in my gender presentation, my desperate need to feel loved and desired was amplified and resulted in my publicly engaging in erotic acts as artwork. I was physically assaulted on the street more than once. I experienced daily harassment about my gender. I was so afraid, constantly afraid. It was like being in fight or flight mode constantly, for almost ten years. I learned to look at the floor, to avoid people's eyes, so they wouldn't see me.

I no longer see this as liberatory. I am not attempting to describe anyone else's motivations for creating porn or erotic art but my own, based on my experience of rigorous self-examination. I believe there are infinite possibilities of erotic expression and am not making a value judgment on the content or producers of those works.

I see my own early erotic artwork as resulting from the lack of support I was given as a young child expressing transgender desires. I see it as a result of the ways my early caregivers abandoned and harmed me. I see it as a result of a transphobic world that responded to my outward expressions of gender transition with violence, and my own lack of knowledge about how to care for myself in that process.

In my twenties and thirties, I often re-created unhealthy relationship dynamics. These were amplified by my gender transition, as I began to experience more violence on a daily basis, and, in turn, I relied more on my partners for physical and emotional safety. My needs were inappropriate and unsatisfiable. I lacked boundaries. I remember one of my partners telling me at the time that I needed constant validation of her love and that she couldn't provide what I needed. At the time, I was hurt. I felt judged.

I was often treated as less than cisgender women—treated as an object, an experiment, or a proof of radicalism by cisgender women. In these experiences, it is hard for me to differentiate between the prevalence of transmisogyny and my own traumatized decisions in choosing partners. I now see how I put myself into many situations, emotional and sexual, which were a result of not valuing, respecting and caring for myself. From a lack of nurturing as a child, I did not know how to love and protect myself.

Years of this, combined with the instability and emotional demands of graduate study toward a PhD, led me into a profound depression. At just the moment I finished graduate school and completed the gender-related surgeries I needed, my life felt worthless and my intimate relationships brought me more and more misery and agony.

Seven years later, I have a much deeper understanding of the ways that my desires for partnership and intimacy have also been shaped by my childhood trauma. My desire for gender transition did serve as an important guide for my politics. That desire was powerful and unwavering in the face of oppression and violence on the institutional and individual levels. Additionally, that desire led me to learn about queer, antiracist, and anticolonial politics in an effort to better understand my own heritage as a mixed-race first-generation Colombian-American woman born in the United States.

I see now how my long-term partners in relationships did provide me with a great deal of emotional support, and I am profoundly grateful for their care and patience. Often, being in a relationship with a trans woman can mean putting yourself into a small degree of the danger she is facing. On too many occasions to count, I had partners stand up for me verbally or even physically, putting themselves in harm's way for my safety. Additionally, I had partners who provided emotional and financial stability through some of my most difficult times. I will never forget these kind acts of generosity.

Today I am profoundly grateful for the healing I have found in the past few years. Once I was stable in my career, I was able to shift my focus to emotional healing. Thanks to a nonhierarchical, spiritual community of women that I encountered, I began to be able to see the connections between my childhood trauma, the violence I had experienced, and my own choices. I have, in recent years, finally been able to build a deep self-love and self-respect that I did not learn from queer communities or radical political communities, where I often felt further devalued, excluded, and objectified. I have found a refuge in people committed to healing, service, and sobriety, and this has given me the tools to question my desire and my part in putting myself in situations that caused me to feel devalued.

By finding a supportive community, I have come to understand how my desires in intimate relationships have been shaped by trauma and have often re-created those traumas. I agreed to contribute to this anthology with the hope of sharing my experience and strength in finding new, healthy forms of desire and intimacy. Now I see that I have to actually love *myself.* Through devotion to self-care, meditation, and the practice of self-love and directing lovingkindness, or metta, toward myself, I am starting to feel a self-love that provides me a basis to feel love for others and receive love that is more than just validation.

In her essay "Situated Knowledges," Donna Haraway put it simply when she said "we are not immediately present to ourselves."[3] This is especially true for survivors of trauma and for people who have generations of trauma history, such as the traumas of alcoholism, abuse, war, and colonization.

Now I try to treat myself and my heart with the utmost care. I enter into romantic and intimate situations with

---

3   Donna Haraway, *Simians, Cyborgs, and Women: The Reinvention of Nature* (New York: Routledge, 1990), 192.

careful awareness and regularly check my reality with people who I trust to be able to see reality clearly and tell me the truth. I take my time and get to know people on an emotional and spiritual level before entering into deeper levels of intimacy with them. I no longer engage in acts that make me feel disembodied or devalued. I am learning how sexuality can be a sacred act, part of a healthy sharing of two realities, and how desire can emerge from care and love, instead of from objectification.

It has been a long journey to be able to build dignity, self-respect, and a capacity for intimacy, and I have a long journey ahead, but I feel more centered, grounded, honest, and happy than ever before in my life. Without a doubt, my artwork, political activism, writing, and teaching have deepened profoundly as a result of my new awareness. Now that I take significant time to sit with and understand my feelings, I find myself able to discern far more shades, combinations, and refractions of my inner life, and that nuance goes into my art/activist/theorist practice.

I once believed that sex and romantic partnership were the most important things in life. I built up a false logic to justify that, but I also found much support for that thinking from both capitalist and radical communities.

Today I believe that justice, honesty, kindness, community, and family (chosen and multispecies family included) outweigh the importance I place on fleeting desires. When Lorde says "having experienced the fullness of this depth of feeling and recognizing [the erotic's] power, in honor and self-respect we can require no less of ourselves," I understand her use of the erotic as a grounds for the struggle for global justice for all beings, emerging out of the experience of true intimacy with myself, the world, and others, and accepting no less.[4]

Now I'm that girl who meditates every day, on my knees by my little statue of Guanyin, with my dog Roja nearby, who is learning what it means to be intimate with herself so

---

4   See Lorde, "Uses of the Erotic," this volume, p. 28–29.

she can be intimate with other people. I found more communities dedicated to liberation through the dharma, meditation, and social justice, which have helped me find more peace and self-love. I still have that Jem and the Holograms shirt. I still love hacking new worlds into existence. Now I love that earlier version of myself, and I can also hold her in compassion. I'm working on being a transformative educator, an artist engaged with my communities, and a good writer. I feel like I'm just starting to see other people's eyes for the first time.

PLEASURE AFTER CHILDHOOD SEXUAL ABUSE

Amita Swadhin

Amita Swadhin is gentle and uncompromising. It's a rare combo. She puts her finger directly on a wound, but only to say—this is not right. This cannot continue. Her work with Mirror Memoirs to support healing from childhood sexual abuse is massive and deeply necessary. Here is a part of her story.

"Did you like it? Did it feel good?"

My father's words, directed at me. We were sitting on the floor in the bedroom I shared with my sister, fully clothed after he had raped me again. I don't remember his face or the sound of his voice in that moment, but I remember his words. I remember the feel of the ugly dark brown slightly shaggy wall-to-wall carpet that he'd bought with his employee discount against my fingers as I ran my hands back and forth, back and forth. I remember staring at his face, trying to assess what he hoped—no, expected—to hear. I remember knowing the violent encounter would only be prolonged if I said the wrong answer.

"Yes," I said.

"What did it feel like?"

"Like … shooting over the moon and through the stars."

He smiled. My face remained blank, per usual, but my gaze was glued to his body, watching, waiting, eyes following his back as he walked out of the room. Something in me relaxed slightly: I had passed the test. The ordeal was over. For now.

I was six years old. I already had a penchant for lying with panache. It was a survival skill.

My father raped me at least once a week—and often more—for eight years of my childhood, beginning when I was four. Whenever my body would show my true feelings through tears, I got hit in the face until I stopped crying. And then the rape would continue. Whenever my body would show my true feelings through resistance, like hitting or kicking, I got pinned down and raped more violently. My father's abuse including forcing me to watch porn with him regularly. Most of the scenes he forced me to watch were in the "incest porn" genre—VHS tapes depicting "daughters enjoying sex with their fathers." I never knew whether the people in the videos were actors or whether they were actually fathers and daughters. I never knew where he acquired these tapes. But I knew with certainty: I hated those videos. And I hated my father.

Given that my parents were married until I was sixteen, my father's violence continued in so many ways even when he wasn't actively raping me. He was inescapable. And so, by second grade, I had learned to protect myself by acquiescing. Submitting. Appeasing. And somewhere along the way, unbeknown to myself, I got really good at dissociating: when my father was nearby, and certainly when he was attacking me verbally, physically, or sexually, I was far, far away in all but body.

To complicate matters, whenever my father's violence was not directed at me but we were in the house together, I was in a constant state of hypervigilance. My father was a bomb that detonated again and again, and my mother, sister, and I were his constant targets. In his moments of stillness, I wondered: was he coming for my mother or my younger sister, both of whom I felt a responsibility to protect? Was he just moments away from coming to find me and attack me again?

Neurobiology teaches us that no animal, human or otherwise, can survive in a constant state of hypervigilance. Our systems simply cannot support being flooded with stress hormones 100 percent of the time. Dissociation was my body's autopilot response to hypervigilance. I survived by finding ways to self-soothe. When most of your time is spent dissociating, it's hard to tell whether you're engaging in activities because you truly find them pleasurable or simply trying to escape reality. When you're constantly in survival mode, it can be easy to confuse thrill-seeking activities that stimulate euphoria and adrenaline due to the threat of danger with pleasurable activities that help one be present and centered and authentically connected to one's sense of self. When I think about my early experiences of what at the time felt like "pleasure," I realize now, on the cusp of being forty, that authentic pleasure was something I didn't experience until much later in my life, after my father was removed from our home and I had some room to breathe (literally and figuratively).

I grew up in a suburb of New York City, just twenty minutes from the George Washington Bridge. Our town was a blue-collar town, about 50 percent families of color and 50 percent ethnic white families. My family lived in an apartment until I was eight and then in a modest house from fifth grade until my parents got divorced the summer before my senior year of high school. There were plenty of children to play with, in both neighborhoods. Most of my friends were other kids of color, mainly African American, all types of Asian American (especially other children of South Asian immigrants), immigrants (and their recent descendants) from the Caribbean, and the type of white kids who knew which countries their families were originally from (mostly fourth- and fifth-generation kids). It was the early 1980s, a time when children were still allowed to roam neighborhoods on their own during daylight hours. Plenty of time for thrill-seeking, escapist adventures in good company.

In elementary school, self-soothing and trauma release and resistance looked like this:

Go outside and play with your friends in the neighborhood. He never hurts you when you're with your friends. He never comes looking for you outside. Neither does your mom, as long as you're home before the streetlights come on.

Stay close to the boys, they are more wild and more fun anyway. You aren't supposed to be dirty and wild like the boys. You love breaking this rule. Run around with them. Scream with them. Climb trees and hang upside down. Play red light, green light. Play freeze tag. Poke glow worms, and catch frogs, and cut earthworms in half. Watch the two halves wriggle away from each other. Wonder if you have killed something alive. Pour salt on slugs. Watch them die. Feel nothing. Pour water on ant hills. Watch the ants die. Feel nothing. Ride your bike fast, fast, so fast you fly off stairs and feel the wind in your hair. You might get hurt. This possibility is thrilling. Spend an entire summer building a bridge of discarded plywood and a shopping cart across the creek that runs behind your apartment building. When you finally make it to the other bank, you encounter a chain link fence. One of the boys runs home to grab his father's wire cutters. You make a hole, all climb through, and you run, fast, fast, so fast you barely notice the small band of old white men in the distance, shouting at all of you, running toward you, golf clubs in hand. You laugh. Gleeful. You are trespassing. You do not get caught, by anyone. You climb the fire escape with the boys. Jump from apartment building rooftop to apartment building rooftop. Enjoy the look of fear on your mother's face when she comes home and sees you in action. You have the power to strike fear into your mother's heart. You feel triumphant. Your sneakers are always dirty, your hair is always disheveled, and your knees are always skinned. You cannot be controlled. At least not by her. Only by him, and only then, in private, by force.

As you approach eight years old, you play with the girls

too. It's no longer acceptable to play with boys all the time, your mother tells you. Or maybe you just understand by watching everyone else. You hate Barbie, but My Little Pony is alright. House is better. You like the sensuality of playing with girls. The way it feels to brush and braid each other's hair. To giggle nonstop. The way it feels to make friendship bracelets and beaded jewelry. The way you can feel each strand, each bead against your tiny fingers. You can feel. You love the precision and concentration girls can engage in, creating entire role-play worlds together with nothing but some stuffed animals and the great outdoors. Your best friend and you dig a huge, deep hole just east of the kickball field. You work on it every day at recess, for weeks. You two have decided you are digging to Australia, not China, because it seems more accurately on the other side of the world. The hole gets filled up by the custodians one weekend, but you don't care. You have found a friend who shares your secret desire: escape. You write love notes to your friends, give them cards and chocolates on Valentine's Day. You love playing hand games at recess, relish the feeling of lungs full of song, punctuated by hand slapping. In your own way, you try to tell. Wonder if it's happening to them too. Look sideways at everyone's father during slumber parties. When you play house, you are the husband. You tell Leah you could make her pregnant so she can give birth to a Cabbage Patch doll, and she says okay. You tell her to lie down. You lie down too, with the soles of your feet touching the soles of Leah's, heads pointing in opposite directions. You place your foot on top of her vagina and rub her through her clothes, just once or twice. "That's where babies come from," you say. She nods like she already knows. It doesn't feel good or bad. Just factual. A reenactment. She passes the Cabbage Patch doll between her legs.

You always understand exactly what is happening to you, even when you don't know the words to tell.

It's hard to talk about pleasure when most of your life before leaving home at seventeen is a careful balancing act: hide the trauma, hide the truth, learn how to pass in the world as a "normal" kid, a kid who isn't being tortured at home. Make your escape plan. Aim your compass at a distant destination: something called "college." Act accordingly. Believe your father's shame is your own. Act accordingly. Survive. Survive. Survive.

By middle school, you spend all your time watching TV, talking on the phone, playing board games with your friends, fighting with your sister, going to the library and Girl Scout meetings and orchestra practice and oratory club practice, and reading, and even going to church with your friends' families. You are never really alone, because even when you're alone, you're escaping into a book or a song or a show or a conversation. You don't know how to be still. When you're still, the flashbacks come.

It's true, some of these moments include fun, and even sensuality, in the company of your friends. You love your friends. You get in trouble in seventh grade for giving half-heart best-friend necklaces to three different girls. You were always emotionally polyamorous. (One best friend would never have been enough to get you through the magnitude of your childhood.) You lay your head in one of your best friend's laps, and she massages your temples, rubs each of your eyebrows in the direction that follows the hair. Your friends play with your long, silky hair, a lot (before that eighth-grade body wave ruins it). You hug each other frequently. You play truth-or-dare, and as you hit eighth grade, the dares more frequently involve Ouija boards, trying to contact "the spirits," prank calling 1-800-MATTRES, and public nudity stunts like mooning passing cars. Gaggles of tightly wound white, Arab, South Asian, East Asian, African American, and Afro-Caribbean middle school girls surviving together and getting their kicks where they can. Your backyard is dominated by an in-ground pool, and in the summer you cannonball off the diving board, enjoying the sharp feel as you hit the water, the feeling of being held by the water before you surface again. Your friends teach you about fashion, and you try to stay on-trend. You try to keep up. Blend in. Fit in. Be normal.

You wear things like ripped jeans with lace patches, and black sweaters with giant random neon words—"HOT" in high-lighter pink, blue, yellow, and green. You wear slouchy socks and slap bracelets, delighting in the knowledge that they are banned, and you get away with them in school anyway. You, after all, are a hall monitor. You love Halloween and dress up every year: homemade costumes of Raggedy Ann, Peter Pan, a scarecrow, and, one year, a present (yes, a gift-wrapped cardboard box over your shoulders and a bow on your head). Your family cannot afford the frivolity of store-bought throw-away costumes. You love pretending.

But does "escape" really count as "pleasure"? Is it possible to experience pleasure when you can't even experience yourself? Where is the room in which to experience yourself, to know yourself, to be an authentic human being, when everything about your public sphere life is a lie (or at least includes a giant and critical omission), and everything about your private sphere life is about surviving torture?

In middle school, you also start what you now know is reclaiming and integrating the trauma. You do not understand it as such at the time. You go to the public library and borrow all the V. C. Andrews books at once. *Flowers in the Attic.* *Heaven.*[1] All the series feature incest as a seedy, glamorized, central plot line. The librarian cocks an eyebrow and asks, "Does your mother know you're reading these?" You laugh on the inside, knowing your mother doesn't know you at all. You barely know yourself. "Yes, it's fine," you say, poker-faced. They know you at this library, you volunteer to help with the younger kids in the children's section, and you play Oregon Trail and Carmen Sandiego on the computer every day. You get to take home all the books. Back at home, you find yourself reading your mother's smutty romance books about pirates and damsels, the ones she tucks behind the upper right corner of the bed frame. Your mother doesn't know you know

---

1   V. C. Andrews, *Flowers in the Attic* (New York: Simon and Schuster, 1979); V. C. Andrews, *Heaven* (New York: Pocket Books, 1990).

her bed better than she does. You get raped in that king-sized waterbed all the time while she is at work. On days when you have the house to yourself, when it is not Thursday so your father is not on his day off, and your mother is still at work, and your sister is across the street playing with her friends, you pull out the pirate books and lie on the water bed and touch yourself as you read. Your breath quickens. You don't ever have an orgasm, but something about this forbidden and stolen space and time, this curious solo exploration; feels like an act of resistance. It is your defiant and private assertion: your body is your own, at least part of the time. You quickly tire of the pirate books and find your father's stash of VHS porn. Of course you skip the nauseating incest porn, but a number of tapes interest you: things that look like something approaching consensual sex between two adults. Sexual cartoons too. You devour them. You aren't turned on, per se. Rather, trying to understand this thing called sex. You know you have never had sex. What happens to you is not sex. But maybe one day you will have sex, and it will be on your own terms, and it will be fun, and you will be powerful. But first you have to understand: what is sex?

You get your period on Christmas morning when you are twelve and a half. At first it seems an inconvenience, but as you sit on the toilet waiting for your mother to come in and show you where the pads are, you realize it might be a gift. Periods mean you can get pregnant. You know your father does not want you to get pregnant, because he often pours Dettol on your vulva and then washes you in the bathtub after he rapes you.

The rape stops. There's no conversation, no admission of harm, but for a long time the lingering threat of violence. You think you might be "safe" now, thanks to your period. But you are worried about your younger sister's safety.

High school begins. You are thirteen, in ninth grade, and soon you will be navigating unwelcome state involvement in your family (thanks to your disclosures to your mother in an attempt to protect your sister).

A lanky guy in eleventh grade asks you on a date. You say yes, conditionally, if his friend and your friend also come along. You are curious to experience a date. You don't like him, per se. You like the attention, and you hate not keeping up with your classmates. He brings you red roses and a teddy bear when he picks you up for the movie. The roses are pretty enough. The petals are soft and somewhat fragrant. Mostly you feel an absence of feeling. He puts his arm around you during the movie. You stiffen. He releases his arm. You relax. This is not like things with your father. You have agency here. Over the year, you realize boys your own age seem intimidated by you. You enjoy this reality. And their attention. Mostly you are restless. You channel your energy into the debate team, the school newspaper, the orchestra, student government, the morning announcements. You have secret crushes: one on the boy who lives around the corner from you who you've known since fifth grade and one on your debate team partner. You say nothing, give no indication. You are terrified of rejection, mostly believing that you are ugly and undesirable. Damaged. Frightening. You focus on your grades. And sometimes your friendships with other college-oriented girls. You start dressing in clothes from the Gap outlet: ecru sweaters, hunter green jeans, and oxblood penny loafers. The less control you feel at home, the more tightly wound you are at school.

You genuinely enjoy going hiking at Girl Scout camp, canoeing on the Delaware, learning first aid, winning debate team matches, and singing in choir. You like making handmade gifts for your friends. You sleep with a stuffed animal, a gray cat that looks like the one from *Pet Sematary* (but cuter). Perhaps these things count as pleasures. Mostly you spend your time being numb or terrified. Your father still lives in your house.

The summer your mother finally has the police remove your father from your home and files for divorce is the summer he beats her and threatens her life on a daily basis, is the summer you are as usual away, is the summer you get your first kiss. His name is Derek, and he is a white boy from Parma Heights, Ohio, a west-side suburb of Cleveland where your grandmother lives. Your summertime best friend Marlena is dating Derek's cousin—she's been dating a string of boys since you were in middle school. She thinks you're getting a bit old to have never been kissed, and you agree. You hate being left behind. Soon after, you can't remember what Derek looked like, but you do know you weren't attracted to him, and you remember how smug he was because he was a very experienced kisser. You clearly recall how satisfying it felt to give him honest feedback when he asked, "How was it?" and you answered, "I didn't like it: too wet, and you shoved your tongue at me. I don't think you know what you're doing." You are fifteen years old.

The next summer, your grandmother helps your mother pay for an ostentatious sweet sixteen party. (When you think about it now, it seems modest, but at the time it was more than you've ever spent on a party, ever.) Your mother rents the local Lions Club hall with wood paneling and orders catered food and a two-tiered custom-made birthday cake. She even hires a DJ, some dude from the local Indian community who does weddings and birthdays and anniversary parties. There are table cloths and balloons and centerpieces and a disco ball and metallic streamers dangling from the ceiling. You get your hair cut into a bob, buy a short black dress from the post-prom discount rack, and dance all night in stockinged feet. You smell like rose oil from the Body Shop. While doing the Electric Slide in this room full of fifty people who have come to celebrate you, you feel a flash of what might be genuine happiness. It is fleeting. But it is there.

In a few weeks, you're back in Ohio and have a crush on a boy you met at the roller skating rink. His name is Brian, and, although he's white, he's from California and just moved to Ohio last year because his parents got divorced. He is less … provincial than the kids you've met in Ohio. With Brian, you learn more about what you actually like. It feels good to put on cherry chapstick and softly kiss while sitting in his lap with your legs wrapped around his waist. It feels good to feel his hands against your skin, rubbing your nipples below your bra. It feels good to hold hands on a picnic blanket at a Cleveland Philharmonic concert. But you do not love Brian, and so you do not want to go much past second base with him. When he tells you he'd like to be your long-distance boyfriend when you go back to New Jersey for your senior year, you tell him that's sweet and accept the charcoal drawing he's made for you. You hang it on your bedroom wall and stare at it while you break up with him over the phone a week later, telling him that long-distance really isn't your thing, you need to focus on your college applications. You look at it all year long, to remember. You feel like some seal has been broken. You go to eighteen-and-under dance clubs with your friends and sneak into Indian American college parties at Rutgers. Guys always ask you to dance, and you always say yes. You don't quite like the feeling of them mashing their pelvis into yours and holding you there, swaying. But you like the attention.

The summer between high school and college, your grandmother pays for you to travel to western Europe on a student delegation with People to People. It is an expensive trip, just a year after an expensive party.

You know it is guilt money.

Your grandmother is a social worker who works with children who have survived sexual abuse and other forms of trauma. She never picked up on your own survivorship, never knew until all was said and done. Your shame is outweighed only by your mother's shame, that of your mother who does not disclose the violence to her mother or sister until your father is removed from the house by the police. When social workers, prosecutors, and police officers intervene in your life in ninth grade, your mother pleads with you not to tell your grandmother or aunt. It's easy for you to agree: like most Hollywood celebrities, childhood trauma has made you a great actor. But your rage catches up with you the summer before your junior year, the summer you finally gain a home without a terrorist father lurking in every corner. Your story comes spilling out of you, and you tell whoever will listen. When she finally learns the truth, your grandmother is full of despair and rage, a heap of guilt.

You desperately want to travel, to leave your suffocating suburban life behind, so you accept the guilt-money trip with gratitude. Traveling feels like running, and you, after all, win medals in the 400-meter race. In Europe, you get drunk with other teenagers for the first time. You skip curfew with the other recent high-school grads and climb out the window and down the trellis on the side of the building. By now you are familiar with the high of thrill seeking. Mixed with alcohol, it is intoxicatingly irresistible.

And then, just a few weeks later, it is time for college. Once you arrive, there is no premade goal about where you're going next. You do not know how to function without a goal. You are forced to confront the uncomfortable truth: you do not know much about who you really are. Without this authentic self-knowledge, it's hard to create life goals. There is only trial and error.

Pleasure emerges in the form of enjoyable and consensual sex with a boyfriend you are madly in love with. Heartbreak follows, a year or so later. It is in the post-heartbreak period that you can access authentic information about who you are and what you like. This truth will prevail for decades to come. You learn to cherish emotional intimacy with your friends.

Eventually life will teach you to value that love as sacrosanct and perhaps even paramount. With your platonic and even romantic (but not sexual) friends, you learn how to play in safe environments and relationships for the first time in your life. You and your friends throw yourselves an un-birthday party, complete with party hats, noisemakers, and a chocolate cake. You discover the joy of hot tubs. You discover your queerness. You drink too much. Again and again. You make mistakes. You mistake mutual attraction for love. You make poor romantic and sexual relationship choices. You break your heart open. Again and again.

It will take years, two decades, for you to become sober, to learn to meditate, to be able to just be. Alone. With yourself. To cross the threshold from loneliness to solitude. To learn that love is abundant but compatibility is rare. To learn there is a difference between hedonism that enables dissociation and disconnection versus joy and pleasure that enable presence and intimacy. You are here: college. The finish line of your childhood. But it is only the beginning of the rest of your life.

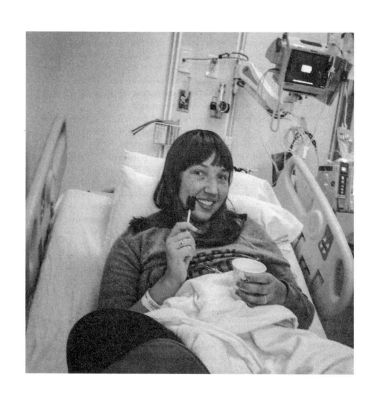

FUCK CANCER

A Conversation with Alana Devich Cyril

I met Alana Devich Cyril through her beloved Malkia Devich Cyril, who I have been comrades with for years. I fell in love with Alana as Malkia did, as the couple shared pictures from Hawaii vacations and Kendrick Lamar rap-offs. When Alana was diagnosed with late-stage cancer, I became part of the larger community in the world that is holding the couple as they grab life and love one day at a time. Alana is clever, hilarious, honest, and incredibly brave. She directed a documentary called My Life, Interrupted, *about her dance with cancer.*

amb. *What was your relationship to pleasure before your cancer diagnosis?*

Alana. There's a Kurt Vonnegut quote that captures it for me: "We're here on earth to fart around and don't let anyone tell you different."[1]

Before my cancer diagnosis, I always liked to describe myself as a bon vivant. I really took great pleasure in delighting in things—food, drinks, art, sex, people, places, all of it. If I was pressed to identify my purpose in life, I thought maybe it was to enjoy things.

---

1   Kurt Vonnegut, *Timequake* (New York: Putnam, 1997), 219.

amb. *It seems like as soon as you learned you had cancer, you also began strategizing and practicing pleasure in so many ways. But I know that might just be perception. How soon after your diagnosis did you get conscious of needing/cultivating pleasure?*

Alana. When I was first diagnosed, I was also really sick. I was sleeping most of the day and couldn't swallow anything that wasn't puréed. So there was an element of just doing what I needed to do to get through each day. After the first couple rounds of chemo I started to feel a lot better, and I remember trying desperately to do things that I would enjoy, despite still being pretty sick.

I remember stubbornly making Mac invite a group of friends to the Exploratorium After Dark night while I was on chemo.[2] My friends kept checking in to make sure I'd be up for it and then I couldn't leave the apartment because of some unfortunate chemo-related pooping. My friends were good sports about it—they all came over, and we had an impromptu party at home. Then I pooped so much I broke the toilet, and we had to call a plumber. Poop party extravaganza!

Mac has really made it a point to keep reminding me to find things I delight in. I'm lucky to be with someone who really prioritizes making room for me to live my best life. When I start to get overwhelmed by my circumstances, Mac is really good at making a surprise karaoke party happen. I get a lot of pleasure from karaoke.

When I was on my first chemo cocktail, I fell into a deep depression, and pleasure was not accessible to me. That was hard. I didn't see the point of living. I was on chemo to extend my life, yet my life was the worst it had ever been. My whole personality was changed. At some point, my oncology team realized that my anti-nausea medication was actually causing the personality change. I stopped taking it, and the very next day I started feeling human again.

---

2   Mac is Malkia Cyril, director of the Center for Media Justice and lover extraordinaire.

amb. *What is cancer teaching you about pleasure?*

Alana. My body has always been a great source of pleasure for me—whether it was sex or exercise or an amazing meal, I've always been a very embodied person. Cancer is the first time where I've really had a hard time being in my body. It's the first time I've been deeply uncomfortable—or even paralyzed—for long stretches of time.

Two things strike me:

When I was in the hospital for a month as a result of my brain hemorrhage, I stayed having fun. I was in really good spirits almost the whole time. It was like a crazy adventure, and I was up for it. Mac and I celebrated our second anniversary in a hospital room in Oahu, when I couldn't move the left side of my body. It was like nothing I had experienced before. But Mac was there, and the nurses loved us. One of the nurses brought us a cake for our anniversary, and she covered my hospital bed with rose petals. Part of me wants to attribute all of that to this amazing nurse, but she also must have really resonated with something in us.

However, I often feel very betrayed by my body now. It can make it very hard to experience bodily pleasure. For a while, sex was simply off the table because it was too hard for me to manage feeling into my body on top of everything else going on. But recently, I decided to just give it a try, and I was like, "oh right, I love sex!" So it can be a little reach and some extra effort to be open to pleasure—that applies to any kind of pleasure—but when I make that leap, it's so amazing.

amb. *I know you love brunch, ice cream, internet animals, and sharp humor. What are some of your other pleasures, and why?*

Alana. I love good music, especially really good lyrics. I love to see live music, theater, performance art. I love film. Historically, I love literature, but reading isn't as accessible to me these days. I love sharing an amazing meal and good conversation with friends. I love sex. I love obsessing about really random things. I love admiring the moon in all its phases. I love making people laugh.

amb. *This may be too personal, in which case, tell me shut up …
but I feel so aware of how Malkia looks at you and sees your beauty
and sensuality every single day, allowing everyone else to see you
through that lens. It feels like that would be good medicine as your
body goes through the challenges of cancer. Is that the case?*

Alana. Mac makes me feel like a sexy beast, no matter what. Sometimes I agree with him, sometimes I don't. It reminds me of my humanity as I manage cancer. It helps me have more compassion and love for myself and others. It makes me feel like a superhero, honestly.

amb. *Have you read Audre Lorde's cancer writings? She also
seemed to share this commitment to pleasure through transition,
and I wonder if she has influenced or encouraged you from the
ancestral realm?*

Alana. I read her *Cancer Journals* a few months after my diagnosis.[3] What struck me the most from it was her commitment to doing whatever it would take to continue her life's work. I honestly found it to be difficult to relate to—I'm someone who has always struggled with understanding my purpose.

Part of me hoped that maybe this cancer diagnosis would activate some secret purpose-filled part of me that was sitting dormant, but that hasn't really happened. What has happened is that I've started a blog and am working on a documentary, and I grow my love for Mac every day. So, in a way, I've been able to rekindle some creativity that hasn't had much attention in many, many years. That feels connected to Audre in some way.

---

3   Audre Lorde, *The Cancer Journals* (San Francisco: Aunt Lute Books, 1980).

amb. *What do you wish everyone understood about pleasure?*

Alana. I think we are on earth, in these humanly bodies, to experience pleasure—among other things.

I also do believe the saying "everything in moderation," with the emphasis on the word "everything."

And, finally, I believe in pleasure as a practice. You can fall out of practice, but life is so much better when you're exercising your pleasure muscles.

CARE AS PLEASURE

Leah Lakshmi Piepzna-Samarasinha

Leah Lakshmi Piepzna-Samarsinha is a prolific writer and teacher in the realm of disability justice and care work. Every time we talk she changes something in my foundational sense of myself.

When I think of care and pleasure I think of:

- Me and my partner hanging out in bed during a "bed day," constantly communicating about what hurts and what positions our bodies need to be in, offering to make each other tea or bringing over the chips. Spooning, reading, telling stories, making out and napping, in the middle of a massive pillow pile. We aren't trying to cram ourselves into an able-bodied vision of what sexy or a relationship is; it's totally okay for us to rest, chill, care for ourselves and each other. Our care needs are not some gross secret walled off from date night.
- Or my friend whose multi-decade-old disability care collective helps her get on the toilet, shower, and dress every day, and people laugh, gossip, hang out, and have a great time—it's the place to be! When I show

a video that she made about her collective to the care webs workshop I teach, there's usually awed silence. Afterward, someone always says, "I've never seen someone be so joyful and unashamed while getting help getting on the toilet."

• Or last weekend, when two disabled femme BIPOC friends and I went on an accessible hike and had a blast.[1] The care that allowed this joyful-ass space to happen included everything from one friend getting a guidebook of accessible hikes and researching routes, to the ways we strategized together when all of a sudden the trail had no curb cuts, to our stopping every five minutes to take a breath (because one of us has lung tumors and one of us was using a manual wheelchair that day and I have asthma), to how my friends were chill when I got hit with sudden food poisoning and had to squat behind a not-so-private tree and have a really bad shit as bikes whizzed by. "This is where access intimacy gets real!" I yelled, and we all laughed.

These are a few examples of the many joyful intersections of disability justice, care, and pleasure that I'm really fucking lucky to have in my life. But I know that for most people, the words "care" and "pleasure" can't even be in the same sentence. We're all soaking in ableism's hatred of bodies that have needs, and we're given a really shitty choice: either have no needs and get to have autonomy, dignity, and control over your life, or admit you need care and lose all of the above. Also in the mix is the fact that some of us come from immigrant, Black, and brown communities and have worked shitty, badly paid caregiving jobs for years, which hasn't made giving or receiving care uncomplicated. Many of us have been taught that needing care is a weakness we cannot afford and have survived through needing absolutely nothing. A lot

---

1   BIPOC: Black, Indigenous and People of Color.

of our communities still look down on disability or mental health as weakness and stigma, and we know that if we show ours, we can lose a lot—dates, credibility, social capital, jobs, kids. It's no wonder I've heard many friends say, "I could never show my partner(s) *that* disability, illness, mental health thing, it's not sexy, it's too embarrassing." For my part, I spent decades curating myself so only my "normal" parts showed—on dates, in the social world—and never showed anyone my damn care needs. I did it because it was the best way I knew to survive. But it also made me deeply believe that those parts were disgusting and unlovable, which meant that I was too.

For much of the past decade, I have been part of a disability justice community whose members have dreamed new ways of creating and accepting care as a pleasure, not a chore, and experimented with creating joyful spaces where we care for each other as queer, disabled people of color. I'm proud of the work we've done and the impact it has had. I also want to complicate it. There can be nothing more badass than a bunch of crips loving and caring for each other. And: community isn't utopia, we can fuck each other over or just be too exhausted or mad to be there, and some of us don't have community at all. Care isn't always orgasmically pleasurable: people need to be able to get what we need and go to the bathroom whether or not it feels like a dance party. I've heard plenty of folks who work with personal care attendants say that they don't want their care workers to be friends—they want them to be professionals who get paid well and treat them right, where there are labor laws and mutual respect.

I want there to be a diversity of care tactics. And I want everyone to be able to create wildly intimate, healing relationships where your care needs are present in the room, not crammed in the garbage. I want everyone to have access to this joyful, dangerous, wide-open pleasure, because it's the vulnerable strength we all deserve.

SUB-SECTION

THE POLITICS OF WHOLENESS IN MOVEMENTS

Tomorrow belongs to those of us who conceive
of it as belonging to everyone, who lend the
best of ourselves to it, and with joy.
—Audre Lorde, "A Burst of Light," 1988

THE PLEASURE OF LIVING AT THE SAME TIME AS BEYONCÉ GISELLE KNOWLES-CARTER

It took years for me to integrate my love of Octavia Butler into the rest of my life—to recognize that my love of her writing and imagination wasn't a pastime but a future.

My love of Beyoncé brings me a similar kind of immense pleasure that actually enhances my wholeness and opens possibilities.[1] They are both Black women who shape/d the narratives that held them, and the world around them, though in most ways Beyoncé couldn't be more different from Octavia. Octavia was awkward whereas Beyoncé is diva, Octavia was private whereas Beyoncé makes most of her work about her

---

1   If Beyoncé worship is offensive to your system in any way, I just want to remind you that you can skip ahead. Because it's gonna be a praise-ful few pages.

intimate relationships, Octavia was delightfully contrarian whereas Beyoncé is, in her own words on *Everything Is Love*, "everybody type."[2]

Beyoncé and I are both Texan-born Virgos with Scorpio moons and Venus in Libra. But that's where our overlaps end—*she* is Beyoncé. She's the queen my anarchic heart continues to choose. I choose her because she works so hard, and she is willing to learn in public, to politicize without rigidity, to exert her will on the public square.

Beyoncé is a mama to three children, and we get to see her with them, weaving them, and her husband, into the grand art production of her life. She is a prolific creative force focused on her own transformation, on transcending ceilings and barriers. A pop queen, a culture queen, Beyoncé's primary public function is to dazzle us with talent.

She only has power because we love her.

Claiming her publicly, in a way, was a key step in the process of coming out as a pleasure activist. My comrade Karissa Lewis recently reminded me of a moment, at a gathering of Black organizers, the morning after Beyoncé dropped her self-titled album. I stood in front of people I respected and let it show that I was beside myself for this Black woman—and I felt like everyone else should be paying attention to her as well.

I knew I liked Beyoncé back in the Destiny's Child days, but my respect and eventually love grew as she did. I began to appreciate how meticulous she is, how hard she holds and raises her standards, how each of her massive pieces of work is distinct from the last, how she stays learning and innovating, transforming in public.

She's grown from "Cater to You" to "Don't Hurt Yourself." She's grown from "Speechless" to "Listen" to "Sorry" to "Freedom" to "Boss."

I am fascinated by how culture shapes politics, how culture shapes our daily lives. Beyoncé takes responsibility for

---

2   The Carters, *Everything Is Love* (Parkwood Entertainment, 2018).

culture shaping and shifting. I love that every time she releases something, a thousand people need to write think pieces about what she means by it. I love the grace and precision with which she holds her responsibility in shaping culture and how she has dominated every corner of her field.

I love that when I go to her concerts, they are self-love gatherings for the attendees. While the world outside rages, we come to these spaces that are centered on Black women loving themselves, and we find each other and find release. I love loving a Black woman pop star this unapologetically, in public, and still demand that anyone I meet takes me seriously in the work. Claiming Beyoncé opened up a path toward my wholeness.

The following few pieces are some excerpts of my Beyoncé love notes.

Beyoncé: The Conference Call

Maryse.[3] I heard some folks talking about burlesque, and, yes, what resonated with me was feeling like, yes, this is what I want to grind to. But also, as a former sex worker, it was so good seeing this woman who doesn't *have* to show herself or her body to be successful, to make the choice to show herself in this way, powerful and liberated in her sexuality. She draws on stripper culture but in a way that is also respectful of people who actually do the work. While also at the same

---

3   After Beyoncé dropped her self-titled album, I hosted a conference call to discuss the work. The call was full of other writers, artists, burlesque dancers, mamas, organizers, academics, women, and trans participants. Not everyone spoke up, but those who did were honest and nuanced.

time being critical of all the things people have to go through to get to that place to do that work, to be desired.

Mahogany. I just want to say this is great you are having this call, to get together as women and process a woman's success and also have a safe space for talking about all this bottom bitch feminism, pardon my French. I love that she is talking about being sexy and being married women [chorus: Yes]. A lot of times, marriage is not explored as a safe space to be sexy. I get to show you how I love you, and I get be a freak with the person I am committed to. And, yes, there are some contradictions.

Unknown. I am calling from Trinidad. I watched it all and have taken it all in. I have been taking in some of the dialogues and pieces on Facebook, but being outside the U.S. context has given me space to see how I enjoy this album. There is something I feel being spoken through her in a spiritual and ancestral way. I haven't seen in my lifetime a Black woman's sexuality being expressed in this way on the world stage and world platform. At this time. There is so much, it is so powerful that it is happening in an age of social media. There is a dynamic of theory from academia and praxis coming from those who don't operate in that space [chorus: Yes!]. I feel like one of the things, from being outside the academic space, just emerging and immersing myself here, as a dual citizen, having this album speak to me from outside of that academic space, which had limited my ability to feel these things, happy about my sexuality, in my body, that maybe my sexuality and the ways I express it is mainstream. I feel that somehow there is something larger happening.

Beyoncé's Grammy Performance Was a
Gilded Afrofuturist Dream

A moment of reverence for the exquisite symbology of heal-ing that is Beyoncé in the last moment of the performance.[4] After the last woman, a white woman, surrenders to her (which, in most parallel universes, would have foreshad-owed her inevitable slaying of the awards)—we are left with Beyoncé, timeless and holy, face-to-face with the camera, her full mother-breasts gleaming, her nails sharp enough to pro-tect against any who would harm her family, her face that of a woman who has learned the sacred witchcraft of healing, who has grown a universe in the landscape of her broken heart.

This performance is, like the best Black speculative work, a spell we cast for a liberated, abundant Black future. The healing we need will require the creative abundance of so many Black women stepping into our wholeness.

Lemonade. Masterpiece.

it's Black love
the next chapter of Her visual album, with

---

4   This essay first appeared as adrienne maree brown, "Beyonce's Grammy Performance Was a Gilded Afrofuturist Dream," *Motherboard*, February 15, 2017, https://motherboard.vice.com/en_us/article/d758bq/beyonces-grammy-performance-was-a-gilded-afrofuturist-dream.

direct responses
to partition and jealous and drunk in love
and blue and to herself
just then
across both the visuals and the lyrics

"grief sedated by orgasm
orgasm heightened by grief
god was in the room
…
sometimes when her nipple was in his mouth
she'd whisper oh my god
that too was a form of worship"[5]

Black womanhood and our pain and
our irresistibility and our grief
from serena's perfection
to the mothers of the slain

the adoration of the natural world
water everywhere
moon to flood
reflection to truth

the journey all over Black america
the love of Black girls and griots
the use of witchcraft, magic, dreams and
spells to heal the heartbreak

transformation, transformative justice
the power of love, vulnerability, walking away
until you can be seen in your wholeness—
truth and reconciliation
"there is a curse that will be broken"[6]

---

5   Beyoncé, *Lemonade* (Parkwood Entertainment, 2016) compact
disc and DVD.

6   Beyoncé, *Lemonade*. This poem first appeared as adrienne maree

Lemonade Screening

We offered blessings to young people, received blessings from our elders, laid on hands and called in ancestors, offered love for those struggling through this pain, called in fat and disabled bodies for the next evolution, generated compassion and sisterhood for all of us who have been Beckys, and scream-leapt through a ton of testimonial and ecstatic praise for our own strength, transformation, resilience, and vision as Black women.[7]

We spoke of orishas and transformative justice and forgiveness and shame and loving ourselves and open relationships and queer love and Black excellence and Prince and complexity and solidarity and intergenerational healing and so much more.

---

brown, "*Lemonade*. Masterpiece," April 24, 2016, http://adrienne mareebrown.net/2016/04/23/lemonade-masterpiece/.

7   Two days after the album dropped, Celeste Faison and I hosted a screening and conversation at Solespace Community Shoe Store in Oakland. These are some excerpts from the reflection.

ON FEAR, SHAME, DEATH, AND HUMOR

A Conversation Between
the Rocca Family and Zizi

The Rocca Family is the name for the top-secret collaborative art-practice work of Ola El-Khaldi and Diala Khasawnih with Rocca the cat as their pussy power. They perform the Zizi Show under the names Taita O and Zizi.

Seven years ago, they traveled through space and time from the faraway (some refer to it as Jordan for highly politicized quasi-practical reasons) and landed with their cat Rocca in San Francisco. On November 30, 2016, they locked their San Francisco home for the last time and embarked on their RF USA 2017 Road Trip. Through its practice, in search of home perhaps, the Family uses all its folkloric know-how and food powers, trusting in humor, to make friendships and talk about immigration, family, freedom, and the meaning of life.

Along their life journey, the Rocca Family found Zizi, a philosopher without concrete definitions and inclined to mood swings, who is not afraid of discomfort or anger. While she might make references to ideal worlds and imagined realities, she also makes up truths and brings forward lies. Zizi is a playground, a space for the Rocca Family to be silly, a platform to challenge their own fears. Zizi is their uninhibited character, their act of resistance, their voice of anger.

Rocca Family (RF). Zizi, we heard that you are traveling around the globe, giving workshops on fear. We are now on a road trip trying to face fear, fear from seeing the other and the other seeing us, fear from being stopped from our right to movement from one place to the other, fear from going back to a place that became too small for us, a place that is getting smaller and smaller in accepting us. We are dreaming of expansion, of no limits to where we look, we are searching for freedom, freedom from fear. Zizi, is that possible? You always talk about fear as a tool for survival—is it possible to be fear-free?

Zizi. No. No, my darling Rocca Family, you shall never be fear-free. The best you could hope for is to befriend fear. Think of it as such, imagine if you can take the adrenaline or whatever hormones that fear makes the body produce and invest this as a stimulant, a drug, toward deeper and more radical living. How exciting it can be to feel your heart racing and you start to smell your sweat = alive!

Indeed, fear is important. How many spankings would you have received if you did not fear Mme. Suzette? That was a bad example, but Zizi has found that it often hits home. Also, other fears help keep us alive and well. However, as you know, my karbujeh,[1] most fears that control our lives are mythical.

As my bbff recommended, when faced with fear, imagine the worst-case scenario and experience it in your head. Bring the fear into proportion. As a matter of fact, bbff told me it was I who had recommended this remedy for fear. (naturally)

I congratulate you for facing fear rather than running away from it. Even if you forgot your raincoat.

---

1   My sweet.

If you see my auntie the lazy crocodile, do not feed her. Nor the bear. Be bear aware. Now. That is a space that allows for fear. If you allow fear to control you, chances are you will turn around and run away from the black bear, and it will chase you down and eat your toes. Befriend fear, pause, take a deep breath: is this black bear a terrorist busy munching berries? Start walking back really slowly and create more distance between you, because bears like space. That is why you do not find them in the center of human urbanistics, where oxygen hardly has space.

RF. Zizi, we would like to talk about shame, do you ever feel that? Or do you even know what it means? We are trying to cleanse ourselves from it; it's hard, very hard. We shave our heads, grow our bodily hair, show our big asses and big thighs. We also have sex with each other and with others; we have many loves, our definitions of commitment are very diluted, we don't believe in the one, we feel deep pleasure in all these practices, and this is how we learned to resist and survive. But we want to go deeper and feel no shame at all; do you think we are doomed? We strive for a shameless existence, Zizi, but we carry the burden of holding the name of our families, our histories, a certain existence that we were born with; how do we change that?

Zizi. Zizi never ever feels shame. What a shame is shame, anyway? However, interacting with the earthly two-leggeds, I get the idea. Deep and silly like snot. It starts with the body, and for many it stays there. How can the two-leggeds fight shame or cope with it if the foundation is shame? If the body they carry is shame, the body they are—blood, veins, flesh and skin, bone and snot and inherited trauma—embodies shame. (Shame/fear/modernity.) Fighting body odor, calling sex sleep, storing farts, black plastic bags for monthly period secrets, childbirth is called beautiful, soaps, perfumes, haircuts, Brazilians, perpetual stunned arches for eyebrows, baby pussies gaping cold at the world, waxing is getting clean, bras, corsets, tight shoes, high heels, smaller noses, bigger boobs, sharper ass curves.

Perpetually faking it.

Shame, shame, shame.

يا عيب العيب ويا خجل الخجل وما عيب، يا روكّا فاميلي، إلّا العيب.[2]

Beauty is in hiding behind shame. Beauty in bad lies and poor imagination. A cosmetic surgery industry, and no one buys horns or antlers or hooves or zebra stripes or roaring climaxes! (Tongue-splitting absolute maximum ceiling! Rolling my eyes.) Starting from there—steep uphill to freedom. Lightness. How can the two-legged really understand nature if they are so far from it within and without?

Zizi's mantra for this one is (everyone sings after me):

أنا كرشي كبير وبحبّه كتير[3]

again:

أنا كرشي كبير وبحبّه كتير

أنا كرشي كبير وبحبّه كتير

أنا كرشي كبير وبحبّه كتير

Rub the bellies. Love the bellies. Reveal the bellies. Scratch the bellies.

(Do this twice a day for the rest of your life and you may have a chance to cope with shame.)

RF. Zizi, you speak as if you know better than anyone, that you have the magic of just knowing, that you have the secret of all secrets; you always say "there is a secret inside a secret

2 *Shamiest* of shame, *embarassingliest* of embarrassment. Nothing is shame, O Rocca Family, but shame.

3 I have a big belly and I love my belly. [repeat]

of a secret," that you are beyond everything and everyone. We, on the other hand, are trying to practice humility, we want to become nothing, we believe that if humans reach a point where they know they are just a moment in time, then we can all just relax and just be and enjoy our cigarettes. We just want to reach the point where we know and believe that death and birth are the only guarantees, and love, for sure love. Does that get on your nerves?

What if we pause and say that without humility one cannot love or maintain love? By love, we mean creating a safe and solid space for the people we care about to be themselves, to allow for a mutual growth for everyone involved, to be extremely sensitive.

Zizi. My dear Rocca Family, if you plan on repeating and/or quoting and adhering to the Zizi, please learn your lessons right. Zizi says:

The secret is a secret inside a secret, and it can only be truly obtained if you do nothing and everything.

Pahleeze.

Let me remind you of what Zizi declared cosmically some time ago or never: Everything Zizi says is possibly the truth and also probably a big lie. Zizi never promised to declare fiction from reality. And Zizi continuously as long as Zizi lives will remain true to changing her mind. My dear Rocca Family, those who claim they know are full of BS gone bad. One can, at best, claim to know to the best of their knowledge.

We seek. And continue to seek. Until it all goes silent.

And Zizi likes you saying: "We, on the other hand, are trying to practice humility, we want to become nothing." You may have chosen a tough journey. You continue by saying: "We believe that if humans…" Zizi recommends you drop the "believe" notion. How about you suggest, try, attempt (maybe trust) this or that, rather than believe? There is very little space for humility in belief.

The pleasure hidden secret like a whisper in the sharp pain of freezing breath venturing into your lungs hiking up the mountain of all beauties. Literally. Or is it breath sharply taken in, gentle like a whisper, sharp like glass, to defrost your lungs in the freezing winters? Does it matter, the difference? The pleasure deep in the pain of witnessing your breath in front of, in the presence of, magic, beauty, ancient nature before and after your birth and your death.

As for love: How dare anyone ever claim the life of another? In any shape or form? Via love or hate? Via human trafficking or marriage? The channel does not matter. You hardly own yourself let alone any others.

أولادكم ليسوا لكم أولادكم أولاد الحياة.[4]

Fucking period.

No claim of anything. Not their bodies. Not their hearts. Not their times. Not their freedoms.

And maybe just maybe if you truly believe this, you can be free.

No one can own you.

And you are free to share your love.

Share your time and body, share your wine and laughter.

Share your dreams and worries.

Understand the individuality and the communality as well as the commonality of life, pain, and death. And, in between, be open to love, joy, and promise.

Respect the mind in its sharpness and loss.

The mood in its light and darkness.

The wealth in its abundance and poverty.

And the mess that comes with all that.

RF. In your lectures, you ask repeatedly, "Are we too scared to live?" So Zizi, are you not scared of death?

The Rocca Family, in our practice, we try to encourage turning pain and guilt into accepting the pleasures that are in front of our eyes, that we don't need to go far to seek pleasure, many bodies to feel, many hearts to get warm with, many

---

4   "Your children are not your children. They are the sons and daughters of Life's longing for itself" —Jubran Khalil Jubran.

waters to swim, we try to live and not think of living as a dream, a future plan, but to accept our existence in its simplest form. Maybe we are scared of talking about the future, because in the future there is death. In your world, is there a future? Zizi, our homelands are burning, are disappearing; does it mean we are disappearing too?

Zizi.

الحياة لحظة.[5]

Are you scared of death?

Wildfires eating up acres of life reducing it all into ashes are fundamentally a problem of the earthly humans living near them. They lose their homes and belongings, clothes, and photographs. Maybe even lives. And that is a problem because they do not see themselves equal to the tree or to the bird or to the coyote burning, losing, rebuilding. The wildfires are rebirth. Life in death. Like in hurricanes and tsunamis. For everyone except man. Because man is arrogant. Man is separatist. What if we were all trees? We grow and experience wind and sun and rain and hunger and thirst and satisfaction; we give birth, we give shade, we offer homes, we make memories, and we burn so others can live. There is real pain in loss. Real pain in being lost. Real pain in bleeding wounds and burning skin. Real pain in unrealized dreams and broken families and hunger and rotting, untreated wounds of the flesh and of the emotion/psyche. Life brings us pains—lick them.

Zizi sees humans treadmill-running, bored out of their wits, in their pursuit of immortality at the price of living. The fountain of youth in the strict diets and bulging hysterical eyes and taut skins and guilt and shaming and foolish choices and inhumane priorities. Waking up early to witness a sunrise that will never be again versus going to the gym—something's gone real wrong. Even worse, if one does not even see the sunrise as it is happening on one's way to the gym (self-absorbed,

---

5   Life is but a moment.

high buildings, pollution fogs, whatever the reason). On one's way to the fountain of youth, is one already dead?

Are we scared of death or dying? Is the fear of dying the wrong side of the coin? Love for living the other side? What is the value in answering those questions anyway?

RF. Zizi, how do we maintain our sense of wonder and curiosity without feeling exhausted? Why do we fear losing it? We try to hold on to it very strongly, every day, every moment we seek the unknown, we follow the unknown, we want more and more. How do we separate greed from wonder?

Is this a question because we come from a place that we are no longer curious about? Have we lost curiosity in home?

Zizi. It is time for that cigarette.

The end of curiosity is death. Be exhausted. Be tired. Be curious at any price. It is sometimes okay to take a break and float in the mainstream using a traditional structure. Tradition has lots of wild within it, can offer a parachute just in case you needed it, a foundation to rest on—but never ever make it your home. Start by never living in the same place for more than two years. Always have guests, turn a blind eye to dirty dishes, and always ask why a certain law is in place and break it.

RF. What do you say to my unrelenting need to do the dishes as soon as I finish lunch and/or before I go to bed? I just cannot sleep with dirty dishes in the sink.

Zizi. You are a fool. That is what I would say. You are using the dishes as a distraction. Go for a walk and think carefully, what are you so afraid of?

RF. What if curiosity is a commodity and the need to always be in awe is a sort of addiction?

Zizi. Are you there yet? When you arrive at too much curiosity, call me. Curiosity is about listening to the answer when you ask a question. Curiosity involves sitting back, being quiet, and listening and watching. And then curiosity is about falling asleep to a world of wonder; go for the rides in dreamland and tell your dreams (only the interesting ones) to a fellow curious. Curiosity is also about sitting back with your emotion and living it. If you get too excited with your curiosity, grab a drink, go out for a smoke, take a break, be lazy, be slow.

Some Zizi teachings:

> *Life brings us pains, lick them.*
> *Life brings us unknowns, chew them.*
> *Life brings us germs, take them. Sip them.*
> *When it is most challenging, consider offering*
> *your body.*
> *Seek the monster under the bed. Let there be pee.*
> *Embarrass yourself.*
> *Surrender to Zizi tonight, and you shall be free.*

THE POWER TO MAKE LIGHT

A Conversation with Dallas Goldtooth

Dallas Goldtooth is the Keep It in the Ground organizer at the Indigenous Environmental Network, and a founder of the political comedy troupe the 1491s and was a trustworthy spokesperson on the ground at Standing Rock, which was a radical mass action to stop a pipeline from being built on Indigenous-held lands.

amb. *One of my theories is that, right now, movements are spaces that people rarely want to enter or stay around because our tone is so serious, so dire, that people are just like "I'm already fucking hopeless, and you look burnt out and tired, and why would I come spend time there?" Dallas, you use humor to draw people in. Was there a time in your life when it was like, "Oh, I'm fucking hilarious. I'm gonna do something with this." You know, was it sort of like, "I'm gonna go be a comedian—oh wait, I've gotta still be an activist."*

Dallas. There's never been that eureka moment. I remember back in fifth grade, we were playing volleyball at school, and it was this little charter school, nothing but Indians. And I remember taking a deliberate fall—a very exaggerated fall—because it garnered laughter. And I knew what I was doing. I knew that I was doing it for attention, but also it was a moment that made me feel good because it elicited a response from other folks—like the response that they got out of it. And the thing about organizing is … and I'm careful about who I speak it to or how I say it … is it's a form of manipulation. You are using information. You're using tactics to manipulate a situation or a response from people for the benefit of a movement or the benefit of your community or for the benefit of yourself. Comedy is of the same sort. Storytelling is the same process. You're using the gift of speech or an action of your body to elicit a sort of response and manipulating emotion. You're tapping into the core source code of who we are as human beings. I think there are so many people that rarely use the transformative power of humor and lightheartedness of stories.

But it's very dicey. It's very careful, because it could really go into like kitschy, hipster-like new age—like, "let's just talk about love and peace and the transformative power of crystals and energy," and all this shit that just turns people off. A good number of people.[1]

I am confident enough that I know what I'm good at. I know what my strengths are, and I know my weaknesses. My experience of making people laugh and loving that. I like the idea of making people smile. So you have that.

Then there's this other experience of me being a six-foot-two big-ass Indian and going to college at Cal. And being hella aware that I fucking intimidate by just walking into a room. That walking down a street—if there's women coming down the street on my side, I'm fucking hyper-aware that I'm a big fucking scary person.

amb. *Because of the socialization that they're walking with?*

---

1   amb: I love crystals and energy, for the record.

Dallas. Yeah, and legitimate concern, like, based off real-life experience. So it was just ingrained, you know, growing up in the movement and being around people, being aware of, like, "Oh, shit, I'm gonna cross the street. I'm'a make the conscious decision that I'm gonna remove that and move—step away."

I realize I started doing something that I was not aware of. When I walk into a room, I'm aware of how they see me. I'm aware of how I see myself. I would fucking amplify the goofiness. I would amplify like—I'm already naturally just likely to make light of a moment. But I would amplify that to be more accessible, to break down that concern. So you're like, "Oh, I don't have to be fucking scared of this dude or intimidated because he's fucking weird and kind of goofy." And that was the result of just trying to make people, make it more accessible, so I can do my work. And after a while I realized, I was like, "Oh, shit, that's what I'm doing, oh, okay. Well, I'm gonna do that in a mindful way."

At Standing Rock was that moment where it was like me wanting to be contrary to the narrative that you have to be a fucking angry-ass protestor. Or an angry-ass, down-ass motherfucker, like, with a "fuck the police" kind of narrative. And I'm like, I wanna go a different route. Like, I think that sometimes we get caught in the spectacle of it, doing it for the spectacle and the dogma of what it means to be, you know, against the machine. And that was a challenge. I think there were a lot of people that pushed back at me. There was a lot of critique of me. Of how I went about it. You know, people saying "you're not down enough."

amb. *I imagine that people also are, like, are you taking this seriously enough? But then, people also wanna follow you. Your lens is an accessible lens, an enjoyable lens.*

Dallas. Yeah, no, totally. Every step of the way I love complicating the narrative. Our job is to complicate our own narrative, our own community narrative, the world narrative as much as possible, just because it's so complex. And the fact that you could have, like, the most hardcore anarchist sorts of folks who were there like … they still have a life, and they fucking find things funny. But there's the spectacle.

amb. *But it's like that's gotta be offstage.*

Dallas. That's offstage. When you're onstage, boom, "this is who I am, and I'm hard, hard, hard." I'm like, fuck, you don't have to be—you wake up hard? You know? Like …

amb. *[laughing inappropriately] I mean, some people do.*

Dallas. Yeah some people really do. I just love the challenge of trying to exhibit the complexity of everybody.

amb. *This is part of our wholeness—being able to laugh at these things.*

Dallas. Exactly. In Standing Rock, the other thing was that the kind of generally agreed upon tactic was the numbers. The strategy of having people there but also having the numbers with us because we're in a fucking rural-ass area and you can only … there's only so much that fifteen Native folks can do until we're all fucking arrested and locked up. And so we had to make it accessible. We had to basically create a narrative that was accessible by all different levels. And "Water is life" built upon that.[2] That was a role that I didn't really plan. But it's like a conscious effort. How do you make this successful? And also, like, the real-ass shit of misinformation and how destructive that can be. It's like, all right, my role is to give reliable, as best as I can, information and do it in a way that's also accessible. And humor is a part of that.

Like, right in the heart of it, I'm like fucking sitting there and I'm like, man, you know what, I wanna just fucking

---

2   *Mní wičhóni*, translated as "Water is life," is the narrative framework of the #NoDAPL struggle. For Dakota, it is the spiritual *casus belli*, reminder of their original instructions to defend the sacred.

livestream me doing some sledding down the hills and show-ing people having fun because that's what happening in the camp, like, people were having fun. People were enjoying themselves, but yet the camera comes on and they play the narrative. They played into the dogma of it: We have to be hard. We have to be serious.

amb. *There's something about being an Indigenous man, being an Indigenous leader and bringing that humor ... it's like, oh, this is actually one of our survival strategies. I had not really worked with Indigenous organizers before Ruckus.[3] And then coming to Ruckus and being like, "Oh y'all are clowning me. And you're clowning each other. Oh, everyone's just laughing." I mean, like, it's all fun and games in direct response to how intense the trauma and pressure is. Does that resonate?*

Dallas. It resonates strongly. Honestly, I feel like Native com-munities would not have gotten to where we are if it wasn't for the power to make light of the situation. And through that lens of humor and laughter critique the world around us. We didn't have the agency to change the situation, we at least have the agency to critique it through laughter and humor.

Native folks are some of the most cynical people on the planet, you can't help but be when you're going through the shit we've gone through. And you know every funeral, every dark moment, I think—from our community, the role of the spokesperson, or in our language the Évapaha, is the MC, and there's an art to it.

In our communities, my specific Dakota communities, you had your elected leaders, but then there was the spokes-person. And they were the speaker on behalf of everybody, and it's still ... that tradition carries today. Everything they say is fed to them.

---

3   I worked at the Ruckus Society, which trains organizers in nonviolent direct action, for five years. I currently sit on their board.

amb. *It's being fed through the community process?*

Dallas. Yes. But their role is to take that but then also using the art of MCing to make light and make it accessible. Every funeral has some of the funniest jokes and laughter. That's the transformative nature of humor and comedy. I think it really heals us and helps us let go. Anger is extremely powerful. And it can transform amazing things. But it also has its obstacles. It sets up walls. The counterbalance to that is laugher. And we have to not be afraid to use that.

amb. *I study somatics and what happens in the body. It's like trauma gets stuck in the body, and it just stays there waiting for you until you release it. And I think we always think, oh, that release has to be weeping for days or whatever. But I've experienced some of the biggest releases of my life actually in laughter. There's a collective aspect. Where with crying it's something you often go off and do alone, laughter you do with others too. In the conversations we're in about decolonization and taking Indigenous leadership ... we have been in this conversation forever, since first contact. At a certain point, if Indigenous people can't laugh at white folks in their learning process ... that seems like one of the ways that y'all are able to stay in relationship.*

Dallas. I mean, the colonial experience is nothing unique to us as Native people. It's worldwide. So there's that connective tissue between all of us. So using that experience, transforming it into something funny and really exposing it for how dysfunctionally funny it is, it helps. It breaks down those barriers between our communities and brings us together.

I see something that's so dysfunctional, I'm like, that shit's hilarious in its own way. There's the construct of what a Native man is. What we as Indian people, how we've constructed what an Indian man is ... is hilarious. And the comedy that we do, that's probably our biggest target, ourselves. Because we do such hilarious, stupid shit that ... let's call it that, show the absurdity of dysfunction.

amb. *Yes. And there's some unlearning that can happen there, right? We don't have to take ourselves so seriously because so much of this is a construction. And we can reconstruct it.*

Dallas. Put it in terms of theater: we've constructed these identities, these masks that we don't realize are fucking hilarious masks and whether it's the ... a mask of what is a man or a mask of what is an activist, anarchist, radical or mask of a feminist—they're all masks that when you start breaking it down, like, look, those are actually fabrications that are quite funny and absurd. Maybe not necessarily funny but absurd in ways. It's an absurd fabrication of our social conscience— we're fabricating our reality. And we can't help but do that. It's ingrained in who we are 'cause we're self-aware, and so, in the process of being self-aware, we create these ... we fabricate these identities.

amb. *And they're hilarious. I'm like, we have this whole miraculous life and then we spend so much of it developing rigidity and developing, like, okay, here's the one way to do this. I'm grateful to you for constantly throwing your rocks up against the windows and being, like, the house is made of glass. It's still made of glass. It's still made of glass.*

Dallas. And it will continue to be made of glass. That's the balance in that. For Indigenous humor, that's the recognition that the comedy balances out the fabrication. The humor balances out what we create for ourselves. And that is a balancing act that will forever go on until we serve our purpose, whatever it may be. The idea that one has to overcome the other is an absurdity in itself.

amb. *I often think "what is dinosaur humor," you know? What was dinosaur humor, those moments where you're like: we're going extinct, let's enjoy it. Even if this is the end of the world, right, or the end of the world as we know it or the end of our species on this planet or whatever. Just do the fucking best you can and be* *the best person you can, put up the best fight you can, but then you also have to be able to laugh and release. Laughter increases our time. If you have time to tell a joke, you're not too rushed.*

FLY AS HELL

A Conversation with Sonya Renee Taylor

Sonya Renee Taylor is the founder of The Body Is Not an Apology, an international movement committed to cultivating global Radical Self Love and Body Empowerment.

> *We believe that discrimination, social inequality, and injustice are manifestations of our inability to make peace with the body, our own and others. Through information dissemination, personal and social transformation projects and community building, The Body Is Not An Apology fosters global, radical, unapologetic self love which translates to radical human love and action in service toward a more just, equitable and compassionate world.*[1]

Sonya and I got to speak in Oakland on April 16, 2017— Sonya came straight from church, and in the process of letting her in, I locked us out of the apartment I was staying in. The image of her jimmying the lock open in her carnation-pink Sunday

---

1   "Mission, Vision, and History," The Body Is Not an Apology: Radical Self-Love for Everybody and Every Body, 2018, https://thebodyisnot anapology.com/about-tbinaa/history-mission-and-vision.

best, finding a way, fully in her beauty and power, will forever be the essence of Sonya to me.

amb. *Sonya, please give me your pleasure bio.*

Sonya. I have always been drawn to what's deeper, what's sticky—I'm a Scorpio. I want to dig in to what can be dug into. There is hedonism in there. I'm driven by desire, pleasure, and passion. And I want to know the underside of it, what it can create. I think that inquiry is what's created all this uncovering. It's what began to compel me about poetry and the arts in general. I often say I came out of my mother's womb with jazz hands. I always loved the immediacy of pleasure in art, having someone experience that moment with you.

When I discovered performance poetry, I got to experience that times a million, the pleasure of experiencing language in real time, of communicating that message and having it received in that moment, was super powerful to me. I was like, "oh, what can be done with this? What can we conjure?" I think that the work of language is that it is aiding and abetting us toward what we are supposed to be living into, either by a sense of deep alignment or deep discovery ("I am up against this thing which isn't true in my everyday").

The Body Is Not an Apology came out of a poem that came out of a conversation with a friend. She was afraid she might be pregnant, and I asked her why she was having unprotected sex with this person she didn't really care about. She has cerebral palsy and said finding sex wasn't easy. And I said, "the body is not an apology," and, oh, there it was between us. She is either going to shift because of it or not, and I was there having spoken these words. I was left with a poem. And it kept illuminating all the ways I was not in alignment with what I was speaking. So I was compelled to get in alignment. I had to figure out what had me still operating like an apology when I was saying otherwise.

That led to a selfie in my phone—I felt fly as hell in this selfie, but there was some voice in me saying it was inappropriate, too much, too fat, too Black, too ugly, et cetera. That feeling of listening to that voice was chafing up against those words, "the body is not an apology."

I'm glad that I use my powers for good cuz otherwise I would be an evil cult leader. I posted it and asked people to tag themselves in it with #thebodyisnotanapology. The next morning, twenty people had tagged me. We started the Facebook page. Our digital reach now is about 250,000 a week. It's a happy accident.

I share the story and speak of a transformative portal. I speak radical vulnerability, radical honesty, radical empathy—those three things together created this moment.

amb. *When did it shift from "I" to "we"?*

Sonya. I started off saying I wanted to start a movement. I want to sell the world on living in our bodies without apology. It was always "we" in my mind. About seven months after I launched the Facebook page, I was like, I think I need people to help me. I can't moderate it by myself. So I put out a call for interns. An unapologetic posse coordinator and a social media intern to help with the Facebook page. That continued to grow. People wanted to submit articles on these ideas. I put out a call, and we made a Tumblr, had eight writers there. Someone else wanted to start a support group, we said yes. A team just coalesced around the idea.

Then, in 2014, it became clear that it had become a large enough entity that it needed to be formalized. We would get suspended from Facebook on the regs, they would take it down. I also realized I was losing control of the brand—I hate that word, but—people were putting the language on everything. Today we're a web-based magazine, do workshops, and a community-building platform. How do we learn? This work is interdependent work, learning with our bodies and the bodies of others.

amb. *What have you learned about your body in that journey?*

Sonya. I learned the way that I was bartering myself.[2] I saw my body as both shame and currency. How can I get what I want from you using this? At the same time, deeply not believing that this was enough. Like, let me sell you something *I* don't want. This work has given me the chance to dig into that. "Why do you want to give yourself away, Sonya?"

amb. *Do you remember when you were taught the body was supposed to be an apology?*

Sonya. I think everyone is exposed to it in different ways. The Taylor women have big boobs, big butts, all that. It was celebrated and regulated. You can be that, but be on a diet so you don't get too thick. I didn't develop early, but when I developed, I developed. D cups all of the sudden. I learned then about the body as currency; there is an attention that gets paid to me. While also getting the message that I was inherently flawed as a Black girl, a bald girl—I got traction alopecia in the third grade, bald spots. I got teased mercilessly.

I posted the selfie, and that same year I felt like, I am a liar. I tell people to love themselves and then slap on this wig that I don't dare to be seen without.

amb. *And how did you learn it was not an apology? Somehow you knew it was true before you could embody it ... how?*

Sonya. My mother, who passed four years ago, was an excellent embodiment of contradiction. She always affirmed this notion that we were phenomenal and beautiful. There were ways she would be in her body that let us know it was okay to be in your body. I have a poem about my mom unbuttoning her pants, and she'd had two C-sections by the time she was seventeen. She had a jiggly, scarred belly, and it taught me

---

2　The choir sang out here!

it was okay. There was a seed there, and even though other things were sprinkled on top of it, that seed was going to break through eventually.

amb. *What do you want the legacy of your work to be?*

Sonya. I want people to see that what we create in the world is a reflection of what is inside of us. We cannot make that in the world that we have not made inside of us. Radical self-love is how we get to a just, equitable, and compassionate world.

ON THE PLEASURES OF WARDROBE

A Conversation with Maori Karmael Holmes

Maori Karmael Holmes is a curator, filmmaker, designer, and cultural worker. She is the founder and artistic director of BlackStar Film Festival. In addition to BlackStar, her curatorial projects include Flaherty NYC (2017), KinoWatt (2011–2012), Black Lily Film and Music Festival (2007–2010), among others. As a filmmaker, her work has screened internationally and been broadcast throughout the United States. As a designer, she has collaborated with film and theater directors, including James Avery and Carol Mitchell-Leon. Her previous professional positions include the Institute of Contemporary Art (Philadelphia), Leeway Foundation, and Washington City Paper. *Maori studied costume design at the graduate level at California Institute of the Arts (CalArts) and earned an MFA in film from Temple University.*

amb. *Maori, tell me about your relationship to clothing.*

Maori. Clothing is super important to me. My family has a long relationship to clothing in that my paternal grandmother was a seamstress, and my paternal grandfather was a haberdasher. My maternal grandmother, also a sun in Taurus like me, was an avid shopper. Like a lot of African American folks, it was always important for my family to be "clean" and "cool."

I have been obsessed with clothing and adornment in some regard since I can remember. One of my earliest memories—and this is a bit contested with my mother—is of me announcing, around five years old, that my mother was "fired" and no longer able to pick out my outfits.

amb. *Precocious.*

Maori. I also remember keeping a daily journal in second grade at school in which I drew my outfit each day rather than write text. The summer before eighth grade, I got a part-time job just so I could buy clothes. I was overjoyed when I finally turned sixteen and could legally work at the Gap! In high school, for special events like prom or homecoming, I would often sketch out my dream outfit as a kind of vision board, and then I would go out and find it. One of my favorites is from tenth-grade homecoming when I wore a silver slip dress [and] silver platform sneakers and had my hair in bantu knots. That entire outfit had been an idea in my head first.

I have been torn in my relationship to clothing, professionally, since high school, always feeling like I was "smart" and should do something that required more analysis or would help people. I am often returning to fashion under secret cover. Immediately after I'd finished my undergraduate BA in history, I applied to a BFA program in fashion design at Otis but then decided not to go. Then, in grad school studying Film, I found myself taking a ton of extracurricular coursework in costume design, and then eventually I pursued a second MFA in costume design at CalArts (which I also didn't finish).

My close friends know I'm obsessed, and I have a lovely collection of exhibition catalogs from museum fashion shows—which are my favorite kind of show.

Have I answered this question?

amb. *Yes, beautifully! You know, you changed my relationship to clothes. I feel like I'd flailed about in the hit-or-miss realm for many years, certain there was nothing out there for me due to my size. Now I get dressed in what I think of as happy style, adorning myself until I feel joy. You told me things like accessorize to really show my personality, have high-quality basics that I felt great in, and great shoes, great boots. Can you share with readers some of the guidelines you offer for constructing a wardrobe that thrills and delights the wearer and the world?*

Maori. That means a lot for you to say. I remember well our conversations around getting dressed. I always feel joy when I see you.

I have spent countless hours shopping with and for friends. I am never trying to instruct folks in any one way to dress—even when I worked retail I would often direct my customers outside of the store I worked in … but I am trying to help them uncover who they truly are—deep down—and find it in their attire.

I haven't yet developed specific guidelines, but I do think our wardrobes should consist of things that we absolutely LOVE. That make us feel good and that bring us joy. Due to the popularity of Marie Kondo, I think folks are beginning to acknowledge this concept of inanimate objects and our spiritual relationship to them, but it is something I have been thinking about for quite some time.[1] Like, how do you help someone actually SHINE and uncover their best self? That is what I'm thinking about when I help friends find clothes.

I care a lot about fashion and knowing what is on trend, but I think it's awful to try and impose a set of rules or articles on a person.

---

1   Marie Kondo is the author of *The Life-Changing Magic of Tidying Up: The Japanese Art of Decluttering and Organizing* (Ten Speed Press, 2014).

One of my favorite shopping jaunts was with a friend who is masculine of center. She had a big-time fund-raising job and wanted to look professional for meeting with donors and was also looking for the perfect attire for a special event. Another friend was trying to get her to "look sexy" and wear heels and carry much too femme-y bags and wear more fitted pants (in the wrong cut). I could see that she was uncomfortable. So much of what she was hearing was that she wasn't "doing it right." I feel like I spent much of our shopping trip (and our consultations afterward) ensuring her that her inclination to wear more masculine cuts and apparel could still be professional and make her look *sharp*. This was over ten years ago, before we were more aware of tailors like Bindle & Keep and custom tailoring at Suit Supply. When we finally found a suit with the right cut and shoes she loved, she lit up in the dressing room mirror and later, I heard, crushed her meetings with donors. To me, that's what clothes should be about.

I am often perplexed by folks who feel like clothes don't matter. They absolutely do. For those of us who are able to see, we respond to visual cues.

amb. *And those who can't see can still feel texture, quality, fit, mood, confidence.*

Maori. I believe that choosing to ignore that is a mistake. At the same time, I don't think we should be forced into boxes based on how we look, but we should understand that how we look can impact how others respond to us. It is a kind of social chemistry.

But, back to answering your question … although I don't yet have a formal practice for working with folks, these are the things I think about when I shop, things I often suggest to my friends while shopping:

Do you *love* this?
Did you scream with delight when you saw this online/in-store/across the street? Are you going to be thinking about

this for the next week 24/7? Sometimes that *is* the test—to leave something and come back to it.

Do you *need* this?

Like food, sex, and exercise—clothing is functional as well as delightful. For the item in question, do you actually need it? Do you have anything like it already in your closet? A good friend recently shared with me that she keeps everything she owns on twenty beautiful hangers. If something else comes in her closet that means something has to go. I think she's onto something. In the past, I would often find myself shopping when I was sad or anxious and buying things that I would never wear again.

On the flip side, sometimes you do need an item. How can you infuse LOVE into that item? I find that small details matter to me (interior linings, button quality, stitching) and if I have to buy something specific, then I try to find the most "interesting" version of that thing. For someone else, the quality of the fabric is more important or the source of the production.

How does it *fit?*

Way too many of us, seduced by fast fashion and advertising, stuff our closets with things that are "on sale" that are ill-fitting. Many of us whose weight has changed hold onto clothes from our past until we can "fit in them again," or we take something home from a sale bin or discount outlet in a size we know we can't fit into today as "inspiration."

I have polycystic ovary syndrome (commonly referred to as PCOS) and gained a lot of weight in my early twenties in a very short amount of time. I had been building a collection of beautiful things and suddenly couldn't wear any of them. I moved around with bags of clothes for nearly a decade with the hope of wearing them again. Right before a cross-country move, I took stock of all of these things and realized these bags were psychically weighing me down and that I needed to release them. So I did. It wasn't easy, but what I learned in the process was that I would find other beautiful things. Always.

It should feel good going into your closet. Facing a bunch of stuff that doesn't fit quite literally doesn't serve you.

I don't even want to get started on shoes.

How does it *feel?*

I swear that there is an energy to clothes when I see them—if I am listening and open. Sometimes you find yourself drawn to a garment that looks like not much on the hanger, and then you put it on and you realize it was calling you. I like to pay attention to that.

amb. *You mentioned how African Americans have a standard on being "clean" and "cool"—I agree, I feel like Black people work through so much related to class, combating white supremacy and setting culture with our clothing. Can you speak to any particularities of being a Black fashionista and dressing other Black bodies?*

Maori. I mentioned that my paternal grandfather was a haberdasher—he and his business partner replicated Italian-style suits for an all-Black clientele in the 1940s in Los Angeles. I didn't know him, but I have also heard stories that he was someone who was meticulous in his dress—all the way down to matching his underwear to his outfit. I can relate to this attention to detail and love that it clearly was passed to me through Spirit. I also know that so much of this concern with appearance is an attempt to be more acceptable as a member of a marginalized community and isn't unique to Black folks in the United States.

I don't necessarily consider myself a fashionista, but I do recognize my specific aesthetic references stemming from my mother exposing me to events like the National Black Arts Festival in Atlanta when I was very young, her subscription to the *Essence* magazine of the 1980s and early 1990s, and coming of age at the height of so-called conscious hip-hop. My affinity for bangles and mixing of prints and bold earrings all come from this. At the same time, I also find myself particularly drawn to Japanese and Scandinavian designers, and I am not sure how much this has to do with my own Black body or is purely aesthetics.

amb. *I used to feel that as someone working to change the world I didn't have time or energy for fashion or shouldn't care. Have you experienced this?*

Maori. Yes! Somewhat, although it is less about time and energy versus "deserving" or "justice" around having beautiful things or caring about them instead of being focused on "the movement."

I find this to be an experience I have shared with other folks in the field as well. It's a secret "Ooh, I like your bag," which turns into a full-on dish session about secretly shopping and feeling badly about it. A lot of the stuff I shared earlier has to do with my ongoing conflict around fashion being seen as vapid or capitalist versus my actual passion for the dressed body. I often wonder, if I hadn't been exposed to certain writing or activism at such a young age, would I have taken a different direction professionally.

amb. *I am selfishly glad you didn't, because you are bringing such glamour and style into the realms I live in, which need it.*

ADORNMENT AND BURLESQUE

A Conversation with Taja Lindley

Taja Lindley is a multimedia performer—she first caught my eye as half of the comedy rap duo Colored Girls Hustle. I bought all their swag because it was aesthetically perfect. The next time I came across her work, it was burlesque and theater. I get very excited by Black women living as radical pleasure artists and was excited to learn more.

amb. *Taja, tell me about all the pleasures that you cultivate and generate in your life.*

Taja. I made a commitment about six years ago that I was gonna allow joy to be my compass, that I was literally going to allow it to direct me where I should go and wanted to go. In 2011, I was working a movement job, and it just wasn't satisfying for me any longer. Now I have an articulation around healing justice and what tools we probably could've used to support that internal infrastructure and interpersonal relationship work, but at the time I didn't. And I was simultaneously discovering my creativity. When I look back on my life, I realize that I've been an artist my whole life, but I didn't really claim that for myself until around 2011, when I started being more intentional about my creativity.

So carving out time for it, committing to it, putting it in a calendar, like really holding boundary and space for it in my schedule and in my life. And actually, my creativity was the thing that burst my life wide open, that just did that thing that Audre Lorde talks about regarding the erotic. I just wasn't satisfied with mediocre experiences in my life. I wasn't satisfied with being places and doing things that I didn't like to do, and while a part of me felt a little selfish, because a lot of our movement work can be based on this idea of sacrifice, I just kind of resolved for myself that I would find the intersections that worked well for me between my creativity and my commitment to my people. I quit my job and had some resources to be creative with all my time. And I spent a lot of time healing myself, engaging in practices that felt good to me: meditating, doing *The Artist's Way* by Julia Cameron, journaling, going on artist dates.[1]

Around this time, Colored Girls Hustle, which is my small business, was just a baby. She still feels like a baby, but she was literally still being birthed, and I really committed myself to leveling up with her. So I came out with a collection of jewelry and began to articulate the ways in which adornment means something to me.

Another way I cultivate pleasure in my life is the ritual of getting ready. I love getting ready. I really enjoy the process. I really enjoy arriving in my body and my self and sculpting myself and choosing the various ways in which I'm gonna express myself through makeup, through clothes, [and] when I had hair, through hair. It's an intentional, pleasurable act and ritual for me.

---

1   Julia Cameron, *The Artist's Way: A Spiritual Life to Higher Creativity* (New York: TarcherPerigree, 1992).

Growing up, my mom and her sisters, my aunts, they loved getting ready. We lived in Atlanta, and my mother was young when she had me, so she was still a young woman doing her thing. So her and her sisters would get ready to go out to the club. It was a whole affair. First of all, we only had one bathroom, so they each had to take turns.

The music was playing, they're doing their hair, asking each other their opinions on, like, "what do you think about this outfit?" "Should I do this?" "Does this look right on me?" And, you know, complimenting each other. It was a whole sisterhood ritual of getting ready. The women in my family enjoy looking good. My apple didn't fall too far from the tree in that sense. I enjoy sequins. I enjoy getting ready, the process of it, the arriving. I really appreciate that process.

I cultivate part of that through Colored Girls Hustle. Colored Girls Hustle does many things, but the way it started was through creating adornment, handmade adornment. I arrived at the name because I was thinking about really aligning my work with my passion, my purpose, and my pleasure. For me, the hustle was about that alignment. It's not about a scarcity framework, it's about doing work that has meaning for you, and it's about fulfilling your self-expression and your highest potential.

I want people to also look good while doing it, you know? I think that expression is really an important part of our ability to manifest the things that we were gifted with. I made some pins. One of my little catchphrases is that "jewelry is a product, and adornment is a practice, and Colored Girls Hustle is in the business of adornment."

We're in the practice of adorning our bodies. Things that, like, really reflect the intentions of who we are and what we stand for. Now, what that's evolved into, the earrings I've produced recently, they each come with a name and an intention. Like Expansion. It's about you in the universe. Elevation, we're all on the come-up. Sunrise, it's about your glow-up. Each earring carries an intention, and even the words that I put on buttons or T-shirts or stickers, it's about affirming your life, your walk, and your hustle. And so that's one of the ways in which I cultivate pleasure.

I organize my life around pleasure, so it's hard for me to stay in a space, an organization, a job if it doesn't feel good. And I think that may sound flighty.

amb. *To me it sounds like intelligence, but go on.*

Taja. It's a way that I move, because I don't want to make it seem like I have a problem with being uncomfortable, because I also know that discomfort is part of an experience of moving through a growing edge.

For example, being a performance artist, I get scared before I get on stage, but it's really exhilarating, and it requires me to pull from that space that Audre Lorde talks about. I really have to unblock myself and become a channel and a medium for what needs to move through me so that I can deliver the ritual of performance. And it's exhilarating. I have to confront parts of myself that I wouldn't otherwise in daily life because I am doing the work of performance art. So I really try to move with what is feeling good. And be really mindful of when I'm not feeling good. I've quit jobs that created "security," you know, biweekly paychecks and health insurance, because I was like: this is making me unhappy. And my reaction to this is making me unhappy. I need to switch up who I am inside of this and also where I am so that I can feel good and be good inside of my life.

amb. *We are kindred in this.*

Taja. The last thing I'll say about cultivating pleasure—burlesque is a really big part of that. It's not my main genre of performance. I identify as a multimedia interdisciplinary performance artist, because it's performance, it's visual, it's installation, it's some shit in between. It's a little amorphous, but people are very familiar with my performance work and less so the burlesque. The burlesque stuff has not been at the forefront until more recently. But I really enjoy being an ecdysiast, that's what we call it: an ecdysiast. The art of the striptease.

amb. *Okay: pleasure vocabulary!*

Taja. Burlesque informs my work conceptually. Like, even for my piece *This Ain't a Eulogy: A Ritual for Re-membering*, I employ beauty as reverence, you know? It's a performance piece honoring ancestors whose lives were taken because of state-sanctioned violence. In the *Bag Lady Manifesta*, my costuming, what I'm doing with trash bags, it's an item that we know we're supposed to throw away, but for me, repurposing them or recycling them, one, it's a call for what we need to do in our communities and in our world, and it's basically a metaphor for oppression. How [do] we transform our reality to create beauty and reverence? How do we hold on and also repurpose the shit to create the world that we wanna live in?

But also I really appreciate beauty because, for me, beauty and pleasure are freedom rituals. Sexual and sensual self-expression is a part of it, but taking my body and telling my own story with it, especially inside of a state, a nation that is concerned with writing my histories and writing my body as legible in certain kinds of ways or illegible in certain kinds of ways, it's powerful. I get so much joy from doing it. And I've actually made more space for just doing straight-up burlesque in my work because I like doing it.

amb. *You started transitioning into the second question, which for me is all about your relationship to your own body and did you always feel "this is a place of joy and pleasure for me," or has there been some claiming or reclaiming? What has your relationship to your body been, and what do you feel like it is now?*

Taja. I've experienced trauma against my person, against my body. There's things that I carry from childhood abuses, and I think our bodies have memory. That's connected to, but not the same as, the memory that's in our brains. There's a bodily experience. I experienced a really interesting physical breakthrough my first time doing solo performance work. The site where I experienced abuse and trauma, which was around my throat, my neck, I did a piece where I was specifically addressing that, and I could feel something break open and loose in performance I had never felt before. That was a real thing that was living inside of my body, and I still carry that with me.

Burlesque has been an interesting experience, because I learned burlesque inside of a setting that was all women of color. We got to talk about the ways in which our bodies are objectified or hypersexualized or our autonomy invisibilized. We got to discuss all of that while learning the three Ps of burlesque, which I think are like pose, parade, and peel. We're talking about this political shit, and we're, like, learning how to peel a glove and coming up with burlesque names and developing an act. My burlesque is not humorous; my first burlesque performance was very political. It was a ten-minute act, which, mind you, in burlesque is a long-ass time. It was called Miss Black America. I collaged like thirty songs together in different ways to go on this journey from the council of respectability condemning me to me finding my pleasure in my body to owning my crown and sexuality.

I really appreciate the folks that I know in burlesque, because a lot of my community is Black and Brown, and a lot of burlesque is not necessarily that. Like, we're out here, but you know there's a lot of ways in which Black and Brown bodies can be marginalized or not included or tokenized inside of burlesque performances and at cabarets.

amb. *Yes! I'm also interviewing Una and Michi Osato from brASS Burlesque for that reason.*

Taja. Actually, one of the cofounders of brASS was my teacher, Miss AuroraBoobRealis.

amb. *Beautiful. And that also leads into the next question. I think political lineage can get very complicated, like who's in my political lineage? But I know for me it has been so healing to be able to say, oh, Octavia is in my political lineage, and Audre is in my political lineage. These are people who shaped me so much, and I'm carrying that work forward, and it actually feels the same way that, you know, when I think of lineage or bloodline. It's like these are the people who are the lineage of my work, my brain, my thinking, my beliefs, my body. So I wanted to ask you: who are a few of the people that are in your political lineage?*

Taja. Definitely Audre Lorde. She taught me a lot about just living from a place of passion and that the body has information and knowledge that we should not only consider but hold in high esteem. I would say Patricia Hill Collins, who wrote *Black Feminist Thought*, which actually informed my concentration, which was called public policy and knowledge production with a focus on health and women of color.[2] I was specifically interested in epistemology, and I actually came across that word while reading her work because she was questioning whose knowledge is valid and where does knowledge come from and who gets to decide what's legitimate. In a Black feminist tradition, our experiences matter. It's not just being book smart or having done research, but, like, do you have the experience?

Malcolm X is a big part of my political lineage too, because I grew up with a lot of racist-ass shit in my high school. And I became known as being militant because I was so pro-Black. That's where I read *The Miseducation of the Negro* and Malcolm X's autobiography because I just needed some space to make sense of what is wrong with these people in my environment: what the hell is going on here?[3]

---

2   Collins, *Black Feminist Thought*.

3   Carter Godwin Woodson, *The Mis-education of the Negro* (Trenton, NJ: Africa World Press, 1998); Malcolm X and Alex Haley, *The Autobiography of Malcolm X* (New York: Ballantine Publishing

Oh, and Nina Simone! Her songs have been featured in my work. As I do more research on her and learn about her stance and the moves that she made as a person at the intersection of being an artist and an activist, she has really inspired me, and she's one of many ancestors that are on my altar.

amb. *Beautiful. This is awesome. What's one thing that you think every human needs to feel?*

Taja. Self-actualized.

amb. *The last questions are: What are you proudest of in your own work? What are you proudest of that you've achieved in your life so far?*

Taja. I'm just so grateful to be able to do the work that I'm doing in the times that we're in. Figuring out how to be a multidimensional human being inside of a system that wants us to choose just one aspect of ourselves. Being able to be an artist and put a lot of time into that. Cultivating such beautiful communities who are reflections of me in different ways, and I'm just so grateful that I get to be alive during this time. I remember thinking in high school when I would read about the civil rights movement and just being like, damn, I think I was born at the wrong time.

amb. *Yes! I totally felt that!*

Taja. I was like, dammit, I think I was supposed to come down here earlier, what's going on? And then: now I look around, and I'm, like, "girlll."

amb. *You were not late for your whole life.*

Group, 1965).

Taja. Right, not late at all. There is so much more work to do, and I'm grateful to just be alive and doing that work.

BURLESQUE AND LIBERATION

Michi Osato and Una Osato

Michi Ilona Osato and Una Aya Osato are sisters, performers, writers, and educators who use burlesque to explore their identities as queer femmes of color. They are co-founders, with Dawn Crandell (aka Miss AuroraBoobRealis), of brASS Burlesque: Brown RadicalAss Burlesque, a multidisciplinary performance troupe based in New York City. brASS uses their unique perspectives as femmes of color as a lens to the myriad issues they are faced with in society. Through celebrations of their politicized bodies, they are making politics sexy and empowering audiences to value their own stories and use their creativity toward collective action.

Una, aka exHOTic other, aka Norms, is a queer femme Japanese self-loving anti-Zionist Jew. She is a performer, writer, and educator from the far, far east ... of NYC. Her love for fully embodying her politics led her to burlesque. ExHOTic other has performed in dozens of venues, from New York City's iconic Joe's Pub to the bright lights of Vegas for the Miss Exotic World and Burlesque Hall of Fame competitions. Una is also an award-winning actor and playwright who tours her work nationally and internationally, while, duh, eating orientalism for brunch. Since graduating from Wesleyan University, she has created six award-winning shows that she performs in theaters, festivals, conferences, clubs, universities, community organizations, classrooms, and prisons.

Michi, aka sister selva, the 2015 Queen of the Texas Burlesque Festival and winner of the Thursday Audience Choice Award, has spread her seedlings all over the stages of New York City—from Joe's Pub, to CIUSA, (Le) Poisson Rouge, the Joyce Theater, Lincoln Center Out of Doors, Sesame Street, and all over the blocks, avenues, and impassioned dance floors. A student of acupuncture and Chinese herbal medicine, she loves exploring the many branches of healing that are rooted in self-love, community love, and justice for all people, creatures, and Mother Nature herself.

The sisters were asked to write about radical burlesque as a tool for liberation and working together as sisters. But they weren't at all sure how to functionally write together (sisters!), so instead they just sat down and had a conversation about these topics.

Sister/Sister on Burlesque

Una. Why do we do burlesque/how is it liberatory? Okay, I want to start off our convo by answering the question I just asked.

Both. Haha.

Una. We know the road to liberation for all peoples is a long one and something we might not see in our lifetimes. I feel like burlesque creates moments of liberation, moments of experience. Burlesque gives us space to feel all emotions and to recharge together, in our bodies together, not just online but viscerally together. It's about finding freedom onstage, in my own body, while others watch and experience. It's not just about rehearsing the revolution, it's about creating cracks that show our bodies that we can experience freedom, we do. Sometimes that happens while we're onstage, sometimes it happens while we're dancing on the dance floor, no one else looking but us. These moments and experiences can be public or private, or private in a public setting, but more important is that they happen. For us to be fully present in our bodies, where we want nothing else but to be right there letting the divine speak through and of us. Where we want nothing of the audience but to witness and hope/know that their own freedom is wrapped in ours and the freer we each are, the more present and fully embodied we are to work for our collective liberation, toppling down borders, prisons, and all other systems that cause violence and keep our people from being free. All while we take off our clothes, showing some titties, ass, and armpit hair.

Michi. Yeah! I feel like, in general, what we are doing when we are creating is envisioning or practicing for the world we want. So to have those moments on stage where we and the audience are living in, inhabiting a different world, where that *is* our reality, gives us a physical memory of it to be able to have the strength to keep working for it, for the world we want to live in.

I was just recently watching the old Slick Rick "Children's Story" music video and found it so interesting that in a moment when the lyrics were talking about the horrors of police violence, the visual story was one in which Slick Rick was outwitting the cops and getting free, and I was so grateful to watch him do that, I needed to see him win. That didn't negate the reality he was speaking to, but, paired with the reality, [it] gave this feeling of power and comedy and slickness that the cops literally couldn't even handle.

Una. Yeah, totally! So, what current burlesque/organizing projects are you excited about that we're working on?

Michi. That feels like a leading question.

Una. We spend so much time working on it, I thought we should mention it here ...

Michi. True, fine. *COMPOST BIN!*

Una. *COMPOST BIN!*, the sexiest name we could think of for a monthly burlesque/cabaret show! Why do you think it's important?

Michi. Well, I think, as people living in a world with so much injustice, in a city where we spend so much of our energy working to afford to live, many of us compartmentalize to be able to hold the pain and contradictions, to be able to keep going. As queer people, as people of color, as activists and organizers, we face the injustice and work day after day holding the pain, anger, and stress of these realities. So, as artists, we have created *COMPOST BIN!* as a space for our communities to both dream *and* create the world we wish to live in. While in *COMPOST BIN!*, our minds are opened to ideas and visions of liberation, and our bodies feel what it is to live in a world where we are all loved, valued, and free. Leaving the show, our bodies have the physical memory of existing in a world that holds all the contradictions with fierce love, reminding us of the world we work for. In *COMPOST BIN!*, storytelling is a cathartic transformation shared between incredible artists and inspiring audience members, each working outside of that space as teachers and organizers.

Una. Yes! See, that's exactly why I wanted you to talk about it!

Michi. In thinking about burlesque as a liberation practice, I've also been thinking about that just because you are taking your clothes off doesn't mean liberation is a given. In some ways, I feel like burlesque has everything to do with liberation—the stripping down, stripping off, freeing, revealing of bodies or truths, the use of satire and political critique. I feel like the structure offers a lot if you are trying to get free.

But, you know, just because I am on vacation doesn't mean I'm relaxing! The body might be there, but if the mind and heart aren't there with it, then it may not feel like a freeing, self-loving experience. I feel like what makes it a liberatory practice is a lot in the intention we bring to it. Like in ritual, there are deliberate steps to help induce a state or experience, the structure offers all these gateways, but you have to actually bring your own intention as you walk through it, so just taking your clothes off doesn't mean you're going to be liberating yourself if you're still—

Una. Hating the body you're in, or doing it just to please the audience.

Michi. Yes, yes. *But*, burlesque does offer us these opportunities to practice it, because it's not like the first time you get on stage and get naked for an audience that it's just gonna be all easy, breezy "I love myself and I'm at peace with systems of oppression that have made me internalize the hatred in the world" and so on and so forth! Sometimes, even when we are performing sexy self-love liberation, we may not feel that way. But doing the performance will remind us that part of us *does* feel that way, and by performing it, practicing that love for ourselves and all people, I feel like it can strengthen our ability to get there.

Una. And it's especially vulnerable because it's our bodies that are up there. Doing burlesque is not like a play we wrote that someone else is performing. We're up there, embodying the story.

Michi. You have mentioned that it's been a journey to pace yourself and not take your clothes off all at once. People think of burlesque performers as these super sexually comfortable people, but I feel like you taking all of your clothes off at once is in some way being afraid of your own sexiness. Do you want to talk about that?

Una. Yeah, it's like, here, I'm aggressively showing my body before you can reject me. When I was younger and liked people who didn't like me back, I found that all the power I felt like I had was in being able to confront them, asking them directly "do you like me?" They would be like, "Umm, I don't even know you to know if I'm into you," so that wouldn't go very far.

I think part of sexiness is the exploration of it in relationship to ourselves and other people. Part of what burlesque has done for me is help me discover what my unique sexiness is to me, on my terms. It's been super profound to see and learn that sexiness is different for each person. When you're like, "Damn, that person is sexy!," I think it's because they've tapped into what sexy is for them, and it continues to evolve and change, but they have a deep connection/understanding with themselves.

It's connected to organizing too. There's something about the honesty and knowledge of the self required when you have to have a relationship with the audience. There are other kinds of performance, where you can hide behind the "fourth wall." There's art that people can just view, they don't have to see you. But there's something about the relationship built between the audience and the performer that requires you, or us, to be rooted in yourself and what your sexy is and what your funny is, and also not get stuck in that. You have to be able to laugh and cry and experience the whole range of emotions together. Any relationship requires that too. It's a constant evolution because no healthy relationship ever gets stuck in one thing; it continues to grow as we all do.

Michi. That's interesting, to think about the way you have to connect to an audience in terms of organizing. Like, there's a difference between dictating how people are supposed to feel and react as opposed to actually listening and having to adapt.

It's an interesting thing as performers, what we choose to put our bodies through. I feel like we intentionally bring joy into the work we do, but it's not an ignorant joy, it's because we believe in joy. We also don't shy away from bringing anger and sadness and confusion, but I think the idea is that to be whole, free people, we need to be able to access and experience all of our emotions, to allow all of them to move through us and not be stuck or stagnant or forced into only one. So many of us are forcibly separated from a range of our emotional experiences, because of systemic inequality, because of the ways our ancestors learned to experience the world and the way their ancestors learned. Sometimes it feels like so many fucked up realities are imposed upon us, that there is so much pain and anger and sadness and injustice, so of course what feels urgent and relevant to express is that. But that is part of the robbery, stealing from us our ability to live joyously and with peace. So creating space where we're actually bringing that to ourselves and to the room is really important.

Una. It's also what makes it all sustainable. We have to find joy and laughter. Our movements need to be able to hold all of us and all of the things we feel. This is essential for us to want to continue.

Michi. I feel like endings to pieces are really hard in this sense. I often think of dream hampton talking about how we don't need "happy endings," we need endings that are envisioning our liberation, envisioning these things, not just re-creating our sadness and pain and lack of power.[1]

Una. It also reminds me of this Grace Lee Boggs quote: "History is not the past. It is the stories we tell about the past. How we tell these stories—triumphantly or self-critically, metaphysically or dialectically—has a lot to do with whether we cut short or advance our evolution as human beings."[2] Sometimes it's important for it not to be neat, to show

---

1   dream hampton is an American cultural critic and filmmaker from Detroit.

2   Grace Lee Boggs was an organizer and philosopher. Grace Lee Boggs, *The Next American Revolution: Sustainable Activism for the Twenty-First*

that we're still questioning. And art can be the perfect place to show/share/hold the mess of the world that isn't neat.

Michi. I think part of it is that you want to inspire people to believe there's possibility and hope, and we're strong, and that's in each of your endings.

As a younger person finding my own self and my sexy, it did matter, to be able to costume myself and to go out in the world, and to continue to do that, even when there was backlash for it. There was backlash in the street, from verbal harassment, to stalking, to being attacked as a young woman alone late at night. There was backlash from my peers, being called a ho or a tease, backlash from my partners telling me I was asking for trouble or disrespecting them. There was backlash from my bosses, being pulled aside and literally forcibly undressed and then redressed—for me, continuing to dress how I felt powerful and beautiful and sexy was a performance for myself in a lot of ways. I needed to continue to go out in the world to do it—it wouldn't have been enough for me to just have my sexy indoor clothes and my appropriate outdoor clothes. It's funny, how that's a confusing thing for people … when they see burlesque performers as just exhibitionists or femmes as objects seeking a male gaze. While there is something about other people being present and witnessing, it is not the same as it being *for* them … We're dedicated to working and creating in this world, and we deserve to enjoy living; there's no point in living it out miserably.

Una. The joy in the process is just as important as the joy at the end that we're striving for.

Century, with Scott Kurashige, foreword by Danny Glover, and new afterword with Immanuel Wallerstein (Berkeley: University of California Press, 2012), 79.

WORKING THE POLE

A Conversation with
Suguey Hernandez

Suguey Hernandez is an organizer who has crossed my path over the years because of shared loves and common friends. A while ago, I started following her on Instagram and was excited to catch the beginning of her journey with pole dancing. I have been continually impressed by her commitment to sharing the sexy embodiment journey in spaces that her community and family will see, claiming that wholeness.

amb. *Suguey, thank you for giving me some time. First—where are you from?*

Suguey. I was born and raised in a little town on the central coast of California called Nipomo (foot of the mountain in Chumash territory), but I am from a Mexican village called Atapaneo via Uruétaro, which translates into "the place where all beginnings commence" in Michoacan/P'urhepecherio.

amb. *Wow, that's a name. An intention. And … what inspired you to start dancing on a pole?*

Suguey. Because FEMMES! Honestly, though, I had just quit my job at a union where life had become semi-depressing, codependent, and definitely unhealthy. You can say that I had hit rock-bottom with the burnout and the heartache of having to leave work that I was deeply passionate about, but my heart knew there had to be another way of balancing out my work and personal life.

I was also going through a deeply transformative experience in my relationship with my mother, who essentially disowned me when I came out to her in 2009. It was a time of revival, renewal, and a deep sense of self.

I saw myself reflected in my friend Amaryllis DeJesus-Moleski, who is a femme and, like me, partnered with a trans person. She invited me to be my most magical self in the pole studio. On top of that, a good friend of mine, Donna Jane Walton, actually owned the studio in downtown Oakland and invited me with open arms. Both of these womyn, who I deeply identified with as queer chingonas, helped heal my aching heart and recovering body with their words of encouragement and affirmations. With their love and tales of their own deeply transformational experiences, I took the plunge to enter the pole studio in my little shorts and tank top, ready to face all of the fears.

amb. *How did you feel in your body before you started?*

Suguey. I felt so insecure. I grew up with a Mexican mother who constantly judged me, fat-shamed me, and told me that I would be much more beautiful if I just lost some weight. I constantly struggled with my weight and how I looked in the mirror. I knew that I used food and specifically sugar as a way to cope with my emotional issues, to cope with stress from work. I became codependent on that nurturing feeling. Often I would look into the mirror and experience dysphoria between two people: one who loved my curves, my thighs, and booty, and the other, who was constantly on a mission to lose my belly fat or arm jiggle. It was very hard for me to imagine myself dancing on a pole next to all those women who were very thin and so damn strong! I was like, you want me to do what with what now? Trippin' ... little did I know that I was going to embark on a journey that would teach me how to love and trust myself.

amb. *What has changed?*

Suguey. I AM A MOTHERFUCKING QUEEN! And I remembered that that's always been who I am! Okay, sorry ... in all seriousness, I am so completely grateful for this art form. I found so much within myself. A renewed sense of self. A deep appreciation for my body because thick thighs save lives! Am I right? Literally in pole, thick thighs are a plus.

I also realized that I was going to need to love my body so hard, harder than I could imagine, so that I could trust it enough to hold myself up in the air. I mean holding your entire body weight while you're upside down is not an easy feat physically, and it's an even harder feat mentally, so I had to find this deep synchronicity between my mind, heart, and body for them to all say in unison, "Suguey, we can do this shit."

Also, it would be remiss of me to not mention that I found a sexy beast deep within me! I was able to become acquainted with my most sensual self who loves to booty-shake and dance it out. This was something that I had been in touch with before but hadn't tapped it in a way that pole helped me to. Constantly I was battling that societal teaching that I was a ho or promiscuous or all the bullshit that womyn are taught to believe when they tap into their sexual beings. I even found myself being, like, I will purposefully post this video of me being my most sensual self so that my tias and cousins and friends will see how many fucks I give.

In return, it was actually the opposite, my friends specifically were so inspired and happy for me. They wanted to know how I found this new sense of self. They too wanted to swing on the pole and twerk on their knees. Soon I found out that I wasn't only doing this for myself, I was doing it for every single womyn who was ever told they were fat or ugly or not sexy or unable. I was like, c'mon sisters, we doing this! We outcheea!

amb. *What do you say to people who think they cannot pole dance (asking for a friend)?*

Suguey. In my most passionate and affirming voice: "Pole dance is for *everyone*, especially *you*! And if you don't believe me, just give me an hour, your most positive attitude, and we got this, friend!"

Honestly, though, you may not be up in the middle of the air going upside down right away—shoot, even I can't do that sometimes. But with consistency, hard work, and trust, you can twerk on the pole and do your best body roll, and with time, you will be dancing away! You will get strong AF,[1] and with every class you will find a renewed sense of self, confidence, [and] increased strength, and every time you look into the mirror, you'll be, like, "Hey, boo!"

amb. *I am encouraged. For my friend. So how does pole dancing connect with social justice?*

Suguey. During a time of intense surveillance, when our bodies are policed along the border and in our communities—and while living under a regime that reads Latinx bodies as criminal, illegal, deportable, and as disposable labor, a society that renders women/femmes of color as the primary receptors of physical and emotional violence … in this time, expressing embodied joy, practicing revolutionary love, self-care, and having mindfulness of our well-being and health are the most radical acts we can perform. This is also a time when queer bodies are under intense policing and subject to violence—sometimes the only option for true freedom that

---

1   AF is a shortcut way the youth say "as fuck."

queer Latinx have is creative expression. I find my freedom in an embodied praxis of self-love through dance. Pole gives me the pleasure and possibility to just *be* in a society hell-bent on hating me for being brown, femme/female, Mexican, and queer. Taking care of my spirit and heart and body in this way allows me to continue doing the work that matters—whether it's organizing in the streets with our communities or advocating for our enfranchisement through formal means. Pole allows me to shout, "I'm here, I'm free, my body defies your boundaries and boxes, and I can and will be happy!"

PLEASURE OVER SIXTY

A Conversation with
Idelisse Malave and Alta Starr

I met Alta Starr and Idelisse Malave when they were at the Ford Foundation and Tides Foundation, respectively, so I initially knew them as funders who were working to shift the relationship between movements and philanthropy. Once they left those jobs, I was excited to discover that Alta was a gifted poet and Idelisse an incredible visual artist. Both have gone on to do organizational development and coaching work in addition to their creative work. They are both committed to lives of pleasure and have taught me a lot about pleasure as we age.

amb. *Hello, my loves. I imagine us sitting together at a dining room table. On the table, there is a bottle of good red wine and a bottle of Macallan 18 Year. And maybe an elegant vaporizer with some OG Kush for me. It's sunset, we have a view over Harlem, and I am so excited to have this time with you. First, what is your choice from the gifts on the table? And how did you learn to love that particular delight?*

Ide. The good red wine! Definitely an acquired taste, and now a luscious pleasure. The first time I tasted wine was when I was nine and playing at a friend's house. It was some Jewish holiday, and her parents had Manischewitz. Looked like grape juice to us, and we helped ourselves. Certainly as sweet as Welch's. No wonder I had to acquire a taste for the "real" stuff.

Alta. The sunset. Your faces. Your eyes. Nature—trees, sunrises and sunsets, animals—has always opened my heart and made me feel good. And feeling good makes me feel affectionate and see and feel the expression of life, in those I'm with, especially when we got that soul-kindred thing working.

amb. *Okay, good. Enjoy. Now can you each tell me what feels most important for people to know about who you are?*

Alta. One of my teachers in grad school called me a "disciple of joy." For the purposes of this conversation, that's enough.

Ide. Perfect, Alta! Then, I'm a joyful old bitch committed to being fully herself.

amb. *What has been the greatest pleasure of your life?*

Ide. So many pleasures. Questions about the "greatest" or "number one favorite" always stymie me because you can—and do—have the chance at more than just one. But, I'll play—sort of. I'm torn between "loving" and "seeing." Loving—children, parents, lovers, friends. The feeling of deep connection and warmth for another person, the energy it releases in your body, mind, and soul, the way it takes you over. The other pleasure vying for the number one spot is "seeing." The delights of just absorbing something or someone with your eyes, of knowing it or them in that way. You can be going about your business, not really noticing much around you, and then, suddenly, you really see, pause, really look and take it in. It's why I love the visual arts and to paint and draw—trying to capture that experience of delight in being fully present. Now that I think of it, both loving and seeing are about connecting and transcending—your bound-aries blur, and you're part of something bigger than just your-self. So maybe the greatest pleasure is transcendence.

Hmm. Was I supposed to talk about sex? Sex is also tran-scending, right?

Alta. The greatest pleasure in my life has been discovering, or rediscovering, that life itself is made out of pleasure. I want to be clear that I don't mean that everything that happens in life is pleasurable. If only! But rather, the very fact that we expe-rience life, that there is this steady hum or pulse of livingness and awareness with only one purpose, living more, reaching greedily for more life—connecting to that and feeling it is pure pleasure for me. Feeling my livingness and the sweet pure livingness of others—my loved ones, trees, my dog, the ocean—catching and surrendering to the heartbeat and pulse of life, in all its varied melodies.

Yes, pleasure is a physical, erotic, heart-filling, and spiri-tual thing for me. At its most mundane edge, maybe I'd call it delight. Feeling tickled about something, like the way my dog (a somewhat new part of my life) draws the oohs and aahs out of folks we pass on the street. Delighted, tickled, a sweet yummy feeling in my stomach and heart. And then there are all kind of ways that get bigger, or more intense—hearing live music, like recent tributes to Abbey Lincoln and Thelonious Monk, all the irrepressible dancing at the edge of losing the through line that makes music jazz. I don't know what to call that: joy, fulfillment? Music fills me up and spills over, spills out, stretches me to be bigger, intuit, and connect to more, hear the sounds light years away, of which these performances are only echoes.

Art, books, poems, woods, laughter with friends, slow groove sex or a giggling quickie, movies, plays, a perfectly iced and lemon-tinged glass of seltzer, helping another feel and celebrate this free life, knowing someone for years and still being surprised by them. Writing, for the freedom of it. And on and on and on.

When I was twelve, I had a German Shepherd, Sheik, a regal and demanding dog, who would go running with me most days, for the fun of it. That sensation of running all out, in the company of a powerful, equally delighted animal, especially in the fall, when browning leaves would pile up against fences and park benches, that sense of aliveness burning through me is one of my hallmarks for pleasure.

One more thing: where's pain in all this? Pleasure, for me, doesn't exclude or deny pain. The same self, the same inclusive awareness that allows me to experience pleasure, may retreat or cramp up in the face of pain (physical or emotional) but returns, and so far, is always bigger and able to absorb or metabolize it. What do I mean? A light example: say, I drop a can of baked beans on my toe! OWWWWW! And, of course, sit and cradle the toe in my hands and squinch up (you know, squinch, all tight), and breathe, and get curious, invite my awareness to be with that pressure and cramp and burning ache, and so far, every time, that awareness changes my relationship to what hurts. Of course, the pain of personal loss or of our suffering world asks for an even larger and steadier awareness, anchored in that livingness that neither loses nor suffers.

amb. *Mmmm, thank you both, such richness here. So, I thought about interviewing y'all because of a very particularly conversation.... Idelisse, you are the cohost of an incredible podcast called* Two Old Bitches, *which is just nonstop awesome conversations with women over fifty. Alta was a guest on the show and ended up speaking about the wonders of the Mona Lisa Touch, "a new procedure based on a unique concept and designed to restore the trophic conditions of the vaginal and the vulvar area."[1] Can you give us some insight on how you knew this podcast was needed?*

---

1   "How Does MonaLisa Touch Help Atrophic Vaginitis?," Greater Boston Urology, January 17, 2018, https://www.info.greaterboston urology.com/blog/gbu-blog/2018/01/how-does-monalisa-touch-help-atrophic-vaginitis.

Ide. It's so easy to overlook older women and to think of aging only in terms of loss in this country. But I know that aging is about "becoming" and unfolding, with the bonus of lots of experience and a heightened sense of freedom. I think of aging as ripening, not withering. When older women are sidelined, everyone loses.

With *Two Old Bitches*, Joanne Sandler and I get to hear and share older women's stories about how they are living and have lived their lives, often reinventing themselves along the way. There's a surprise in every conversation we share, some unexpected bit that challenges preconceived notions about older women or reveals another unfair obstacle they face as they age. Storytelling is so powerful, and asking questions is such a pleasure! The women we interview are so game—they answer our questions, no matter how unexpected, serious, or frivolous. Like Alta telling us about Mona Lisa Touch! We laugh a lot. And one of the surprises of the podcast has been the number of younger women who listen. It inspires them, they say, and their listening inspires us.

amb. *Yes, it is such a gift, there is so much in there that I, as someone about to turn forty, find really useful and aspirational. So Alta, you were a guest on that show, and you spoke about how you have been reclaiming your pleasure. It felt inspiring and clarifying, like a conversation that isn't had in public often enough. So, first, can you each tell me a bit about how that conversation came to be—did you plan to go where you went with it?*

Alta. I absolutely did *not* plan! What came out was the result of feeling so comfy and kitchen-table-like with Ide and Joanne. I was an early interview, I think, and Ide and I had been in conversation about the unfolding of the project for a while. Of course, I was up for the interview and thought I had many things I wanted to celebrate and share.

amb. *And how does it feel to have that interview out in the world?*

Alta. A bit weird. It was fun, and I don't mind that there's a somewhat permanent record of my delight in life, including sex. On the other hand, there are moments when I think about all the things that I didn't say, perhaps more serious, and wish I had. Then again, the side of me that showed up in the interview hasn't had nearly as much airspace in recent years as my more sober serious-biz personality.

amb. *What do both of y'all wish people knew about pleasure over sixty?*

Ide. Our sense of "aliveness"—know what I mean?—doesn't dim with age. Passion, in all its guises, doesn't disappear. Death is the end, not being old. Older women can take their pleasure where they find it. A "why the fuck not!" mind-set helps, and most of the older women I know have that attitude. Think it was Alice Walker who wrote, "Resistance is the secret of joy."[2]

Alta. It gets easier and easier to live as pleasure! It's a kind of shedding all the irritations and bumpiness—Oh god! The *drama*!—so little of that matters. Ease. Focus. Clear purpose. Absorption in living, in the sense of being present with what is, in the expanded self that makes room for it all. Life, moment by moment, is delicious.

amb. *Do you have a daily practice for pleasure? Do you recommend such things?*

Ide. I don't have an intentional practice. Wait, maybe I do. My mantra this year is "if it pleases me, I will." I invoke it regularly to encourage myself to live it up.

Alta. Getting present, noticing how far I am from being present, and where I went. Yes, I recommend building the muscle

---

2   Alice Walker, *Possessing the Secret of Joy* (San Diego: Harcourt, 1992), 20.

of feeling pleasure, because I've noticed the world conspires to keep our attention elsewhere. When I was college (almost fifty years ago), I realized that I had an accurate external barometer of my emotional state (since I wasn't that skilled then in knowing it from the inside out!). If I hadn't listened to music in a couple days, I was off my feed, askew to the world and my own feelings. And I could get home, back to myself, by making playlists, that sometimes took me way down deep into grief or anger but always home, back to presence. Bottom line, I've practiced noticing what works rather than what's not working, feeling gratitude, letting myself be awed and know it—by beauty, by mystery, by human creativity. If, as was true for me and many, many folks I know, it was a struggle to survive and there was lots of trauma and pain, we get really good at checking for danger or either clamping down on and avoiding, or being overwhelmed by, moods that accompany suffering. They are familiar and so well-practiced that they might as well be hardwired. It can take intentional practice to rediscover the pleasure of just being, of life itself, right now, right here.

amb. *And, final question—if you were to articulate a pleasure principle, some fundamental truth about pleasure, what would you offer up?*

Ide. Perhaps my mantra: "If it pleases me, I will." I don't mean free license to do whatever I want regardless of the consequences to me or others. Pleasure is deeper than that—it encompasses our values.

Alta. There's a slogan for the general strike in Paris in 1968 that I've always loved, which has come to have even deeper meaning for me: "Love without limit, play without restraint, live without dead time." We can trust our livingness, which is pleasure, and if we are true to it, pleasure frees. If we are true to it, if we let pleasure free us, we become all the more attuned to creating freedom and ensuring it for everyone.

THE WORK OF PARENTING

Autumn Brown

Autumn Brown is a mother of three living children, a facilitator with AORTA, and cohost of How to Survive the End of the World, *our podcast. She teaches me most of what I know.*

Pleasure in the work of parenting is abundant. It is hard to describe, best revealed through a series of scenes.

The reverential interest of Siobhán, age seven, and Máiréad, age five, watching their father Genjo transplanting tender Hog Heart tomato starts, explaining that the most fragile part of the plant is its tiny root system, which peeks out from the peat pockets from which they sprouted.

The smell of Máiréad's hair and the warmth of her naked leggy body when she crawls under the covers with me at seven in the morning, pulls my arms over and under her, and settles in for another half hour of restless rest.

Finn is ten now, but when we lost our fourth child, the infant phenomenon, in 2014, Finn had recently turned six. In processing our loss, he wrote a cartoon about a momma dragon and a baby dragon. The momma dragon sustained an injury to her wing. In one scene, the momma dragon stands with her wings spread to show her wound, and the baby dragon stands next to and below her, wings spread in concert. They both look at her wound with frowny faces. Later, she dies while battling a T. Rex, and the baby dragon is forced to escape the scene in terror. The only way he can take flight is by throwing up.

Finn instinctively understands that to play a game successfully with his sister Máiréad he must let her both win and continuously change the rules as suits her fancy. In this area of his life, alone, he is patient.

Siobhán lies in my lap weeping for the death of her teacher's mother, who dies in hospice at a ripe old age. She is weeping for her teacher, and she is weeping for me because she knows this means, finally, that I will die. She is inconsolable. But she is also consoled and secured by my living body, holding her right here, right now.

Siobhán, this past winter, is lying in my lap while I stroke her hair and her face. She lifts her face and whispers into my ear, "Mommy, I feel safe with you." Less than a year prior, she had been terrorized by her school, who more than once called the police on her, at the tender age of six. She knows what it means to feel unsafe and again safe.

These pleasures are not only pleasures, they are also other feelings. But at the base is something that can only be understood in the body, made sense of by the body. That feeling of loving a child with your whole body, being loved by that child with her whole body, and watching children learn to be loved and to express love with their whole bodies.

Love, which is not pleasure but is also pleasure, happens in the body and through the body. Words cannot contain all that the gaze can hold, or the pressure of a particular touch, or the pain of knowing your children will grow old and die, and sometimes be young and die, and most times, be young and learn what it is to die.

RAISING SEXUALLY LIBERATED KIDS

Janine de Novais

Janine de Novais recently completed her PhD at Harvard's School of Education, but all of us who love her know that her intelligence is beyond what any institution can teach—it is intuitive and compassionate, and one of the few reasons I believe race will one day be something other than a wound.

I always gave him massages. From when he was a baby, I cherished his little being so much, all the way to the tips of toes, curve of his cheeks, the particular symmetry of his eye brows, and I naturally communicated that to him through touch. I showed him that hand and foot and scalp massages were soothing.

I also used to "draw his face"—a face massage, that my grandmother taught me, where you trace the features and narrate that as if it is a house. For eyes, you say windows, et cetera, then mouth, you say door, and to the baby's delight, for nose, you say doorbell and "ring!" He very naturally and early on would request these rituals.

When masturbation happened at a relatively early age, his own word for it was "massage." And all I had to do was explain that he should seek privacy for that and ask me any questions. Which he did not, because those of us lucky to have an unburdened relationship to that practice don't have questions about it!

Drawing from the instinct of having had a lot of judgment directed at my body early on, which I internalized, I worked very hard to model for him how to regard his body with acceptance and celebration. When he was small, I did not allow anyone to talk to him about his weight or appearance. Adults say ridiculous things to children, as if they are not embodied actual people. Folks talk about a kid being scrawny, or having or not having baby fat, or gaining or losing weight over a vacation. I tried to monitor that misbehavior, and if I couldn't prevent someone from saying something tacky, I would always find time later to tell him that such and such adult was an asshole for saying that.

I also spoke of anything to do with his physical self with love and acceptance. For example, he fell in kindergarten and broke a front tooth, and it turned gray. The dentist said to wait for it to fall off rather than extract it. I immediately named it "the Leader Tooth" and we created a whole story about it. When the tooth fell out, what I told him was that the Leader Tooth had fallen out. When it was revealed he had a slight curve in his spine we needed to monitor, I told him he was lucky to have a "permanent gangsta lean," knowing he is the kid who would love that. He still relishes his lean. All this has not been about cultivating his vanity but really about giving him a map and a vocabulary and a practice of loving himself, not abstractly but concretely. For him to understand that his body is extraordinary in what it can do.

We have had cyclical sex talks. At ages four, then eight, then twelve, then again around fifteen, and none since. They have always been precise, frank, and age-appropriate, dictated by him. His questions have been great and even instructive for me. He is a very private young man, so now I am told to stay at bay. But I still compliment him anytime I notice something that I find particularly healthy in his engagement with his own body or with the young women and men in his life. I celebrate his body-positive and sexually healthy attitudes, his physical intimacy with his male friends, his feminist ideas, which come so naturally to him, the fierce way he respects the young women he has close relationships with, and their comfort and trust and intimacy with him. I am explicit about how amazing that is, how rare and necessary for him and for them. Without making things awkward, I gently connect the dots—I try to tell him that sex should be a lot like how they hang out in his room watching movies or talking for hours, and that sexual pleasure belongs to him just like love and friendship and ideas and dreams belong.

I think he gets that.

TIPS FOR RAISING SEXUALLY LIBERATED KIDS

Zahra Ala

amb: I was texting a babysitting friend while working on this book. He sent me this message: "Finally got the kids quiet and lights out when the older one comes and says 'It's so hot in the room, and I need to masturbate.' I'm like, 'Okay, knock yourself out, son, that's normal.' But he's like, 'but I'm too hot, is there a fan?' So I turn on the ceiling fan to facilitate my nephew's pleasure and sleep going, and, wow, for parenting with a sexual liberation lens." I was so impressed by this that I had to interview the parent/s who created this result. It turns out it's Zahra Ala, who I have known and admired for over a decade. Here is what Zahra had to say:

- Being a parent who is in touch with one's own pleasure is vital to raising children toward pleasure: mind, body, spirit pleasure.
- Inquire about what makes them feel good, mind, body, spirit.

- Encourage what brings them pleasure. Talk about it, inquire about it, laugh about it.
- Have age-appropriate anatomy conversation on an ongoing basis.
- Normalize the conversation about pleasure. Have it with people who are a part of our tribe to demonstrate that everyone is talking about it, particularly sexual pleasure.
- Have conversations about age-appropriate ways to show love and care.
- Exclaim that we all deserve to feel good in our bodies and always check in about consent: is anyone is inappropriately touching their body, et cetera?
- I also do not hide anything from them. I am affectionate in front of them. They know that I openly relate to and love many people; they meet my loves, I chat with them before I enter a relationship, et cetera.

SUB-SECTION

THE POLITICS
OF LIBERATED
RELATIONSHIPS

Chile, we need all the small shared pleasures.
—Kiese Laymon

RADICAL GRATITUDE
SPELL

a spell to cast upon meeting a stranger, comrade, or friend working for social and/or environmental justice and liberation:

      you are a miracle walking
i greet you with wonder
in a world which seeks to own
your joy and your imagination
you have chosen to be free,
every day, as a practice.
i can never know
the struggles you went through to get here,
but i know you have swum upstream
and at times it has been lonely

       i want you to know
i honor the choices you made in solitude
and i honor the work you have done to
belong
i honor your commitment to that which is
larger than yourself
and your journey
to love the particular container of life
that is you

you are enough
your work is enough
you are needed
your work is sacred
you are here
and i am grateful

LIBERATED RELATIONSHIPS, EXPANDED

In my previous book, *Emergent Strategy*, I offered some principles in development for liberated relationships, relationships that center the freedom and transformation of all partners, romantic, platonic, political, familial, or some combination of these. Here they are, as a reminder:

- Radical honesty. No omissions, no white lies, no projections. Ask the questions you really want answered, speak your truth, and let the relationship build inside all that reality. Just a note from experience, the small lies can be the hardest to stop telling. "No, I don't want to get on the phone right now, can we just text?"[1]; "I'm busy catching up on my reality TV show"; "Real cow milk ice cream"; or "I know I said I didn't want to ___, but now I do." However, the more you practice this, the more you will find yourself spending your waking

---

1   Or sext. I must admit, sexting is a favorite multitask, while watching anime or reality TV.

hours in the ways you want to, the ways that honor the miracle of your existence, which was not given to you to waste in polite avoidance of hurting people's feelings. You will find that you can be honest and kind; you can be honest and compassionate.

- Acknowledge the dynamics, then keep growing. Have an understanding on the front end of the race, class, gender, ability, geographic, and other power dynamics that exist between you. And also remember that these are mostly constructs. Be in the complexity of living inside these constructs while evolving beyond them through relationship.

- Relinquish Frankenstein. You are not creating people to be with or work with, some idealized individuals made of perfect parts of personality that you discovered on your life journey. You are meeting individuals with their own full lives behind and ahead of them. Stop trying to make and fix others and instead be curious about what they have made of themselves.

For this book I'm adding a few pleasure-specific practices that I've learned for liberated relationships:

- Create your own normal. How often do you pleasure each other? What are your go-to moves, positions? What are your growing edges? What do your bodies love? What agreements and safe words and safe sex practices work for y'all? What is the pace by which you want to deepen your connection or commitment? All of this should be up to you and your lover/partner/s—don't live in the misery of comparative relationships. Normal is a myth! There are as many ways to love, desire, please, and be pleased as there are bodies, minds, and imaginations.

- Line up your longings. Chemistry is a special thing, beautifully mysterious. What is less mysterious as we get older are the things that we enjoy doing with our

bodies and our lives. Learn how to name your longings and to assess if your longings are aligned with a
potential lover, partner, friend, or group.

- ○ This is the place where we can do the most unlearning work around how most of us are taught
  to date—you know, that game of "hunting" and
  "catching" each other and then compromising
  in order to get to the marriage end goal? No, my
  loves, don't start with compromise and cunning,
  start with alignment and grow from there.
- ○ This is also an important place to line up pleasure
  behaviors beyond sex. Do you both like getting
  high? Beaches? Baths? Threesomes? Oh, that's sex
  … um, punk concerts? Hiking? In your organizing work do you love debate? Planning? Actions?
  Create a pleasurable culture between you.
- ○ Pleasure shapes our lives through and around the
  challenges we face. The relationships (personal
  and political) that last the longest have a solid
  foundation of aligned longings that can handle the
  tensions of difference and change.
- Change, and be changed. You can do the same all by
  yourself. One of the exciting things about being in
  any relationship is the opportunity to be seen, to be
  known, to let the cauldron of love and honesty and
  intimacy become a container for transformation.
  - ○ Shift away from any mentality that you are there
    to fix each other, and shift into an understand-
    ing that change is constant, and you get the
    gift of witnessing and supporting each other in
    transformation.
  - ○ This is true in your sexual relationship as well—the
    first time you have sex is not the defining dynamic
    of your sexual connection, it's an introduction. In
    the healthiest relationships, sex is deeply satisfying,
    a place for growth and depth, for complete freedom
    and release, and for naked visceral honest exchange.

- ○ Pay attention to feedback that is repeated. When it is repeated from multiple people, it is more likely to be true. If it is repeated from a lover, it is more likely to be a long-term sign of incompatibility.
- ○ Change if you want to for yourself, not to keep someone or stay in a place/organization. Change because it is your path, not to contort into spaces you have outgrown.
- Stay curious. So much of what we really long for can get buried under socialization. As you generate trust with each other, between each other, hopefully both/all partners will be able to be more of themselves, bring more of themselves into the relationship space. Stay curious about each other's longings, desires. When you hear something that may be new, surprising, even a bit scary, see if you can center curiosity.
- Set generative boundaries.[2] Create mutual abundance. I envision generative boundaries as organic fences made of stacked rocks or thick bushes that become home to millions of small creature families. Porous, breathing boundaries that are clear, that mark the space between partners in ways that make them both feel abundant. If you are in a relationship where you can't honestly and easily set boundaries, then there is reason for concern about the health and longevity of your connection; whatever *yes* exists between you is not trustworthy. Learn how to feel your own edges, limits, and needs—the places where you need to be selfish, the places where you need to preserve yourself.
  - ○ Boundaries arise from needs. One major need in any relationship is a recognition of what belongs where. Here are two of my favorite boundary-setting statements:

---

2   These are for relationships that are defined by both/all partners as healthy. In relationships that have abusive dynamics present, generative boundaries may not be safe or possible, and you may need boundaries that are concrete and one-sided.

. "It sounds like you might need some professional support. I love/like our connection/fuckship/friendship/coworkership/romance and don't want to slip into an inappropriate role of healer or coach here. How can I help you connect to support?"

. "There is my work, your work, and our work. I am down for us to do our work, and I will hold down my work, but I cannot take on your work. I deeply support you figuring out what you need to do around that."

o Boundaries arise from requests. This may include boundaries around drugs ("babe, I request that you are not high during my boss's wedding"), sex ("lover, I felt a bit exposed when you shared about our reverse cowgirl experiments over brunch; please don't share that level of sexual detail in public"), or other things. You both/all have the right to request boundaries. The expectation here is that the partner will respond honestly to the request, forming an agreement or inviting a negotiation. "Yes, I can wait until the reception to get high." Or "no, I actually can't even go in the church without a hit or two. How about I just have half a J so I am not high enough to get the giggles?" And you can say, "Okay, but save me some for the reception." I could keep scripting this exchange, but I think you get the point.

Liberated relationships are one of the ways we actually create abundant justice, the understanding that there is enough attention, care, resource, and connection for all of us to access belonging, to be in our dignity, and to be safe in community.[3]

---

3   Dignity, safety, and belonging are identified as foundational human needs in the work of Generative Somatics.

ON NONMONOGAMY

When *The Ethical Slut* was released in 1997, I was in college.[1] I borrowed a friend's copy, which was well worn, with bent pages, even though it was less than a year old. *The Ethical Slut* offered a new realm of language and ideas that aligned with some of the ways my friends and I thought about relationships: we were interested in taking lovers, trying polyamory, having open marriages, and delving into nonmonogamy, though we didn't yet have the language for those desires.[2]

The book encouraged readers to center desire and freedom over long-term commitment and obligation, which resonated with me. As a child in the 1980s, I only saw the traditional God-approved marriage between a man and a woman and the singular pathway to that marriage: date, declare love with flowers, commit to feel that way forever, get married in a virginal white dress, live together, and raise children. Yet, from early on I wanted something else: I often crushed on multiple people at a time. I focused more on dynamic and romantic physical connections than the escalator toward commitment.[3]

---

1   This essay first appeared as adrienne maree brown, "The Pleasure Dome: On Nonmnogamy and Casual Sex," June 21, 2017, *Bitch Media* (blog), https://www.bitchmedia.org/article/pleasure-dome/nonmonogamy-and-casual-sex-hearken.

2   Janet W. Hardy and Dossie Easton, *The Ethical Slut: A Guide to Infinite Sexual Possibilities,* 3rd ed. (Berkeley: Ten Speed Press, 2017).

3   The term "escalator" came to me from my friend David Treleaven.

In the early 1990s, I became aware of pop culture figures who loved more freely. I saw Prince grinding against the air and being in love over and over. And then Madonna and Angelina Jolie made impressions on me because they were seen publicly in relationships with male and female lovers that emphasized sexual desire. I read of Anaïs Nin's affair with Henry Miller. I even remember a moment of rethinking the conundrum Archie faced while stress-dating both Betty and Veronica. I saw that the women were clearly so different from each other and could serve very different needs for Archie.

In my twenties, I experimented with taking lovers, which mostly entailed making a lot of messes—and learning a lot of lessons:

1. People will lie about their availability.
2. Make agreements based on the true nature of the person or people. If spontaneous hookups turn you on, don't agree to a drawn-out approval process with your partner that you have to follow before flirting or having sex with a new person. Or, if you don't want a hierarchy, don't cave to the pressure to call one person your primary partner.
3. It's hard and necessary to say what you really want in a relationship.

I learned that general ho'ing around didn't work for me because it's too messy.[4] But neither did traditional monogamy, which I tried for about seven years.

For a while, I thought that there was a moral or evolutionary superiority to my nonmonogamous worldview: true feminists and anticapitalists had to see that monogamy was about ownership and patriarchy. I thought my lovers

---

4   And because I am immensely picky. This is one of the funniest aspects of being a pleasure activist—when people hear me say this, they think I am down for what- and whomever. The truth is that I am quite picky, and as I gain confidence to be my whole sexy self, I become more discerning about who can gather my attention.

would outgrow monogamy if they really loved me. I even asked monogamous partners to read *Opening Up,* hoping this particular reading assignment would make it possible for me to "keep" them if we just made some adjustments and then added more people.[5] That failed. But this happens a lot when people get politicized around something—we become obnoxious, thinking we can look down on those who don't know or don't choose our path. We lose sight of nuance and honesty.

Some versions of nonmonogamy work better for me, such as being in love with people who encourage my crushes, being in relationships that are transparent about desiring other people, and being respected for desiring multiple genders, but I also recognize and honor that nonmonogamy is not for everyone. I rarely get jealous. While this inherent absence of jealousy makes nonmonogamy easier for me, it is not a requirement. I know lots of people who experience and navigate jealousy in open relationship structures by naming and being gentle with it. There is no shame in jealousy.

With time, I've learned that under the layers of socialization—and jealousy—there's deeper wiring that says yes to one or yes to two or yes to many.[6] And relationships should be formed around that yes rather than what society or books say *should* happen.

And society is becoming a bit more open-minded. While writing this, I grew hungry for modern examples of nonmonogamy in pop culture—and I found examples, but it would be an epic reach to say they're functional.

Claire and Frank have a terrifying version on *House of Cards* where they take lovers like prey and rarely touch each other.[7]

---

5   Tristan Taormino, *Opening Up: A Guide to Creating and Sustaining Open Relationships* (New York: Simon & Schuster, 2005).

6   And even in this deep wiring, there can be shifts over time. Apparently. At least in my deep wiring.

7   This piece was written before Kevin Spacey's unfortunate fall from grace. The rope he threw to save himself was his gay identity. This

Then there's the hot mess *Bachelor/Bachelorette* franchise, where one person dates twenty people at a time, eventually falling in love with and sleeping with three finalists before selecting one for a proposal. Nonmonogamy is not about making people compete for your love and devotion—it's about abundance and not having to let go of the people who help you grow. These reality contestant show relationships rarely work long-term, perhaps because it's hard to focus on one person after the harem experience.

On the other hand, I've been very excited by the way intimacy flows in *Sens8*, where love and desire are ways of knowing others and pleasure is a way of comforting others and making life worthwhile. The eight core characters feel each other's pain and pleasure and have epic orgies.

So far, I don't know any people living that *Sens8* life. In real life, I know married and unmarried couples who integrate their desire for others into their sex life with fantasy, and I know couples who take lovers into their shared bed, and couples who have virtual affairs, and couples who openly date others. I know individuals who choose to be with multiple people at a time, who have a steady relationship and then participate in BDSM communities, who don't place a hierarchy on any relationships, or who have a primary love and then special names for others. I know people who are working to undo the bonds of marriage as the only legitimate way to practice love, pulling love away from the state and capitalism.[8] And I know people who are happily

---

is a bit random, but it makes me think of how many people have practiced shady nonmonogamy because they were so scared to come out of the closet. And you know, I have compassion—closets are full of shadows and shade. Come out on your own time … but come out without casting that shade on anyone you have harmed while in there.

8   "I am an unapologetic marriage abolitionist, which means that I believe that the financial and legalized structural advantages currently attached to the institution of marriage in this country should not be linked to the practice of marriage as such, but should be available to all people who want to collaborate on home, family, support and love on their own terms." Alexis Pauline Gumbs, "'Keep Your

married or coupled, aren't looking for anything else, and feel satisfied.

In my relationship coaching work, I often see people push down their deepest desires because our society measures our success by a relationship, even if it's a bad relationship—being "alone" is still read as a sign of failure. These denied desires become toxic energy that strives for daylight. Desire shifts and changes over time, but my mom always taught me that it doesn't disappear. Opening a relationship in some way can release a desire and allow it to nourish the relationship, relieve pressure, and feed trust and satisfaction.

Nonmonogamy looks different for everyone. The model I've been most excited by recently is relationship anarchy, which operates around a set of principles that can strengthen any connection.[9]

I find this model makes room for all kinds of relationships, increasing the freedom and truth in any formation. It's a deeply feminist model, founded in the equality of all partners and the idea that everyone gets to determine what works for them.

Trust is a core aspect of relationship anarchy and a core part of reprogramming the parts of us that believe we can never trust those we love, that we have to be suspicious and deceitful in the pursuit and maintenance of relationships.

What if, instead, we started from trust, and we kept returning to trust, measuring intimacy by how much it made us trust ourselves and trust those we hold close to us?

Because let me testify—trust feels *incredibly* good. We often take for granted the kind of trust we have for friends and that we can trust our friends to love us and also love other friends, to get different needs met in different friendships. Bringing this kind of trust to our intimate relationships,

---

Sorry': On Slavery, Marriage, and the Possibility of Love," *Feminist Wire*, July 27, 2011, https://www.thefeministwire.com/2011/07/keep-your-sorry-on-slavery-marriage-and-the-possibility-of-love.

9   Principles are listed in the essay "Love as Political Resistance" in this book, p. 59.

whether the needs include sex or just other ways of knowing, means more time can be spent on the pleasure of connection.

HOT AND HEAVY HOMEWORK

At the top of a blank page, write down your ideal structure (monogamy, open marriage, lovers, et cetera) for sexual connection, love, and relationship. Create a map from the bottom of the page to that ideal, showing what skills, conversations, and practices are needed to get there.

BEING SECOND

The other woman has time to manicure her nails
The other woman is perfect where her rival fails
And she's never seen with pin curls in her hair,
    anywhere.[1]

The other woman enchants her clothes with
    French perfume
The other woman keeps fresh cut flowers in
    each room
There are never toys that's scattered everywhere

And when her old man comes to call
He finds her waiting like a lonesome queen
'Cause to be by her side
It's such a change from old routine

But the other woman will always cry herself to
    sleep
The other woman will never have his love to
    keep
And as the years go by the other woman
Will spend her life alone
Alone
Alone
    —Nina Simone, "The Other Woman," 1968[2]

---

1   This essay first appeared as adrienne maree brown, "Being a Second Lover
     Means Loving Yourself First," September 20, 2017, *Bitch Media* (blog),
     https://www.bitchmedia.org/article/being-second-lover-means-
     loving-yourself-first.

2   "The Other Woman" is a song written by Jessie Mae Robinson and

I heard Nina Simone sing this song before I had ever really had a boyfriend. Or a girlfriend.[3] Or even a proper crush. I loved it the way a child loves things she can't comprehend—before I knew about sex, commitment, betrayal, cheating, mistresses. It sounded romantic and sophisticated. At that age, I loved serious poetry, New York City and Paris, stamps, and elegance. I romanticized the "other woman's" independence and allure.

I ignored the final verse.

In high school, I learned that being the other woman was the worst. The "other women," I thought, were home-wrecking sluts who could not be trusted.

But in my twenties, I was, sometimes, the other woman. I knew, sometimes, what was going on, and I made contorted internal assessments that it was okay.[4] I was starved for touch and performing my sexual confidence. I did what I thought was desired and required of me to be a contemporary woman: exercise independence, be sexual, and take what I wanted.

There were a lot of reasons for that messiness. I was insecure in my fatness. I was figuring out sex in an America that demands a virgin-whore in perfect balance. I was nonmonogamous but didn't know yet how to ask for it, let alone practice it. This is the biggest reason I was drawn to the lifestyle of the other woman. In the traditional relationships I'd witnessed, relationships were spaces of obligation and contortion, and what I wanted was romantic and sexual connection. I wanted to feel free to make my own choices, feel great in my body, and get to be exactly myself. Being secondary allowed room to experience connection on my own terms.

One of the hardest and most liberating lessons is learning how to be direct with potential new lovers about whether we're both actually available to have sex. When people cheat,

---

popularized by Nina Simone. Nina Simone, *The Other Woman*, vinyl, 1968.

3   Or a theyfriend!

4   Other times I overlooked questions that I should have asked, red flags I should have noticed, assumptions I let ride.

a lot of crucial information is often left unspoken—like what are the agreements and boundaries with their partner, whether they have told their partner about you or have a plan to say anything, or even if they are ever going to tell their partner that they are cheating.

I don't initiate flirtation with someone if I know they are in a partnership. If they do, I've learned to ask the questions and honor their boundaries, which includes, sometimes, helping them hold their own boundaries.

Another big lesson has been being able to say, without shame, that I really enjoy being a second. You have to be honest with yourself about this or it won't work. A friend, who also enjoys being a second, helped me name what's pleasurable. Here are some key features of being second.

1. Second is not necessarily a numeric thing, it's just being a non-primary lover/partner to someone who is transparent and open with a primary partner/lover.

2. Being a second only works with clear communication. Not perfect communication but clear communication. Being a proper second requires being able to say: What's your relationship status? Is it open? And if it is, live your best life. If it's not, figure out the necessary boundaries.

3. Being a second can be a phase of life—it's a great role to play between big relationships. Or as you're learning how you want to navigate open relationships. Or you might just be second to a particular person. I also enjoy being a primary, an only, or one of many.

4. For some people, second can be an intimacy preference. I really enjoy being the other woman in a transparent scenario. I love doing my own work all week and having someone show up to romance and touch me and then go home. I love knowing my lovers have stability and support and home, that I am only responsible for my/our pleasure. I love having

abundant nonstop sexy time for a few days and then not having to worry about anyone else's needs until the next visit.

5. Being second is very different from what I grew up learning about mistresses/affairs—the goal is not to steal your lover from their partner. You aren't diminutive or pining. You're satisfied.

6. And, in alignment, your lover's goal isn't to keep you a secret, or to become first in your life, to displace your work or other lovers or other commitments. They're enjoying the miracle of pleasure from another body. Ideally, they're as grateful for your preexisting commitments as you are for theirs.

HOT AND HEAVY HOMEWORK

If you're in a committed relationship, reflect on how it could benefit from you or your partner taking on a second. If you're single or nonmonogamous, reflect on whether you might be a budding second.

THE PLEASURE OF DEEP, INTENTIONAL FRIENDSHIP

A Conversation with
Dani McClain and Jodie Tonita

AMB.[1] *Woes!*[2] *Being in relationship with y'all has been one of the great pleasures of my adult life. I spoke of it briefly in* Emergent Strategy *and, of course, had both of you in your own element/ expertise in that book. For this book, I really want to focus on the pleasures of interdependence as it shows up in our love. I am imagining us sitting on one of the beaches, sun everywhere, reflecting on our lives.*

First, can you tell readers how we became woes? What was your journey into this intentional coevolution through friendship?

---

1   I am both interviewer [AMB] and one of the interviewees [amb] here.
2   Woes are friends who are committed to Working on Excellence. This may be how you operate at all times or in all relationships, but in case you don't, "woes" is a way to identify people with whom you have an increased accountability and responsibility for manifesting your best life. This term came to me via Drake.

Dani. I met adrienne early on in college, more than twenty years ago. I felt close to her soon after meeting. We shared a love of writing, of thinking deeply about things. Our work on a labor of love, a campus literary journal called *Roots and Culture* took us from being acquaintances to close friends. Then we went on a random trip to Prague together, spring break of our senior year, and that sealed the deal. There has been so much in the intervening years that has been important and beautiful, through a lot of cities, partners, family changes, and just life happening. I'm an only child, but at the age of nineteen or twenty, I feel like I acquired adrienne as a sister.

Jodie. I first saw Adrienne in Vancouver when she was on a speaking tour for her first book on *How to Get Stupid White Men Out of Office*. A year later we got to know each other at a training for environmental activists and it was there sparks flew (in the hot tub to be exact). I was starved for a justice and equity perspective in the enviro movement and adrienne brought it along with joy and laughter. Over time we became friends and comrades and I eventually moved from Vancouver to Oakland.

Dani. Jodie and I moved to Oakland around the same time. The building where adrienne lived was nicknamed Melrose Place and had a patio where there was lots of ongoing hanging out with neighbors and folks in the community. I met Jodie there—she was friends with adrienne and another friend in the building, Jessamyn Sabbag. I got to know more about Jodie, and we began spending time together. Then she recruited me as part of this wild work retreat near Vancouver a few years later in September 2010.

amb. I think that was the one where we got mad people of color up in the British Columbia forest and the power went out because of a squall? I had forgotten that.

Dani. I got to better understand Jodie's work and build trust with her as part of that journey, which was complex.

Jodie. I remember sending adrienne off on her sabbatical—getting her to the airport was everything.

amb. Oh my god, I remember that! You took me to get a functional, grown-up suitcase.

Dani. When adrienne moved away from Oakland, I feel like she kind of set Jodie and me up. She nudged us to hang more and get to know each other better, since we were both close to her as individuals, and she was kind of leaving us in the friend lurch. Luckily, we did. I think we both identified the ways that life in the Bay can be full and fun but strangely lonely, so we leaned into keeping each other company in meaningful ways, being available for the last-minute drink at the end of the workday, the random stop-by in the middle of a Saturday afternoon to sit on the porch and soak up sun. And somewhere in there the three of us started hanging out together—definitely during adrienne's trips to the Bay but also going on vacations together, planning joint trips to wherever the third person was living, and, of course, our text thread.

amb. I actually remember our first vacation together very distinctly. We went to Orr Hot Springs. It was a big deal to me, because I wasn't quite sure if it would work, all three of us—I was worried about feeling left out since y'all had been living in the same place and I was across the country. But we went to Orr and ended up piled in a bed after soaking in mineral pools all day, singing Beyoncé. It was so easy. After that, Jodie asked for explicit permission to talk about us to each other, to trust that we would speak of each other with the intention of helping each other. I thought that was so radical, to bring that out into the open. The interdependence really kicked off then.

Jodie. I opened up to interdependence around some trauma I was going through, which meant actually needing to count on other people and having people show up for me fully in my most vulnerable state. Being willing to be messy, being overwhelmed, and asking for help. Adrienne, you talking me through my anxiety fears and facilitating some of the process—which I have no memory of because I was completely dissociated. When Dani stepped in to help out with crucial logistics—she saved my whole life, and I was in woe love.

amb. Yes! It felt like each time we were there for each other at a deeper and deeper level, we were falling in woe love.

Jodie. Yes, like really—this person is going to help me like that? And be funny and stunning and on it? After that, I remember sharing some stories of our biggest mistakes, over the course of a long night—that created a surge of dignity that we leaned into and rode. Like, wow—we said those things out loud and we didn't die? We didn't die. Bringing Dani food when she wasn't well. I was like, I really love this person and want her to be cared for. And I remember lots of Dani and Jodie chats about work and love—getting the gumption to set and hold standards together and to grieve what was heartbreaking. I was like, wow, she is going all in and healing the fuck out of that. I was honored to witness, and it gave me so much permission. I survived my next break-up because of that.

AMB. *We have a high level of daily interdependence. It feels like the place I go to be my truest self, for emotional support, to learn. What brings you to the woes?*

Jodie. It's the place where we are fully seen and held and all of the parts of us are welcomed. We're here for each other's greatest longings, desires, and wounds. We know shame's tricks, and they may work on one of us, but the others will catch it and blast it off and bring compassion and tenderness to that place. This is co-evolution through woeship.

amb. Yes, for it me it the first place I go to practice one thousand percent honesty. Like, I am hurt by how someone is treating me, or confused about a work boundary, or I just ate mad ice cream, whatever it is. I would add humility. This is the place where I can be like, I HAVE NO IDEA HOW TO DO THIS. I know I will receive compassion, care, and also be reminded about what matters to me, what I am trying to accomplish in this lifetime, what makes me feel real joy. And I care so much, and learn so much, from what is moving in your lives.

Dani. As far as what brings me to our text thread, I have worked by myself from home for the past five years, and now I'm raising a toddler without other adult support in our home. I do not get a lot of adult time. Nowadays I can't really follow our thread that closely during the day, but at the end of the day, after I put my daughter to sleep, I turn to it to catch up on what's happening in your lives and to update you with what I've been up to or thinking about or challenged by or working on. You really prompt me to be reflective about my life, my life as a woman, as a writer, and not just a mom, which is helpful because it's easy for me to get stuck in mom-only mode in my sharing there. I need those gentle reminders to pay attention to my whole self. I don't have much of a social media presence, and what I do have is focused on work. I'm pretty private online about my life. So this circle of three is where I can "post" and seek responses and support from an intimate group that I care about and that I know sincerely cares about me.

AMB. *And what do you feel like you bring to the woes?*

Jodie. My fierce Scorpio anaconda love and loyalty.[3] My commitment to my own life and dignity now feels very

---

3   What y'all know about that Primal Astrology? See www.primal astrology.com.

woven into my commitment to my woes. If I can't muster it for me, I certainly can for my woes, and they for me. It's a dignity-amplifying superpower.

Dani. Hopefully I bring good, thoughtful feedback to the questions and considerations you pose and share. I bring my attention. I bring my care. I think I also bring a helpful dose of the mundane. Real talk: there is a lot of fabulousness happening in woes-land. There is a ton of travel to fabulous places, a lot of high-level work with some of the baddest organizers and thinkers in the country and world, a lot of freedom around thinking about what's possible in sex and in love. While I used to share in a lot of that fabulousness, my life is different now and probably will continue to be for a while. I wash a lot of dishes, prepare a lot of food, do a lot of nursing, sweep the floor a lot. I'm much more homebound than maybe at any other time in my adulthood. My life has shifted because I can't travel or work as much. I do a lot of thinking about how to best piece together childcare and manage family relationships. I know that family relationships and children are hugely important in your lives too, but I think I bring a dose of what it means to be primarily focused on these things every day. I think we learn from each other in this regard—I remember not to give up on the fabulousness of life, and you both witness what's tough for me and fill in in incredible ways to lend support.

amb. That's true, it has been powerful actually to feel the woeship adapt to the change in Dani's life of becoming a parent. I feel like I bring an attitude of "what do you *really* want? You can have that." A standard for pleasure, permission. I bring a Virgo energy of getting things functional. And I love problem-solving, working through things that feel impossible. I am also fiercely protective of both of you, of your right to be whole. Also, I am funny.

AMB. *We also share a commitment to pleasure, which shows up* *in our support of each other living our best lives and in our woe-cations, aka, wherever two or more of us are gathered. What have you learned about pleasure in this relationship?*

Jodie. I've learned I love pleasure and can notice what pleasures me and create it. Adrienne is a pleasure extrovert and Dani is a pleasure introvert. They both have pleasure superpowers. And I think I vacillate somewhere between them. We celebrate each other's pleasure. Adrienne is so good at naming all of the things to strive for. She gives me stretch goals. I've learned to create spaces that bring me infinite pleasure. I love my apartment—it emits pleasure. I created a collection of little tiny antique frames with all of the people I most love in them, and they are all around the house. There is currently a picture of us woes in Vancouver making our woe sign being transposed onto a six-by-six piece of wood that's going to go in all our houses. It will be in my bedroom. And this super sweet precious little glass antique frame that has a pic of Bel in it. They live in my bedroom. At the foot of my bed, by the window, with all of the precious things. I get to see them when I first wake up. That is so much pleasure. The woes vibranium mugs arrive this week. It gives me great pleasure to imagine sipping tea apart but together. I feel like my woes taught me to live, love, and travel well.

Dani. Our relationships have deepened my appreciation of the set and setting approach to pleasure. I think it's typically used with regard to drug use, but for me it has a broader application. My ability to take risks, stop worrying, relax, enjoy, and accept pleasure is connected to whether I feel safe in and trust the environment (setting) and whether I'm in a good state of mind (mind-set) that will allow me to embrace whatever's going on. Because I trust you two and, because I know that our spidey senses are pretty much aligned, we often create ideal environments wherever we go—in each other's homes, on vacation, whatever. And, again, because we're aligned and I don't have a ton of defenses up or concerns rolling through my head when we're together, my mind-set tends to be really positive when I'm around you both.

Our relationships have reminded me to prioritize pleasure, even when I don't feel like I have time for it or necessarily "deserve" it. You two remind me that my pleasure matters.

amb. I feel like from Jodie I have learned that it is worthwhile to invest in the quality version of the thing you actually need. Like a perfect omelet pan. Or an anti-Zionist home bubbly water machine. Like the pleasures of aiming for perfection in how home feels. And that if you want the ocean, you should go to the ocean. And from Dani I have learned a lot about the pleasures of care, of family. The love and care she brought to her aunt through her cancer, finding ways to ease her pain and focus on her joy … and the pleasure of motherhood, the absolute massive love I get to witness Dani give in how she cares for keeping the world clean and healthy for her child, it's amazing. Also the pleasure of being effortlessly fly, I have relaxed so much more into my fashion by witnessing the breezy Dani ways.

AMB. *We are also committed to making the best life we can for our next generation of nibblings and babies. Can you talk about what this space makes possible for your parenting/auntie work?*

Jodie. I fell in love with my first nibbling by love before they were born, and I was committed to Noah from the jump. Noah was ten when I first met adrienne, and our friendship provided a space where I could share the shape and meaning of this relationship. Noah has always been a source of joy, inspiration, and wonder. Adrienne and my first bio nibblings were born within a month of each other—one of our many life parallels. Sharing that phase of our lives has been incredibly validating. Woedom honors my role in all of my families, and that acceptance is like sunshine and water to the beautiful garden that is my network of intimacy and relationships.

amb. Yes, and it has helped to have this other familial space in which to check in around stuff—to understand especially around boundaries of auntiehood. We are lucky that our nibblings are being raised by people who we are mostly aligned with in terms of their choices. And then Dani, watching Dani choose and move toward her child. All of us falling in love with her before she existed.

Jodie. Watching Dani choose motherhood and be blessed with her child has been one of my greatest joys. Having Dani's back and supporting her dignity amidst the demands of parenting is a privilege. Watching her daughter grow and cheering on her best life is a gift from the gods. Dani's an incredible mother, and I am so grateful that she is writing about how we raise liberated Black children in these times.

Dani. I'm an only child, so my daughter doesn't have biological aunties or uncles on my side. She has a fabulous aunt on her dad's side. She also has you two, and that is incredibly important to me and to her. In January, when we all made the trek to Jodie's home, adrienne came to me in Cincinnati to make it easier to take a long plane ride west with my daughter. That's love. Jodie had toddler-proofed her home to make it easy for the little one to roam around and feel immediately comfortable, which she did. Because you both have been coming around since she was first born, she knows and loves you. So I was able to leave her with you two while I did work interviews. I can't stress how huge this was, what a gift it was to me.

amb. Your child is the gift. She is so smart and unique and self-determined and interesting. And watching the two of you together, the connection between you is palpable; this is how every child should be loved.

Dani. And I love that you two just invite yourselves to come to Cincinnati to be with us. I may forget to issue a formal invitation, but without fail you'll say, "Hey, how do these dates look for you?" And then you come and slide right into our rhythms and help me and love up on her. It has made parenting so much more joyful and doable. You're a central part of the community that is encircling us with love and care, and I deeply appreciate that.

AMB. *I feel like each of us have said at different points that woeship has saved our lives—I know it's saved mine. Could you share a story of how this connection has saved your life?*

Jodie. We create harm reduction spells around each other. Being able to intervene with trust and care for that person's well-being. We have each other's backs so hard. I text my woes to celebrate all the things, but I can also trust my woes' judgment when I know I am struggling for perspective. I can share it, doesn't matter what, and we can reflect on it. I told my woes about some of the bravest, and possibly pettiest, things I have ever done. I can forget that, but they will always remind me who I am. I am my best bio/chosen family member, ED, auntie, and lover because I work hard with my woes to be one.

Dani. The parenting stuff is mostly on my mind, but there have been so many times before that as well. Bad breakups that were actually moments of profound transformation waiting to happen. You helped me see the opportunity. Helped me trust that it was all for the good. You've helped me get out of jobs that I'd outgrown. Jodie helping me move my entire apartment in a day and a half? With my daughter in tow? Adrienne whisking me off to Mexico to heal and find some pleasure after a heartbreak. I can't imagine going through my aunt's illness and subsequent death without you two. There are a lot of ways the woedom has been a lifeline.

amb. Jodie moving me out of my apartment in Oakland when I was in total denial. She showed up and somehow organized the entire building and, within an hour, everything was packed, heading somewhere. I struggle with boundaries. My love is oceanic, I want to be everywhere. The woes are a place I can trust to ask, is this a mistake? Well … can I still make this mistake? No? Bet. It really is sisterhood. Dani has seen me through my depressions, through the times when I nearly got trapped in a bad life. Jodie has seen me through so much shame. Both of y'all save me over and over. I am tearing up writing this. But the woes keep me focused on my most excellent life.

Jodie. When people ask me what my spiritual practice is, I include woes. This level of interdependence and co-evolution through woedom is a practice that changes you and creates greater possibility.

Dani. The woedom gives me what I think a lot of people believe is possible only through romantic relationship: unconditional love and the feeling of being known.

amb. Well, I am so grateful y'all were willing to share so vulnerably in this way, I know that's more my thing. Thank you for the risk, I love y'all so, so, so much.

PRINCIPLES IN PRACTICE

I am in multiple communities that put an emphasis on practice. In the Allied Media community, we have articulated principles that matter to us, and we have focused on how we embody those principles as a matter of practice. In the Generative Somatics and Black Organizing for Leadership and Dignity circles, we recognize that we are what we practice, and we become what we intentionally practice with our somas, our whole selves. As this book begins with pleasure principles, I would like to land the plane with practices that explicitly bring the principles to life, practices to root us in pleasure activism here and now, and in the future we are shaping. These are practices that make us pleasure activists not just in theory but also in the practices of our lives, awakening a pleasure politics that makes justice and liberation irresistible.

Practices

- *Attention liberation.* Use meditation to learn to have agency with your attention, bringing it to breath, or sensation, or pain, or solution, or transformation.[1]

---

1   Meditation starter kit: Download the Insight Meditation app, start with a minute a day. Use the guided meditations if you find them useful. Read books by Thich Nhat Hanh, Angel Kyodo Williams, Pema Chodron.

- *Practice pleasure in your own body and life.* Notice what brings a yes to your lips, to your center. Make a pleasure journal. Put signs around your house to remind you of your pleasures. Please yourself, please others. Feel pleasure every day. Don't let your body or your heart forget why we fight—to feel aliveness and togetherness. We will grow.
- *Find the ease.* There are aspects of this life that are an uphill battle, and we seem to still be on the ascending portion of that long arc bending toward justice. But we can sustain the struggle if we find all the ease available to us, the places where we can flow together, coast together, and rest.[2]
- In organizing work, *center pleasure as an organizing principle.* This means feeding people great healthy local food that nourishes them when they come to a meeting and working together to meet the needs of the people in the space. Take the time to affirm the people and affirm the learning that sometimes masquerades as failure. Be unconditional in your commitment to movement, be transformational in every area of your life and work, and center pleasure and joy as resistance: laughter, dance, taking time for

---

2   Ella Baker taught us that "we who believe in freedom cannot rest." Ella Baker, untitled speech (Mississippi Freedom Democratic Party nominating convention, Jackson, MS, August 6, 1964). I wrestle with these words all the time, because I believe in freedom and I believe my body is a crucial part of the fight for freedom. So I interpret these words through my work. I do not rest in terms of how I work. I tirelessly show up for movements I believe in, to hold planned or unexpected hard conversations and mediations, to invite transformation in the face of frustration. I tirelessly seek out old and new ways of moving through our current paradigm and into a viable future. But when it comes to my body, I rest. I rest in myriad ways that allow me to show up fully for each facilitation. I ensure that I have quiet time each evening, a bath when there's a tub, at least seven hours of sleep each night. I want to give us more permission to rest our bodies so that we don't burn out our spirits and minds in our lifelong commitment to liberation.

the relationships. When people find movements that meet their needs, welcome them whole, affirm them, commit to their transformation, and actually feel good, they stay, and movement grows.

- *Set generative boundaries.* And hold them.
- *Only say yes when you mean it.*
- *Take responsibility* for your part of this fractal existence, and cultivate pleasure and joy in your life, knowing that authentic pleasure is good for the whole human system.
- *Be absolutely committed to your process*, to doing what you are doing in the best way you possibly can.
- *Be detached from any outcomes.*
- *Be satisfiable.* Learn what enough feels like in your body; don't settle, don't overindulge.
- *You are a miracle. Act like it. Don't waste it.*

SECTION SIX

OUTRO, THANK YOUS

OUTRO

I have begun to see pleasure activism all around me.

When I originally conceived of this book, it was a different time for me, for the United States, and for the world. So much existed under the veil of politeness, functionality, a narrative of order and rules. Struggle wasn't absent by any means, but if you had privilege you could avoid a lot of the violence, terror, and misery. As I am writing this book, every single day contains multiple all-hands-on-deck political, economic, and/or spiritual crises.

There have been days when I doubted if this book still made sense as the next offer I wanted to make to the world. I would dismiss myself, try to dedicate myself to more "serious" things. And then pleasure would save my day or my week or my life. Pleasure reminds us to enjoy being alive and on purpose. Again and again I have realized that our misery only serves those who wish to control us, to have our existence be in service to their own. Again and again I have had to surrender to the truth and freedom of pleasure.

True pleasure—joy, happiness and satisfaction—has been the force that helps us move beyond the constant struggle, that helps us live and generate futures beyond this dystopic present, futures worthy of our miraculous lives.

Pleasure—embodied, connected pleasure—is one of the ways we know when we are free. That we are always free. That we always have the power to co-create the world. Pleasure helps us move through the times that are unfair, through grief and loneliness, through the terror of genocide, or days when the demands are just overwhelming. Pleasure heals the places where our hearts and spirit get wounded. Pleasure reminds us that even in the dark, we are alive. Pleasure is a medicine for the suffering that is absolutely promised in life.

Pulling the essays and interviews together has been medicinal for me, and I hope that something in here helps with your own liberation.

As I was writing this book, I tuned into the ways we are explicitly practicing pleasure as a species, even in this apocalyptic time. There is the explicit pleasure organizing and activism documented in these pages, and then there are the ways pleasure just comes through, the beautiful moments of historically oppressed people engaging in radical acts of public pleasure.

Landing home from a long work trip, both exhausted and invigorated by the work for Black liberation, I was moving through the underground tunnel at Detroit Metropolitan Airport when I saw an airport worker running after two others, all young Black men. They were laughing like kids playing tag, leaping, darting, moving around people and rolling luggage like dancers.

A few months later I was chasing one of my nibblings around a sprayground—those places in cities where the ground is full of fountains that you can run through and step on and splash in. There was a Black teenage girl in a striped bikini who positioned herself right over one of the strongest sprays. The light was settling to late afternoon sun, the water was making rainbows everywhere, her eyes were closed, face calm, smiling, arms hanging to her sides, palms wide and forward facing as if she were receiving a blessing. It took me a second to realize that she was pleasuring herself. She kept calling out to a bunch of younger kids who seemed to be her siblings, "This water is the best place, this is the best feeling!" They ignored her, preferring to risk the water tunnels. She didn't move, and everyone gave her her space.

A while later I realized that she was a teenage mom, that an older woman on the bench surrounded by stroller and diaper bag and piles of kid clothes was the girl's mother, watching a quiet infant while the girl played in the water. Something about this felt especially tender, like a moment I wanted to protect—the safety and freedom that young mother had in that moment to feel pleasure. I want to live in communities designed around that.

Within movement there are significant small pleasures too. I have been facilitating Black liberation work a lot more in the past few years, and one group has developed a practice of celebrating a decision with music—actually putting on a nineties R&B song and singing it together all the way through to cement the decision in our bodies and cells. It makes me thrill when it's time for a decision, to feel our aliveness and laughter and nostalgia and power. The work should, as often as possible given the obstacles we're facing, be a pleasure.

I am completing this book in the spot in my house where I meditate, an old couch at the foot of my bed. Out the window is a defunct streetlight, a grassy concrete lot, some nondescript square buildings in the housing complex next door, and snippets of Detroit's skyline. I feel the pleasure of attention liberation as I sit here. The early morning sounds and sights of the city flow by, but louder than that are the birds who are my closest neighbors. They gather on the lightpost and the mysterious wires slung from here to there, sometimes singular, sometimes as a flock landing at the same time. They are loud in the morning, wild. There are two black squirrels who scurry along the thicker lines, and the birds float up to let them pass, then return, settling feathers, chattering, busy.

In the time of writing this book, my mind has often been as busy as these birds—I have navigated the scarcity that comes with being punished by the IRS, wondered how I was going to pay my rent, get groceries, travel outside of work. I have been working on old, deep trauma that doesn't even have a language yet. I have wrestled with body image and weight gain. I have fallen near and far and out of and again into love. I have cursed cancer and grieved for strangers and friends. I have danced with my depression in the face of personal and global apocalypse. I have wondered how committed I can be to a nation that never planned for me to be more than a slave. I have felt movements fracture and tremble under the pressures of this time.

And I have felt more joy, connection, satisfaction—more pleasure—during this time than any other in my life.

I have had to ask for help, again and again, becoming porous, transparent, and more human. I had to learn how to say what I want in clear words and contend with the answers to my real longings instead of swallowing bitterness about unmet and unspoken wishes. Each day I am more and more a real person—it turns out this is the only way to move through these years that my projected "perfect" selves, which I created to impress others or protect my heart, simply cannot handle. I remember, daily, that none of this is explained and none of it is promised. I remind myself that even when I turn inward to quietly hermit, I am supported by people who love me and honor my boundaries.

I touch my own skin, and it tells me that before there was any harm, there was miracle. When I reach an edge that feels impossible to go beyond, I laugh, softening any remaining rigidity in myself that makes me think I have control. I confess daily, "Here is where it hurts." I let the healing come through connection. When I feel like a failure, I look at my plants, at how they wilt and seem to be dying, and then water and sun and my loving words bring them back to vibrancy. I let water move over me, sun change me, love reach me. I root down into the soil and back into my lineage, which reminds me that everything is temporary but nothing disappears, this is how life is.

I reach forward and up, shaping a world that feels good for me, for all who look like me, for all who love like me, for all who have yet to realize that love is liberation. I let myself work through anger until all that is left is compassion. I cultivate justice within myself, rooted not in vengeance or righteousness but in love and interdependence. I work hard on answering my calling, listening to the bass notes of my life, following underground rivers to find more room for my whole self. I let my days be spent in love, connection, and creation.

I recognize that my sorrow carves out the space for my joy,[1] and that both in this lifetime and in the cycles of my lineage there is so much space that has been carved out by sorrow, and I get to fill it up with joy and pleasure. What a pleasure it is, after all, to be a free Black queer woman. To be a human, self-aware. To be of the earth, with such beauty and interconnectedness.

Pleasure is the point. Feeling good is not frivolous, it is freedom. We can gift it to each other in a million ways: with authentic presence, abundant care, and honesty; with boundaries that keep us from overextending; with slower kisses; with foot massages in the evening; with baby hugs and elder hugs; with delicious food; with supported solitude and listening to our bodies, our shameless desire, and coordinated longing.

Find the pleasure path for your life and follow it. Let it reverberate healing back into your ancestors' wounds. Let it open you up and remind you that you are already whole. Let it shape a future where feeling good is the normal, primary experience of all beings.

That's all. ♥

---

1   I was introduced to Khalil Gibran's *The Prophet* early in life and it has never let me down.

GRATITUDE

Thank you to my woes, dear friends, beloveds, and lovers, who have walked toward pleasure with me, refusing to settle.

Thank you to my team at AK Press, who are infinitely patient, clear, radical, and supportive about helping me share my work with the world. Y'all rock.

Thank you to Lisa Factora-Borchers, who took a risk to bring me to *Bitch* magazine during her time there. I told her I wanted to write for *Bitch*, and she worked with me to conceive of and focus the "Pleasure Dome" column, and then she and Evette Dionne, to whom I am also deeply grateful, worked wonders as editors to help me discover a clear voice for speaking the private into the public sphere.

Thank you to the team at Turkey Land Cove Foundation for the gift of writing time.

ALSO AVAILABLE FROM adrienne maree brown:

Edited by adrienne maree brown and Walidah Imarisha
$18.00 / £13.00 / 9781849352093 / Ebook also available

Whenever we envision a world without war, without prisons, without capitalism, we are producing speculative fiction. Organizers and activists envision, and try to create, such worlds all the time. Walidah Imarisha and adrienne maree brown have brought twenty of them together in the first anthology of short stories to explore the connections between radical speculative fiction and movements for social change. The visionary tales of *Octavia's Brood* span genres—sci-fi, fantasy, horror, magical realism—but all are united by an attempt to inject a healthy dose of imagination and innovation into our political practice and to try on new ways of understanding ourselves, the world around us, and all the selves and worlds that could be. The collection is rounded off with essays by Tananarive Due and Mumia Abu-Jamal, and a preface by Sheree Renée Thomas.

"In this provocative collection of fiction, Walida Imarisha and adrienne maree brown provide boundless space for their writers—changemakers, teachers, organizers and leaders—to untether from this realm their struggles for justice.... Like Butler's fiction, this collection is cartography, a map to freedom."

—dream hampton, filmmaker and Visiting Artist at
Stanford University's Institute for Diversity in the Arts

Written by adrienne maree brown
$16.00 / £12.50 / 9781849352604 / Ebook also available

Inspired by Octavia Butler's explorations of our human relationship to change, *Emergent Strategy* is radical self-help, society-help, and planet-help designed to shape the futures we want to live. Change is constant. The world is in a continual state of flux. It is a stream of ever-mutating, emergent patterns. Rather than steel ourselves against such change, this book invites us to feel, map, assess, and learn from the swirling patterns around us in order to better understand and influence them as they happen. This is a resolutely materialist "spirituality" based equally on science and science fiction, a visionary incantation to transform that which ultimately transforms us.

"A word/heart sojourn through the hard questions."
　　　　　　—Makani Themba, facilitator for the Movement for Black Lives

"Adrienne leads us on a passionate, purposeful, intimate ride into this Universe where relationships spawn new possibilities. Her years of dedication to facilitating change by partnering with life invite us to also join with life to create the changes so desperately needed now."
　　　　　　—Margaret Wheatley, author of *Leadership and the New Science*

AK Press is small, in terms of staff and resources, but we also manage to be one of the world's most productive anarchist publishing houses. We publish close to twenty books every year, and distribute thousands of other titles published by like-minded independent presses and projects from around the globe. We're entirely worker-run and democratically managed. We operate without a corporate structure—no boss, no managers, no bullshit.

The Friends of AK program is a way you can directly contribute to the continued existence of AK Press, and ensure that we're able to keep publishing books like this one! Friends pay $25 a month directly into our publishing account ($30 for Canada, $35 for international), and receive a copy of every book AK Press publishes for the duration of their membership! Friends also receive a discount on anything they order from our website or buy at a table: 50% on AK titles, and 20% on everything else. We have a Friends of AK ebook program as well: $15 a month gets you an electronic copy of every book we publish for the duration of your membership. You can even sponsor a very discounted membership for someone in prison.

Email FRIENDSOFAK@AKPRESS.ORG for more info, or visit the Friends of AK Press website: HTTPS://WWW.AKPRESS.ORG/FRIENDS.HTML.

There are always great book projects in the works—so sign up now to become a Friend of AK Press, and let the presses roll!